Prejudice and Your Child

Second edition, enlarged

KENNETH B. CLARK

Beacon Press   Boston

TO KATE AND HILTON

Kenneth B. Clark is a professor of psychology at the City College of New York, research director of the Northside Center for Child Development, and a member of the Board of Regents of the State of New York. He has been research psychologist for projects sponsored by the Carnegie Corporation (the Gunnar Myrdal study of the Negro in America), by the Office of War Information, and by the American Jewish Congress. For the Mid-Century White House Conference on Children and Youth (1950), Dr. Clark prepared a report on "The Effects of Prejudice and Discrimination on Personality Development in Children"; the research was sponsored by the Division of Scientific Research of the American Jewish Committee. The United States Supreme Court cited Dr. Clark's report in its decision of May 1954, which ruled that laws requiring or permitting racial segregation in public education are unconstitutional.

Contents

Preface to Paperback Edition

We Americans are not alone in facing ominous crises of racial segregation, desegregation and integration; throughout the world today the status of non-white groups in relation to the previously dominant white and Western groups is changing. The obsolescence of segregation and the resultant winds of change are as present in international relations as they are present in the internal social issues facing the United States. The surge of the Asian and African peoples from colonialism to nationhood, the reorganization of the British Commonwealth, the brittleness of relationships between Soviet Russia and China, and the rapid expansion of United Nations membership are all aspects of a pervasive desegregation affecting our world. The democratic idea has become infectious on an unprecedented world scale, a fact which is sometimes obscured by phenomena of nationalism, economic change and cold war ideological distortions. Racial desegregation in the United States is inseparable from this wider historic process, and in fact vitally influences the position of the United States in our evolving world.

In the years since the United States Supreme Court handed down the *Brown* decision in the *School Segregation Cases* on May 17, 1954, that decision has given rise to many significant social, political, educational and intellectual consequences. Most important, that decision has resulted in the admission of hundreds of thousands of Negro children into non-segregated schools in such border states as Kansas, Missouri, Maryland, West Virginia, Oklahoma, Texas, Kentucky and the District of Columbia. This

fact has been obscured by the strident and at times violent reactions to the Court decision, the cries of "massive resistance"
and talk of "interposition," and the resistance — thus far successful — to even token public school desegregation in such states as
Mississippi, South Carolina and Alabama.

One of our nation's most severe and persistent social and political crises since the Civil War has resulted from the Federal
Courts' public school desegregation decisions and from the extreme negative reactions to these decisions which have been
encouraged by some southern politicians. Indeed, the present
issues of controversy and even violence are fundamentally the
same issues which brought on the Civil War: the inviolability of
human dignity and the integrity of a United States which limits
the autonomy of its individual states. The determination of
whether governmental power will be used to enhance human
freedom and dignity or to perpetuate power itself and the social
status quo is a far broader issue of our time than even the social
and political consequences of the *Brown* decision. Controversy
over the *Brown* decision has accentuated other controversies
over the uses of governmental power and has virtually created
an important new controversy over the influence of social science
upon government and law. To this observer, it seems that the
attacks upon the role of social scientists in the *School Segregation
Cases* are closely related to the underlying issue of whether governmental power shall be used to perpetuate itself and the *status
quo* or used to enlarge human freedom.

In re-issuing *Prejudice and Your Child* in this new paperback
edition, at the request of the publishers, I have thought it desirable to bring together in one extended supplement the actual
documents involved in the controversies over the *Brown* decision
and over the role of social scientists in that epoch-making decision. *Prejudice and Your Child* is itself the revised or book
version of the manuscript "Effect of Prejudice and Discrimination on Personality Development," which I prepared for the
Midcentury White House Conference on Children and Youth,

1950, and which the Supreme Court cited in footnote 11 of the *Brown* decision, in 1954. This study of mine was first published in its book form, *Prejudice and Your Child,* in 1955, after the *Brown* decision. Parts One and Two of *Prejudice and Your Child,* which are left unchanged in this new edition, summarize my study and pattern of thought which was cited by the Court in its first citation under footnote 11 of the *Brown* decision.

Since the *Brown* decision followed a long line of Supreme Court decisions in the area of segregation, I am deeply grateful to Professor Philip Kurland of the Law School of the University of Chicago for preparing especially for this paperback edition an essay on the legal background of the *School Segregation Cases.* Professor Kurland's essay appears as Appendix I in this edition. This edition is also supplemented by a printing of the *Brown* decision itself, made exciting reading by the eloquent and simple majesty of its language as it spells out the unqualified rights of human beings to respect and dignity. The Social Science Brief (Appendix to Appellant's Briefs: Statement by Social Scientists) is presented for its intrinsic worth as well as to provide the reader with a basis for judging the controversy over this brief's quality, scientific objectivity, concern for justice, and appropriateness for presentation to the Court. Two of my own papers written since the *Brown* decision are included as appendices in this new edition, in order to provide the reader with a summary of significant developments in public school desegregation, with my most recent thoughts on the role of social scientists in this and similar social issues, and with this observer's estimate of what remains to be done if social scientists are to continue making significant contributions to the democratic resolution of this difficult human problem, desegregation.

September 1962   Kenneth B. Clark

Introduction

One of the most characteristic and impressive things about the American people is their dedication to their children. Ours is indeed a "child-centered" society. Almost no sacrifice is too great for parents to make if it will benefit their children. Parents will work, scheme, attend church, buy life and endowment insurance, move from country to city, from city to suburbs, from one neighborhood to another, from south to north, from east to west — all for the welfare of their children. Divorces have been postponed and marriages maintained because of the children. Schools change their policies from traditional to progressive or vice versa in order to meet the needs of the children. Experts write books to present the latest version of the facts on the care of the infant and child. Parents buy, and sometimes read, these books in order to ensure their children a happy future. Important research projects on the causes, prevention, and cure of polio, muscular dystrophy, mental retardation, and emotional disturbances have been subsidized by parents moved by an emotional response to the picture of an afflicted child who could have been their own. American parents are intensely conscious, if not overly self-conscious, about the welfare and future success of their children. In the main, their activities in the present and their plans for the future are geared to protecting their children from want and foreseeable harm.

When mistakes are made and things go wrong with their children, parents suffer from feelings of guilt even if they did not deliberately harm their children. Often these difficulties reflect factors that the parents do not understand or control; therefore the parents cannot know what is the "right" thing to do.

When white American parents demand that a school board maintain separate schools for white and Negro children, and when some of these parents encourage their children to refuse to attend a school to which Negro students have been recently admitted, they do so not only as an expression of their own racial feelings but also in the belief that they are protecting their children. If these parents understood that, far from protecting their children, acts of this type distort and damage the core of their children's personalities, they would not act this way. If they understood that the opportunity for a child to meet and know other children of different races, religions, and cultures is beneficial and not detrimental; that it contributes to social competence and confidence; that it increases a child's chances for personal and moral stability — then they would demand, in the name of their children, non-segregated public education.

For these and other reasons, it is necessary to have a clear understanding of the nature of racial prejudices and the effects of these prejudices upon American society in general and upon the personality development of children.

Some scholars have pointed out that all complex human societies assign to different groups of individuals positions of different status. The pretext for the different status varies from differences in religion, region, sex, politics, or material possessions to differences in physical characteristics. In differentiating among human beings, the societies decide which are "better" and which are "worse." Then the society excludes and rejects those in the "worse" groups. Finally, these patterns become fixed and unquestioned social customs.

Racial discrimination in America is one example of this tendency to grant preferred status to some individuals and to reject others. In this case the basis for preference is skin color.

Some scholars have speculated on the reasons for prejudice, to discover which came first — the lower status or the prejudice.

In either case the stereotyped thinking almost invariably asserts the inferiority of one group and the superiority of the other. Needless to say, these explanations are satisfying to the group on top and disturbing to the group on the bottom. Some observers maintain that these forms of prejudices are irrational, that they fulfill an emotional rather than intellectual need of those who hold them. It would be difficult, however, to understand social prejudices in terms of whether they are rational. Man utilizes all of his faculties, both rational and irrational, in his struggle to establish an adequate status for himself, and in his attempt to justify his existence and his superiority to others.

Not all human prejudices have bad consequences. Some prejudices may have positive personal and social results. The aversion to poisonous food is a positive prejudice. Such a prejudice reflects the accumulated knowledge of the culture; and it is neither necessary nor reasonable for an individual to try to make a personal verification of what is already known. Moreover, there are prejudices that are neither positive nor negative — "neutral" prejudices, which do not help or harm. An example of neutral prejudice would be the rather widespread aversion to the eating of horsemeat. Horsemeat would not harm the person who ate it; but neither would his refusal to eat horsemeat damage either the horse or the abstainer (so long as he took some other food for adequate nourishment).

In addition to the positive and neutral prejudices, there are destructive and negative prejudices. Among them are racial, religious, economic, and social prejudices, which threaten the integrity of individuals and of whole societies.

Parents and other adults who care about the welfare of children must be concerned with the problem of the types of ideas and judgments transmitted to children. An important aspect of the education of all children in a democracy is teaching them those beliefs, ideas, and patterns of behavior which are most consistent with reality and with personal and social stability. An equally important aspect involves training children to recognize beliefs that conflict with objective reality and with their own integrity — beliefs that are detrimental to themselves and others. Moral and ethical considerations are necessary aspects of sound education in a democratic society. Children cannot be encouraged to substitute personal wishes for social reality without severe risk to the stability of their personalities. Racial prejudices are indications of a disturbed and potentially unstable society.

Racial prejudice in America involves not only a pattern of preferred status for some on the basis of skin color, but also feelings of hostility and aggression sometimes reflected in barbaric cruelty. This pattern cannot exist in a democratic society without arousing deep currents of guilt and conflict.

As Gunnar Myrdal has pointed out, [1] there is a gulf between the American ideals of democracy and brotherhood on the one hand, and the existence of racial prejudice, discrimination, and segregation on the other. The "American creed," which emphasizes the essential dignity of the human personality, the fundamental equality of man, and the inalienable rights to freedom, justice, and equal opportunity, is clearly contradicted by the denial of these to certain human beings because of their race, religion, or nationality background. The struggle between the moral forces and the manifestations of racial prejudice has long influenced American society. At times this struggle seems to have immobilized the constructive role of many of our social institutions, such as schools and churches. Indeed, during long periods of American history, it seemed possible for Americans to adjust, with little apparent difficulty, both to their dedication to the "American creed" and to their discrimination against Negroes. However, the essential strength of the democratic ideology periodically reasserts itself and demands re-examination of our racial practices. Myrdal and his associates have stated that the main trend in American history is toward the eventual realization of the "American creed" and the elimination of racial discrimina-

---

[1] In his monumental work, *An American Dilemma.* (See the Bibliography at the end of this book.)

tion. Certainly the rapid changes and widespread improvements in race relations in America during the past fifteen years would seem to justify this optimistic conclusion.

There still remains, however, the problem of understanding how it was possible for Americans, whose nation was founded on clear statements of democratic principles, to tolerate for so long a pattern of racial discrimination that so clearly violated these principles. To understand this apparent contradiction, one would have to examine the basic motivations involved in America's colonization, development, and eventual emergence as a world power.

All white Americans were either immigrants or the descendants of immigrants. Each wave of newcomers had in common with all the others the fact that the group was fleeing either from economic hardships, from religious or political persecution, or from social humiliation. The people who made up this new nation, therefore, were driven by some basic form of personal or group *insecurity*. This insecurity had to be strong enough to compensate for the disadvantages and discomforts involved in leaving the homeland and migrating to a new world. In time America became the land of opportunity — the land which promised a security denied to the marginal or non-conforming men of the old world.

If one accepts the assumption that this basic motivation of insecurity was inherent in the very foundation of the American nation, then it is possible to interpret the pattern of American culture as a consistent whole. It would seem that the initial insecurity of each group of new Americans not only resulted in a systematic exploitation of the natural resources of the new land, a pushing back of the frontiers, a glorification of work, and the rise of a technology that has practically dominated the culture, but also produced a fundamental concern with the ideas and practices of general equalitarianism and political democracy. The entrenchment in the culture of the expressed ideals of the "American creed" was determined by the past inferior status that had made the old world no longer tolerable. To American white colonizers and immigrants, the "American creed," like American technology, was accepted and sustained in order to obtain a security and integrity that had been previously denied. If this is true, it may offer an explanation of the relationship between the American ideology of equality and the American pattern of social and racial discrimination. An individual in quest of security and status may seek to obtain them not only through positive objective methods — work and personal achievement — but through the denial of security and status to another person or group. The exercise of this power over others may bring with it a feeling of security and status which equals or surpasses any satisfaction achieved by actual personal effort. The white American's espousal of the "American creed" is real and significant to him. It is the expression of *his* desire for equality, status, and security. His denial of these to the Negro is a manifestation of this same desire, and makes him feel he has won a superior status. Seen from this point of view, the "American creed" and racial discrimination are not contradictory but compatible elements of American history and social psychology. Each has the same motivation — an intense drive for status and security.

If the resolution of the American dilemma is in the direction of the "American creed," it will not be because of the power of the ideals in themselves, or because of their apparent contradiction with social realities, or because of guilt feelings. It will be a result of the realistic pressures of changed economic and technological developments, together with social and political national and international events, which will tip the balance in the direction of forcing Americans to adhere to our ideals as the most effective means for maintaining the stability and vitality of our society.

One must acknowledge that it has been possible for America to accept this discrepancy between its moral codes and its violations of them; but one cannot completely discount the potential significance of the ideals themselves. Americans are both practical and idealistic. A basic belief of American culture is that one can work toward progress. Up to the present, the most significant indications of social progress in America have been brought about through material and technological advances. If political, legal, economic, and international pressures demand fundamental social changes in America, the American ideals of brotherhood may help to make the transitional period less disruptive and probably even a challenging and creative period in American history.

Beyond the larger social, economic, and international aspects of racial prejudice, there exist the inescapable human costs. Racial prejudices are not impersonal social problems. A democratic society should seek to eliminate symptoms of man's inhumanity to man because they distort and dehumanize human beings. Prejudiced persons are dominated by primitive fears and hatreds; and prejudices also damage the personalities of the victims. Parents, educators, and other adults concerned with stable personality and character in our children — all those who seek to provide the opportunity for children to enrich their lives and contribute to society as fully as possible — must increase their concern with the problem of protecting children from the corrosion of destructive racial and social prejudices. It may not always be easy for adults to provide these opportunities for children, since most adults themselves grew up under social conditions that fostered racial prejudices. However, among the responsibilities and obligations that parents assume for their children is that of providing opportunities and experiences for growth which they, the parents, may not have had. This obligation is imperative not only in the family's economic and educational advancement, but in the area of social attitudes.

No normal parent would deliberately block his child's opportunity to obtain the preparation he needs in order to meet the demands of the present and the future. Racial attitudes which may not have been clearly inconsistent with the world in which the present generation of parents and grandparents grew up are clearly inconsistent with today's world. Vast changes in transportation and communication have brought distant lands and peoples within easy access and close relations. Narrow, provincial prejudices are no longer appropriate. The contemporary world demands the development of cosmopolitan attitudes toward people who are different. The peoples of Asia and Africa who were seen as exotic or bizarre in the nineteenth century are now demanding the status of equal partners in a world struggling for democratic stability. Our children will not be able to play an effective role in this modern world if they are blocked by our past prejudices and if through these attitudes they stimulate resentment and hostility rather than cooperation and understanding among other peoples of the world.

These are positive reasons for helping our children to meet the demands of our times. The modern world challenges American parents and educators to re-examine educational techniques and methods in order to determine the most effective ways to stimulate and reinforce in our children positive social attitudes which are essential to moral strength and personal stability. The vitality and stability of a humane society are at stake. The concern with the dignity of the human being — with the opportunity for the development of the moral potentialities of all individuals — distinguishes a democratic society from a totalitarian one.

On May 17, 1954, the United States Supreme Court handed down a decision which ruled that state laws requiring or permitting racial segregation in public education are a violation of the United States Constitution. This decision is historic from the legal, educational, and human points of view. It may eventually rank with the great documents that have marked our progress toward the goals of democracy. In simple and eloquent words the Court stated:

We must consider public education in the light of its full development and its present place in American life throughout the nation. . . .

Today, education is perhaps the most important function of state and local governments. . . . It is the very foundation of good citizenship. Today it is a principal instrument in awakening the child to cultural values, in preparing him for later professional training, and in helping him to adjust normally to his environment. In these days, it is doubtful that any child may reasonably be expected to succeed in life if he is denied the opportunity of an education. . . .

We come then to the question presented: Does segregation of children in public schools solely on the basis of race, even though the physical facilities and other "tangible" factors may be equal, deprive the children of the minority group of equal educational opportunities? We believe that it does.

. . . To separate them from others of similar age and qualifications solely because of their race generates a feeling of inferiority as to their status in the community that may affect their hearts and minds in a way unlikely ever to be undone. . . .

We conclude that in the field of public education the doctrine of "separate but equal" has no place. Separate educational facilities are inherently unequal.

This decision was the climax of a long series of legal cases which have challenged the constitutionality of various forms of racial segregation in public education and other areas of American life. The Court's decision also took into account a growing body of knowledge in psychology and the social sciences, the result of extensive research into the development of racial attitudes and the effect of prejudice on the development of American children. The research, which had been carried on by social scientists for many years, made it possible to present to the Court a coherent and systematic picture of the effects of prejudice, discrimination, and segregation on personality development.

In December 1950, the Mid-Century White House Conference on Children and Youth had dealt with the theme of healthy personality development in American children. The research staff gathered and presented the available knowledge on this general problem. The author of this book was given the responsibility for examining all available information on racial prejudice and its effects on the personality of American children. This material was presented as a manuscript, which was used as the basis for discussion of this problem at the White House conference.

In May 1951, the first case to challenge the constitutionality of segregation in public elementary and high schools was heard before three judges in a Federal district court in Charleston, South Carolina. Much of the information that had been assembled for the White House conference was used as expert testimony to show the damaging effects of racial prejudice and segregation on children. This type of testimony was also presented in three of the four subsequent cases. The Supreme Court, in its May 1954 decision, cited the original manuscript in support of its finding that racial segregation in public education deprives children of minority groups of equal educational opportunities and therefore violates the "equal protection" clauses of the Fourteenth Amendment.

In writing this clear and unequivocal decision, the Supreme Court made a major contribution to the progress of racial democracy in America. The decision itself did not, and could not, solve all of the many complex social problems which must be met as various communities seek to make the transition from segregated to non-segregated schools. This decision clarified the legal and moral grounds for non-segregated public education. It also established the legal basis for the elimination of segregation in other areas of American life.

The Supreme Court, in effect, challenged boards of education, public officials, parents, educators, and all citizens who believe in democracy to re-examine American social practices in order to determine whether they damage or enhance the human potentialities of children. The legal power of our government is now clearly on the side of protecting our children. There remains, however, the problem of translating this legal decision into practical and beneficial social changes. This problem is primarily the responsibility of individual citizens in their local communities. Parents, social workers, educators, clergymen, and others must now mobilize their energies for effective implementation of this decision.

In order to do so with a minimum of social conflict and confusion, American citizens should have the same type of objective information that was available to the justices of the United States Supreme Court. It is probably not enough to believe that racial prejudice, discrimination, and segregation are morally wrong. In order to become actively involved in the struggle to eradicate these symptoms of social maladjustment and save our children from their harmful effects, it is necessary to know *why* they are wrong. Responsible citizens must understand clearly what negative racial attitudes are, how they affect our society, and the ways in which they are communicated to our children. When the effects of these forms of prejudice on the personalities of children are clearly understood, then the efforts to immunize our children from their virulence will be more effective.

PART ONE

THE PROBLEM OF PREJUDICE

1. How Children Learn About Race

Are children born with racial feelings? Or do they have to learn, first, what color they are and, second, what color is "best"?

Less than fifty years ago, some social theorists maintained that racial and religious prejudices are inborn — that they are inherent and instinctive. These theorists believed that children do not have to *learn* to dislike people who differ from them in physical characteristics; it was considered natural to dislike those different from oneself and to like those similar to oneself.

However, research over the past thirty years has refuted these earlier theories. Social scientists are now convinced that children learn social, racial, and religious prejudices in the course of observing, and being influenced by, the existence of patterns in the culture in which they live. Students of the problem are now facing these questions:

(1) How and when do children learn to identify themselves with some people and to differentiate themselves from others?

(2) How and when do children acquire racial attitudes and begin to express these attitudes in their behavior?

(3) What conditions in the environment foster the development of these racial attitudes and behavior?

(4) What can be done to prevent the development and expression of destructive racial prejudices in children?

Until quite recently, there were differences of opinion concerning the age at which children develop and express racial prejudices. Some observers (in the tradition of those who believed that prejudices are inborn) said that even infants express racial preferences and that therefore such preferences are natural and spontaneous. At the other extreme, certain observers maintained that social and racial prejudices play little or no role in the life of the child until the early teens. They pointed out that children of different races have been observed playing together and sometimes developing close friendships; this fact, they thought, showed that young children are unaware of racial or religious differences.

Within the past two decades, social scientists have made a series of studies of this problem.[1] They indicate, on the one hand, that there is no evidence that racial prejudices are inborn; and, on the other hand, that it is equally false to assume that the child remains unaffected by racial considerations until his teens or pre-teens.

Racial attitudes appear early in the life of children and affect the ideas and behavior of children in the first grades of school. Such attitudes — which appear to be almost inevitable in children in our society — develop gradually.

According to one recent study, white kindergarten children in New York City show a clear preference for whites and a clear rejection of Negroes. Other studies show that Negro children in the kindergarten and early elementary grades of a New England town, in New York City, in Philadelphia, and in two urban communities in Arkansas know the difference between Negroes and

---

[1]A pioneer work in this field is *Race Attitudes in Children* by Bruno Lasker. Since its publication in 1935, a number of psychologists and other social scientists have studied aspects of racial attitudes in children by more precise methods. Eugene Horowitz set the pattern for empirical investigations of this problem in his study of the development of racial attitudes in children. His results have been supported and extended by the findings of Ruth Horowitz; Kenneth and Mamie Clark; Radke, Trager, and Davis; and Mary Ellen Goodman. Specific studies by these and other researchers are listed in the Bibliography below.

whites; realize whether they are Negro or white; and are aware of the social meaning and evaluation of racial differences.

The development of racial awareness and racial preferences in Negro children has been studied by the author and his wife. To determine the extent of consciousness of skin color in these children between three and seven years old, we showed the children four dolls all from the same mold and dressed alike; the only difference in the dolls was that two were brown and two were white. We asked the children to choose among the dolls in answer to certain requests:

(1) "Give me the white doll."
(2) "Give me the colored doll."
(3) "Give me the Negro doll."

These children reacted with strong awareness of skin color. Among three-year-old Negro children in both northern and southern communities, more than 75 per cent showed that they were conscious of the difference between "white" and "colored." Among older children, an increasingly greater number made the correct choices.

These findings clearly support the conclusion that racial awareness is present in Negro children as young as three years old. Furthermore, this knowledge develops in stability and clarity from year to year, and by the age of seven it is a part of the knowledge of all Negro children. Other investigators[2] have shown that the same is true of white children.

Some children whose skin color is indistinguishable from that of white people, but who are nonetheless classified as Negroes by the society, have difficulty in making a correct racial identification of themselves at an age when other children do so. Soon, however — by the age of five or six — the majority of these children also begin to accept the social definition of themselves, even though this differs from their observance of their own skin color.

There is now no doubt that children learn the prevailing social

---

[2] Ruth Horowitz; Mary Ellen Goodman; Radke, Trager, and Davis.

ideas about racial differences early in their lives. Not only are they aware of race in terms of physical characteristics such as skin color, but also they are generally able to identify themselves in terms of race.

The problem of the development and awareness of religious ideas and identification in children involves more subtle and complex distinctions which understandably require a longer period of time before they are clearly understood.

It is much more difficult for children to know if they are Catholic, Protestant, or Jewish than it is to know if they are white or Negro. In one study (Radke, Trager, and Davis), children were shown pictures of a church with a cross, and of a building clearly marked as a synagogue. The investigators asked the children their reactions to these pictures. Only a minority of children between the ages of five and eight made stable and accurate identification of themselves in terms of religion. Less than half of the Jewish children in this age group identified themselves as Jews, while only 30 per cent of the Catholic children and only 27 per cent of the white Protestant children made correct religious identifications. The relatively high percentage of Jewish children who correctly identified themselves as Jews indicates that for these children there is an earlier awareness of religious identification and probably of minority status.

In these tests, no Negro child identified himself in religious terms. This fact probably indicates that for the Negro child at these ages the dominant factor in self-identification is skin color. The impact of their minority status as determined by skin color is so great that it precludes more abstract bases for self-identification.

A study of seven- and eight-year-old Jewish boys (by Hartley, Rosenbaum, and Schwartz) found that these boys had a generalized preference for all things "Jewish." The children responded to all questions concerning self-identification and preference with such comments as: "Because I am Jewish." "Because I like

Jewish." "Because they are Jewish like me." "Because I like to play with Jewish people."

This undifferentiated preference for Jewishness was found by Radke to be appreciably less among Jewish children of ten and eleven, and even less in thirteen- and fourteen-year-olds. It is possible that as these children mature their increased contact with the larger culture results in a decreased interest in Jewishness as such. It is also possible that this tendency reflects an increase in rejection of Jewishness — indicating the children's growing awareness of the minority status of Jews in America.

The same social scientists have studied small groups of Jewish, Catholic, Negro, and white Protestant children in New York City. These children were asked to respond to the simple question, "What are you?" Jewish children on all age levels answered by the term "Jewish," rarely identifying themselves in terms of nationality or color. On the other hand, a considerable proportion of the non-Jewish children identified themselves in terms of nationality rather than religion.

Non-Jewish children between the ages of 3½ and 4½ were usually not certain what religion they belonged to. Some non-Jewish white children in this age group said that they were Jewish; the fact that they were enrolled in a Jewish neighborhood center may have accounted for their mistaken belief that they were Jewish. At this stage of development, a non-Jewish child in a Jewish setting may conceive of himself as Jewish, and vice versa. These results suggest that the problem of religious identification involves a level of abstract thinking of which pre-school children are generally incapable.

These investigators also studied the meaning of such terms as "Jewish" and "Catholic" for children between the ages of four and ten. They found that at these ages the concepts are understood in terms of concrete activities. Jewish children mentioned "Going to shul," "Not eating bacon," or "Talking Jewish." Catholic children mentioned "Going to church," "Making communion," or "To speak as a Catholic."

Certain conclusions arise from the many independent investigations of the development of racial awareness and identification in children. By the age of four, Negro and white children are generally aware of differences in skin color and can identify themselves correctly in terms of such differences. Jewish children are not consistently aware of their Jewishness until around the age of five. The average Catholic or Protestant child does not begin to identify himself in religious terms until around seven or eight. Thus it appears that the concrete and perceptible fact of skin color provides a basis for earlier self-identification and preferences in American children than the more abstract factor of the family religion.

A child gradually learns what status the society accords to his group. The tendency of older Jewish children to show less preference for Jewishness than younger Jewish children suggests that they have learned that Jews do not have a preferred status in the larger society, and that these children have accordingly modified their self-appraisal. This effect of the awareness of the status of one's own group is even more clearly apparent in the case of Negro children.

In addition to Negro children's awareness of differences in skin color, the author and his wife studied the ability of these children to identify themselves in racial terms. We asked the children to point out the doll "which is most like you." Approximately two-thirds of all the children answered correctly. Correct answers were more frequent among the older ones. (Only 37 per cent of the three-year-olds but 87 per cent of the seven-year-olds responded accurately.) Negro children of light skin color had more difficulty in choosing the brown doll than Negro children of medium-brown or dark-brown skin color. This was true for older as well as younger children.

Many personal and emotional factors probably affected the ability of these Negro children to select the brown doll. In an effort to determine their racial preferences, we asked the children the following four questions:

(1) "Give me the doll that you like to play with" or "the doll you like best."

(2) "Give me the doll that is the nice doll."

(3) "Give me the doll that looks bad."

(4) "Give me the doll that is a nice color."

The majority of these Negro children at each age indicated an unmistakable preference for the white doll and a rejection of the brown doll.[3]

Studies of the development of racial awareness, racial identification, and racial preference in both Negro and white children thus present a consistent pattern. Learning about races and racial differences, learning one's own racial identity, learning which race is to be preferred and which rejected — all these are assimilated by the child as part of the total pattern of ideas he acquires about himself and the society in which he lives. These acquired patterns of social and racial ideas are interrelated both in development and in function. The child's first awareness of racial differences is found to be associated with some rudimentary evaluation of these differences. Furthermore, as the average child learns to evaluate these differences according to the standards of the society, he is at the same time required to identify himself with one or another group. This identification necessarily involves a knowledge of the status assigned to the group with which he identifies himself, in relation to the status of other groups. The child therefore cannot learn what racial group he belongs to without being involved in a larger pattern of emotions, conflicts, and desires which are part of his growing knowledge of what society thinks about his race.

Many independent studies enable us to begin to understand how children learn about race, how they identify themselves and others in terms of racial, religious, or nationality differences, and

[3] Even at three years the majority preferred the white doll and rejected the brown doll. The children of six or seven showed some indication of an increased preference for the brown doll; even at this age, however, the majority of the Negro children still preferred the doll with the white skin color.

what meaning these differences have for the growing child. Racial and religious identification involves the ability of the child to identify himself with others of similar characteristics, and to distinguish himself from those who appear to be dissimilar.

The fact that young Negro children would prefer to be white reflects their knowledge that society prefers white people. White children are generally found to prefer their white skin — an indication that they too know that society likes whites better. It is clear, therefore, that the self-acceptance or self-rejection found so early in a child's developing complex of racial ideas reflects the awareness and acceptance of the prevailing racial attitudes in his community.

Some children as young as three years of age begin to express racial and religious attitudes similar to those held by adults in their society. The racial and religious attitudes of sixth-graders are more definite than the attitudes of pre-school children, and hardly distinguishable from the attitudes of high-school students. Thereafter there is an increase in the intensity and complexity of these attitudes, until they become similar (at least, as far as words go) to the prevailing attitudes held by the average adult American.

The racial ideas of children are less rigid, more easily changed, than the racial ideas of adults. It is probable, too, that racial attitudes and behavior are more directly related among adults. The racial and religious attitudes of a young child may become more positive or more negative as he matures. The direction these attitudes will take, their intensity and form of expression, will be determined by the type of experiences that the child is permitted to have. One student of this problem says that, although children tend to become more tolerant in their general social attitudes as they grow older, they become less tolerant in their attitudes toward the Negro. This may reflect the fact that the things children are taught about the Negro and the experiences they are permitted to have usually result in the development of racial intolerance.

2. Society and Children's Feelings About Race

Who teaches a child to hate and fear — or to respect as his equal — a member of another race? Does he learn from his mother and father? From his schoolteachers? From his playmates? Or does he learn from those impersonal but pervasive teachers, the television set, the moving picture, the comic book? Probably it is all of these that teach him to love or to hate. Studies indicate that such attitudes are determined not by a single factor but by all of the child's experiences.

When white children in urban and rural sections of Georgia and in urban areas of Tennessee were compared with children attending an all-white school in New York City, their basic attitudes toward the Negro were found to be the same.[1] Students of the problem now generally accept the view that children's attitudes toward Negroes are determined chiefly "not by contact with Negroes but by contacts with the prevailing attitudes toward Negroes." It is not the Negro child, but the *idea* of the Negro child, that influences children.

Rarely do American parents deliberately teach their children to hate members of another racial, religious, or nationality group. Many parents, however, communicate the prevailing racial attitudes to their children in subtle and sometimes unconscious ways. Parents often forget their influence on the formation of their children's opinions and frequently deny that they have ever said anything to their children that would encourage race prejudice. A group of southern white children told one investigator (Horowitz) that their parents punished them most often when

---

[1] Eugene L. Horowitz (1936).

they went to play with Negro children who lived in their neighborhood. He concluded that the development of attitudes of southern children toward Negroes has its source in community pressures brought to bear upon the parents, who then transmit them to their children. The particular way in which this happens is frequently forgotten by the parents, and eventually they develop a system of rationalizations to support their behavior and the behavior they impose upon their children.

It is possible that these community pressures are transmitted to children not only through their own parents, but also, as they grow older, through their friends and their friends' parents. Some investigations suggest that the attitudes of parents have a greater influence on younger children than on older ones. From about ten years of age, the child is being more directly influenced by the larger environment; if his racial attitudes and behavior are still consistent with those of his parents, it is probably because the larger environment agrees with his parents.

There is no consistent evidence that parents always play a crucial continuing role in the transmission of the prevailing racial attitudes in their children. Studies dealing with the attitudes of Negro children show that these children generally have negative attitudes toward other Negroes. It would seem unlikely that the negative attitudes of these children toward their own group are a result of the direct influence of their parents. Although some Negro parents have mixed feelings about their own racial status, the average parent would be careful in the way he expressed such feelings in the presence of his children. But some children of a minority group may be sensitive to the unexpressed racial feelings of their parents. An occasional offhand disparaging remark, an occasional overheard adult conversation, may contribute to the development of the child's racial feelings. On the whole, however, it seems that Negro children, like white children, get their negative attitudes toward other Negroes as much from the outside community as from the home.

At a parent-teacher meeting devoted to the development of

racial attitudes in young children, a white mother arose to present a problem. She said that she and her husband, concerned with problems of racial justice, had sought to provide for their children the type of democratic home atmosphere that would foster a sensitivity for and appreciation of the equality and dignity of all human beings. She had friends of different racial and religious groups who visited her home and whom she visited with her children. Nevertheless, her oldest child had come home from the first grade of school with disparaging remarks about Negroes. Once he used a particularly offensive racial epithet. She and her husband were disturbed about this and wanted to know how such a thing could happen and in what ways they had failed as parents. The guest speaker at the meeting pointed out that, once her child left the sheltered environment of the home, he was naturally exposed to other social influences. This child was learning about the attitudes that existed among the majority of his playmates and a few dominant individuals in his class who had been influenced by their parents or other adults.

Certain evidence seems to indicate that parents who are primarily preoccupied with their personal status, and parents who impose upon their children harsh and rigid forms of discipline, are likely to foster in their children intense prejudices toward individuals of another race or religion. Some students claim that children who are personally secure and happy are not as likely to develop rigid prejudices. But other observers maintain that it is misleading to explain the development of prejudices in terms of the personal happiness or security of the child within his family. Many children, growing up in the normal American environment, do not have the opportunity to learn any attitude except one that stereotypes individuals of a different race.

Parents are merely one element of the complex pattern of social forces that influence the child's racial, religious, and social attitudes. The development of racial prejudices in children reflects, among other things, the complexities of his family relationships, the type of community in which he lives (including friends and neighbors), his school experiences, and the religious influences brought to bear upon him.

Racial symbols are so prevalent in the American scene that all normal children eventually perceive them. They observe segregated residential areas, segregated and often inferior schools for Negro children, segregated recreational facilities, and in some areas of the country segregated transportation. They see Negroes often only in domestic service or in other menial occupations. Such observations contribute to the young child's attitude toward those individuals whom the society consistently labels as "inferior."

This is a problem even for the Negro child who grows up in a segregated Negro community. Such children have some contacts with life outside their racial ghettos; their parents frequently work in a subordinate capacity for whites, and the children see the same moving pictures, radio and television programs, newspapers, magazines, and comic books that white children see. From these and other sources they learn that they are considered by the larger society to have an inferior status.

In seeking to understand the origin and source of racial attitudes in children, one should not ignore the role of the mass media of communication. Until recently, the treatment of Negro characters in the movies, over the radio, and on television has contributed to the perpetuation of stereotypes. This treatment has labeled the Negro as either comic, menial, or inferior. But it is possible to overemphasize the role of even the powerful instruments of mass communication. It is doubtful that television, the radio, and the movies can be held totally responsible for the racial attitudes of American children. Rather, the treatment of racial groups by these media reflects the prevailing racial attitudes in the larger culture. The media are mirrors of society.

One Negro father attempted to discourage his ten-year-old son from looking at a television program that presented Negro characters in stereotyped roles. The father said he would be happy if the son did not look at this program, because all of the Negroes were required to speak in a comic southern dialect. The son insisted that he liked the program because "it was funny."

The father replied: "Listen to the way those people are talking. Have you ever heard any of our friends or relatives speak in that manner?"

The son answered in a matter-of-fact way: "Of course not. But this is the way colored people talk on radio and television."

This episode indicates that some children may be able to make a clear distinction between reality and what is presented to them as entertainment. Radio, television, and other media do not, in themselves, determine the attitudes of children; but they may reinforce the developing attitudes of some children.

In understanding the growth and elaboration of racial attitudes in children, one must emphasize that the many institutionalized forms of prejudice are of primary importance. The various types of racial segregation that children observe — must take part in — are crucial in the formation of their racial attitudes. A white child who attends a segregated school from his earliest grades up through high school, or a child who is told that he must not play with Negro children because they are dirty or delinquent, is being taught that there are people who are "inferior" and that he himself is "superior" by virtue of race or skin color alone.

A study of 173 New York City children between the ages of seven and thirteen showed that the judgments of children are more likely to be influenced by the attitudes of their classmates than by the authority of their teacher. The investigator asked these children to estimate the length of lines, to compare one line with a standard line, and to match lines with lines of different lengths. These tasks varied in difficulty. The experiment was designed so that small groups of children were pitted against other groups, an individual child against a number of other children, and a child against his teacher. Always the majority group was instructed, unknown to the individual subject, to give answers that were sometimes obviously incorrect. The investigator found that an individual child, confronted with the fact that the majority of his own classmates were unanimous in making an incorrect judgment, tended to modify his own judgments according to the opinion of the rest. The younger children were more dependent upon the group than were the older children.[2] On the other hand, when a teacher tried to influence the child's judgment by a clearly false opinion, not one of the children followed the teacher's judgment completely. The role of the teacher in influencing the opinion of these children was therefore much weaker than the role of their classmates. Although this particular study was not concerned directly with the problem of racial attitudes, it suggests that children of this age group are more likely to be influenced by friends of their own age than by adults.

There have been no consistent conclusions about the effect of individual teachers and the role of the school in the fostering of good intergroup relations among children. While there might be some question concerning the effects of direct attempts at indoctrination by teachers — particularly when these attempts are clearly in contradiction to observable facts — the influence by subtle and indirect means of adults on children's attitudes cannot be discounted. A school may have an excellent over-all human-relations program, but individual teachers with negative racial attitudes may present such a program in a way that cancels out the positive aims of the larger program. Allport and Kramer, after studying the racial attitudes of college undergraduates, concluded that, although many of their subjects remembered learn-

---

[2] Only 7 per cent of the children between the ages of seven and ten maintained their own correct judgment in the face of contradiction from the group. Of the older group of children, 20 per cent were able to contradict the group judgment consistently. It should be pointed out also that the degree to which the group's judgment influenced the judgment of the individual child depended upon the clarity of the situation presented to him. When the situation was not clear, the judgment of the majority had a greater influence upon the individual. See R. W. Berenda, *The Influence of the Group on the Judgments of Children.*

ing something about racial attitudes in elementary and high school, they could not recall anything specific. About 8 per cent reported that they had learned some "scientific facts about race." These were generally the less prejudiced individuals.

Although many people continue to believe that schools and teachers have a direct influence on the development of racial attitudes in children, this view is not supported by any substantial body of evidence. There have not been enough specific studies of the role of the schools in the development of racial attitudes of children; the real extent of their influence is therefore unknown. A cautious interpretation of the available evidence suggests that the influence of schools and teachers is more passive than active. For the most part, educators seem to approach this problem somewhat in the way in which they approach the problem of sex education. Rather than taking the leadership in educational programs designed to develop more positive racial attitudes, the schools tend to follow the existing community prejudices. The few experiments in dynamic race-relations programs as integral parts of the school curriculum reflect the general inadequacy of our educational institutions in this area. They also show what could be done if teachers and other school officials were sufficiently alerted to their social and educational responsibility.

Given this tendency to passivity on the part of our schools and educators, episodes demonstrating the prejudice of individual teachers may become important factors in the development of negative racial attitudes in children. The following incident took place in a school in a New England city that had a reputation for good race relations. When a teacher was assembling her third-grade class after a play period in the school yard, the children did not want to stop playing and return to their classroom. The teacher was somewhat impatient in gathering the stragglers. One little boy returned breathlessly to the line just as it started to move away. It was clear that he had been playing rather hard, and his face was covered with dirt from the playground. The teacher looked at him and shouted: "Jimmie, look at you! You are all dirty. You look just like a little colored boy." There were two Negro children in that class. As the other children laughed at Jimmie, these two children hung their heads in embarrassment and shame. Thoughtlessly, and probably without venom, this teacher had given her class a most effective lesson in anti-Negro prejudice.

Unfortunately, such incidents are not rare. A teacher in a New York City public school considered it desirable to separate the children in her class according to her estimate of their academic standing. Because this school is in a mixed neighborhood, she had white, colored, and Puerto Rican children in her class. Almost invariably the white children were placed in the first rows, the Negroes in the middle rows, and the Puerto Rican children in the back rows. The teacher insisted that this procedure was in no way a reflection of racial attitudes and she did not believe that the children in her class could be influenced by this pattern. She could not understand that children respond more to the concrete realities they perceive than to the abstract ideas and explanations they are offered. Here they were being taught by the actual classroom situation that certain children with white skin color were "superior" or were preferred by their teacher; and that those with brown skin color or with an accent were "inferior" and were being rejected by their teacher. Unquestionably these and similar situations contribute to the total pattern of children's racial attitudes. As long as such situations are not counteracted by vigorous educational programs by responsible school officials, the result will be an increase in racial prejudice. The influence of racially segregated schools is even more clear and direct. These schools are in themselves concrete monuments to the prevailing racial prejudices in a community. A child who is required to attend a segregated school is being taught that race is an important factor in his education. It is practically impossible for him to avoid including in his appraisal of himself, as this is influenced by his experience in school, the fact of his racial identity. In the case of the Negro child, his attendance at a segregated school establishes the fact of his "inferiority," since he is aware that his school is generally inferior to the one provided for whites, and that he is being rejected and prevented from associating with the other children in the community. In the case of the white child, his attendance at a segregated school demonstrates to him his "superiority" in terms of whiteness alone and teaches him in a concrete way that the rejected Negro attending the Negro school is inherently "inferior."

This situation clearly plays a major role in the total pattern of racial attitudes that these children develop. Democratic education cannot be effective in a racially segregated school. Lip service to democratic ideals is contradicted by the concrete fact of the segregation itself. These schools, therefore, stimulate, perpetuate, and reinforce negative racial attitudes in children and are powerful obstacles to the attainment of genuine democratic education.[3]

What is the influence of the church in the development of racial attitudes in children? One must keep in mind the fact that nearly ninety million Americans are enrolled in some church. Nearly thirty million American children are enrolled in Sunday schools. Much of the educational literature published by the major Protestant churches is designed for use with children and young people, and some of it deals directly with the problem of improving intergroup relations. The moral and religious basis for good human relationships is generally very well expressed, but there is a general vagueness about how a child is to translate these words into concrete daily behavior. The major difficulty in the translation of these moral and religious ideas into social reality lies in the fact that churches themselves are predominantly segregated institutions. There is the dilemma of how to teach children the moralities of brotherhood in racially segregated Sunday schools.

---

[3] The role of the schools is discussed at further length in Chapter 5 below.

Studies of the influence of religious training on racial attitudes have revealed a paradox. They show that individuals who profess strong religious affiliations or attend church frequently are more likely to be prejudiced than those who do not. Although these results are not entirely conclusive, consistent evidence from independent studies strongly suggests that religious training in itself does not make the individual more tolerant toward other races. There is even some suggestion that under the present pattern of religious training it might tend to make him more prejudiced.

There should be further research into this problem. The available evidence suggests, however, that churches and Sunday schools do not now play an effective part in developing positive racial and religious attitudes in children. This may be because the churches tend to reflect the prevailing racial attitudes of the larger community. For the most part the churches, like the schools, do not take the initiative in attempting to develop a systematic program for the improvement of racial attitudes in children. It is clear that such a program would be extremely difficult as long as racially segregated churches exist.

Since there is no evidence that churches actively encourage the development of negative racial attitudes, the children are influenced by other forces in society. Their racial attitudes reflect the effects of these other forces which are not counteracted — even if they are not reinforced — by the church and the Sunday school.

These findings present a significant challenge to priests, ministers, and religious educators. As long as this challenge is not successfully met by American religious education, the church must be considered still another area of our society in which negative intergroup attitudes of children are not effectively discouraged. Religion as generally practiced in America, therefore, must be seen as another passive force which helps keep prejudice alive.[4]

---

[4] The role of the churches is discussed at further length in Chapter 7 below.

Some observers have studied the possible effect of the socio-economic status of the family on the racial attitudes of children. It has been said that poorer whites are more likely to express intense racial prejudice. It has also been said, less frequently, that more privileged whites are somewhat prejudiced. Different classes of whites generally express their prejudices in different ways.

Unfortunately this problem has not been studied extensively. One investigator studied the racial prejudices of seventy-nine university students whose parents owned residential property, were members of a country club, a riding club, or yacht club, and fulfilled other criteria of membership in a higher socio-economic class. He found that these individuals expressed prejudices against Jews, Negroes, and other minorities, and that their behavior was even more prejudiced than their answers to questionnaires. This behavior took the form of social snobbery and rejection rather than overt bigotry.

Most of the studies in this area have concerned themselves with individuals of the middle class, such as college students, or public-school students in middle-class neighborhoods. There have been relatively few studies of the racial attitudes of white individuals in the lower and the extreme upper socio-economic groups.[5]

The studies dealing with the effects of the relationship between political beliefs and racial attitudes provide no more definite conclusions than those dealing with the socio-economic factor. One early study found that students of the average Republican and Democratic families did not differ in their attitudes toward the Negro, but that members of liberal socialist groups were more liberal and tolerant in their racial attitudes, at least verbally. Ten years later, a study indicated that members of the traditional

---

[5] One may speculate on this absence of adequate studies of individuals outside of the "middle class." Does it reflect the degree to which students of this problem have functioned in terms of the American assumption of classlessness — believing that all Americans belong to the middle class?

wings of the Republican and Democratic parties were most con-
servative and most likely to have negative racial attitudes, that
more progressive wings of these parties were less prejudiced; and
that socialists were the least prejudiced.

In spite of the meager evidence, it appears that the political
point of view of the family may bear some relationship to the
racial attitudes of the individual. It is possible that a liberal
political point of view tends to correspond with a greater likelihood of positive racial attitudes. Yet how far do these more
positive attitudes actually influence children? It is conceivable
that children of politically non-conforming parents are more
intensely indoctrinated in social attitudes. This may result in an
intensely protective loyalty to the family, and to its beliefs.

The available studies, then, indicate that children get their
racial attitudes from a number of interrelated social influences,
which begin to affect the child even before he enters school.
This pattern of social and cultural forces from which the child
learns how to evaluate himself and others may include his family,
his playmates, his neighbors, his school, the socio-economic status
of his family in the community, and influences of the church and
the mass media of communication. The impact of any single
influence may vary according to the age of the child, and some
of these influences are more direct than others.

However, there is no concrete evidence that any one of these
social forces, or any combination of them, generally exerts a
significant restraining force on the development of negative racial
attitudes in American children and adolescents. In fact, it seems
clear that these forces, rather than counteracting the development
of negative racial and religious prejudices, reinforce the prevailing racist ideas, encourage rejection, and teach the child to think
of people in stereotyped terms. These attitudes are acquired as a
natural part of the daily life of the child, as he comes to know
the existing values, norms, and attitudes which are essential for
his acceptance in the outside world.

3. The Negro Child and Race Prejudice

"I got a sun-tan at the beach this summer," a seven-year-old Negro boy repeated over and over again to a psychologist. His mother, he said, was white and his father was white and therefore he was a "white boy." His brown skin was the result of a summer at the beach. He became almost plaintive in his pleading, begging the adult to believe him.

His story unfortunately is not uncommon. If society says it is better to be white, not only white people but Negroes come to believe it. And a child may try to escape the trap of inferiority by denying the fact of his own race.

The measure of a social injustice is its consequences in the lives of human beings. Over and above the political, economic, sociological, and international implications of racial prejudices, their major significance is that they place unnecessary burdens upon human beings, sometimes even distorting and damaging the individual personality.

As recently as twenty years ago many scholars believed that a discussion of social problems in terms of moral and human values was outside the competence of the social sciences. Today, however, there is general recognition that it is impossible to exclude moral judgments and human considerations from research in the social sciences. The exclusion of such considerations is a sign not of real objectivity but of a subjective incompleteness.

Of course, the acceptance of the need for moral judgments presents certain difficulties; it requires that the social scientists take

certain social risks. Yet, as Louis Wirth, one of America's most
distinguished social scientists, has said, "Without evaluations we
have no interest, no sense of relevance or significance." And the
social psychologist Theodore Newcomb has written:

> Medical research is not hampered by the assumptions that pain and
> disease are bad. Prejudice and discrimination are also bad. By direct-
> ing our research to the practical end of eliminating them, I think we
> may find not only that our research is better, but also that we have
> moved from illusion toward social reality.

Many contemporary social scientists are no longer afraid that
moral guidance based on objective research need be arbitrary,
elusive, or abstract. Whenever behavior involves two or more
people, moral implications are inevitable. The social sciences
must recognize that one of their major goals involves a search
for description and verification of moral laws. Judgments are
inevitable in man's quest for truth and understanding.

Moral judgments on the part of social scientists frequently require courage, especially when their judgments conflict with
those of men of authority. The same was at one time true for the
physical scientists — but it did not stop scientific progress. In this
area the relentless, independent, and courageous pursuit of
knowledge brought about changes in the judgment and perspective of the more "practical" men of affairs. Today there is a new
concern among physical scientists about whether their knowledge
will be used to help or to harm mankind.

It is impossible for social scientists, midway in the twentieth
century, to deny their moral responsibility to society, without at
the same time denying all claims to scientific responsibility. Such
denials would mean asking society either to shackle social scientists as intellectual peons; or to indulge them in a luxurious preoccupation with irrelevant or futile abstractions; or to ignore
them as intellectual eccentrics who piddle with sophistries while
more practical men grapple with the real and immediate problems of society.

This does not mean that social scientists should do research on practical problems only. This restriction would also limit freedom of inquiry and imagination, which are essential to creative thought and science. Much of our knowledge about the effects of prejudice, discrimination, and segregation on the personality of Negro children came from research that had not been done for any immediate practical purposes. This knowledge has come from a group of independent students who chose to do research on the problems of personality and society — though these students were probably not oblivious to the social and human implications of their findings. Their interest in these problems reflected a basic concern with the stability of society and the enrichment of human experience.

Two researchers, Deutscher and Chein, questioned more than five hundred social scientists in anthropology, sociology, and social psychology who had done work and published scientific articles in the field of race relations. The investigators found that 90 per cent of the social scientists who replied believed that segregation has bad psychological effects on members of the segregated group, even if equal facilities are provided. The majority based their opinion either upon their own professional experience or on the research of other scholars. They said these were the detrimental effects on members of the minority group.

1. Segregation puts special burdens upon members of a minority group by the clear discrepancy between democratic ideals and the actual practice of enforced segregation.
2. Segregation is a special source of frustration for persons who are segregated.
3. Segregation leads to feelings of inferiority and of not being wanted.
4. Segregation leads to feelings of submissiveness, martyrdom, aggressiveness, withdrawal tendencies, and conflicts about the individual's worth.
5. Segregation leads to a distortion in the sense of what is real.

Some of these social scientists said that segregation leads to a vicious cycle: the harmful personality patterns arising from segregation are in their turn used to support arguments for further segregation. A few said that some individuals could be helped by being members of the segregated group; but most of these social scientists maintained that segregated individuals suffer from being segregated.

What of the persons who impose the segregation? What happens, for instance, to whites when they discriminate against Negroes? Of the social scientists who replied to the questions of Deutscher and Chein, 83 per cent maintained that racial segregation has detrimental psychological effects on members of the privileged group. A number of the scholars maintained that segregation harms those who enforce segregation even more than the victims. Although there was less certainty about these results, they may be summarized as follows:

1. Segregation is a symptom of some psychological maladjustment in those who demand segregation.
2. There are pervasive and elusive harmful effects of segregation on members of the majority group — increased hostility, deterioration of moral values, the hardening of social sensitivity, conflict between ideology and practices, the development of rationalizations and other techniques for protecting one's self.
3. Segregation results in inner conflicts and guilt feelings among members of the group enforcing segregation.
4. Segregation leads to disturbances in the individual's sense of reality and the relation of the individual to the world around him.

This study by Deutscher and Chein has had considerable influence. Its findings were cited in a brief presented to the Supreme Court by the Solicitor General and the Assistant Attorney General of the United States in a case involving the segregation of a Negro in interstate transportation on a railroad.[1] The study was also cited in the social-science appendix submitted to the United States Supreme Court in the segregated-school cases. In addition this was one of the studies cited by the Supreme Court itself in the famous footnote 11 of the May 1954 decision, which ruled that state laws requiring or permitting racial segregation in public education are unconstitutional.

In spite of the well-deserved reputation of this study, one must recognize that it presented only the *opinions* of social scientists — not the actual data upon which they based these opinions. How did such a large proportion of students arrive at the same conclusions?

Allison Davis, a cultural anthropologist, maintains that high racial status protects the individual against restriction, punishments, frustrations, and taboos to which individuals of low racial status are required to submit. High racial status also gives an individual the right and the opportunity to be paternalistic and to give or withhold favors and protection. Low racial status, on the other hand, requires the individual to show deference and restricts his open aggressiveness against the dominant group. Davis contends that the effects on the personality become more marked as the individual grows older, and as he comes into contact with larger spheres of his environment.

As we have seen, a child's personality is influenced by racial considerations at the same early age at which he learns about racial differences and begins to express racial preferences. In kindergarten and the first and second grades, children from minority groups have already developed negative feelings about themselves and personal conflicts concerning identification with their racial or religious groups. "Negro children" says Davis, "revealed most vividly and often the feelings of insecurity resulting from anticipated rejection or insult from white children." Negro children are bombarded with opposing forces — including ac-

---

[1] *Henderson vs. United States of America* (October 1949).

quired negative ideas that tend to increase their rejection of themselves as Negroes; the normal healthy forces that give rise to the need for self-acceptance and self-esteem; and finally the forces that result in the understandable, if futile, desire for aggressive retaliation against whites.

An even more specific report stated that Negro children of this age group react to an awareness of their inferior racial status by escape and the conscious search for revenge. American adults might find it difficult to accept some descriptions of the reactions of children between five and seven; but evidence from independent investigators supports these findings and describes similar reactions among even younger children. Negro children between the ages of 3 and 4½ in a Boston nursery school were studied by Mary Ellen Goodman, a Wellesley anthropologist. Asked questions about their racial identification, they generally reacted with uneasiness and with tense and evasive behavior. Such responses were not found among the white children studied. A study by Ruth Horowitz of nursery-school children, two to five years old, in New York City, showed that the ability of these children to identify themselves with their own racial group was part of their ability to identify themselves. The individual child develops an awareness of his own personality through recognizing his own physical characteristics and learning what value others in the society place on those characteristics. This becomes an important part of what he thinks about himself.

The study of the development of racial awareness, preference, and identification in Negro children made by the author and his wife[2] throws more light on the personal and emotional consequences of race and the meaning of race for the Negro child. In addition to the "dolls test," these children took a "coloring test." The investigator gave each child a sheet of paper with drawings of a leaf, an apple, an orange, a mouse, a boy, and a girl, plus a box of twenty-four colored crayons which included

---

[2] See Chapter 2 above.

brown, black, white, yellow, pink, and tan. Each child was tested alone and asked to color the leaf, apple, orange, and mouse. If the child responded correctly, it was assumed that he knew what colors things really are. If the child was a boy, the investigator then said: "See this little boy? Let's make believe he is you. Color this little boy the color that you are." After the child responded, he was told: "Now this is a little girl. Color her the color you like little girls to be." (If the child being tested was a girl, the questions were altered accordingly.) Of the responses to the "coloring test," only those of the children between five and seven seemed consistent enough to be analyzed. There were 160 children in this age group.

These children generally made spontaneous comments as they colored the little boy or the little girl or as they reacted to the questions asked during the "dolls test." (In view of the discovery that children are sensitive to many racial nuances and may have their responses influenced by the skin color of the observer, it may be important to point out that the person who conducted these experiments was of medium-brown skin color.)

In the "coloring test," all of the Negro children with very light skin color colored the figure representing themselves with the white or yellow crayon; these children were reacting in terms of the color they could see that their skin was. These responses were interpreted as accurate. But 15 per cent of the children with medium-brown skin color and 14 per cent of the dark-brown children also colored their "own" figure with either a white or a yellow crayon or with some bizarre color like red or green. Yet these same children were quite accurate in their ability to color the leaf, the apple, the orange, and the mouse. Their refusal to choose an appropriate color for themselves was an indication of emotional anxiety and conflict in terms of their own skin color. Because they wanted to be white, they pretended to be.

When these children were asked to color the child of the opposite sex the color they preferred, 48 per cent of them chose brown, 37 per cent white, and 15 per cent a bizarre or irrelevant color.

It is significant that 52 per cent of these children refused to color their preference either brown or black. This finding supports the conclusions of the "dolls test," in which 60 per cent of these children preferred the white doll or rejected the brown doll.

The discrepancy in the percentage of Negro children who rejected the brown doll compared to the percentage who refused to color their preference brown may be due to the fact that the "coloring test" required a greater effort from the child. It subjected him to a greater strain in indicating his preference. In the "dolls test," he could solve the conflict merely by pointing to a certain doll. In the "coloring test," he not only had to choose a crayon of a certain color, but also had to use this crayon long enough to color the drawing. Many of these children spent a long time in looking at all of the different colors before making a deliberate choice. Some of them picked out one crayon, looked at it, put it back, and chose another one — usually of a lighter color. Their behavior revealed how deeply embedded in their personality is the conflict about what color they are and what color they want to be. Some of these children, who colored the leaf and the fruit and the mouse rather carefully and correctly, revealed their inner turmoil by coloring the picture representing themselves with a scribbling vigor. Others, even when making an obviously wishful, evasive, or inappropriate response, colored the picture with great tenderness and care.

How do northern Negro children differ from southern Negro children in this respect? Nearly 80 per cent of the southern children colored their preferences brown, whereas only 36 per cent of the northern children did. Furthermore, over 20 per cent of the northern children colored their preferences in a bizarre color, while only 5 per cent of the southern children did. A record of the spontaneous remarks of the children showed that 82 per cent of the southern children spoke as they worked, but only 20 per cent of the northern children did so. Most of the remarks of the northern children were concerned with the desirability of one or another skin color. While the same was true of the southern children, a substantially higher proportion of them supported their color preferences by remarks relating to the ugliness or prettiness of one or another color. The only two children who made spontaneous remarks indicating a derisive rejection of the brown color were southern children. On the other hand a substantially higher proportion of the northern children made evasive remarks.[3]

Some of the children reacted with such intense emotion to the "dolls test" or to the "coloring test" that they were unable to continue. One little girl who had shown a clear preference for the white doll and who described the brown doll as "ugly" and "dirty" broke into a torrent of tears when she was asked to identify herself with one of the dolls. When confronted with this personal conflict, some children looked at the investigator with terror or hostility. Many of these children had to be coaxed to finish the tests.

The only children who reacted with such open demonstrations of intense emotions were northern children. The southern children when confronted with this personal dilemma were much more matter-of-fact in their ability to identify themselves with the brown doll which they had previously rejected. Some of them were able to laugh or giggle self-consciously as they did so. Others merely stated flatly: "This one. It's a nigger. I'm a nigger."

On the surface, these findings might suggest that northern Negro children suffer more personality damage from racial prejudice and discrimination than southern Negro children. However, this interpretation would seem to be not only superficial but incorrect. The apparent emotional stability of the southern Negro child may be indicative only of the fact that through rigid racial segregation and isolation he has accepted as normal the fact of his inferior social status. Such an acceptance is not symptomatic of a healthy personality. The emotional turmoil revealed by some

---

[3] Trager and Davis also found a greater tendency for northern children to evade as much as possible this threatening and seemingly painful area of racial identification and preference.

of the northern children may be interpreted as an attempt on their part to assert some positive aspect of the self.[4]

On examination of the various studies of this subject, a number of important facts emerge. As children develop an awareness of racial differences and of their racial identity, they also develop an awareness and acceptance of the prevailing social attitudes and values attached to race and skin color. The early rejection of the color brown by Negro children is part of the combination of attitudes and ideas of the child who knows that he must be identified with something that is being rejected — and something that he himself rejects. This pattern introduces, early in the formation of the personality of these children, a fundamental conflict about themselves.

Many Negro children attempt to resolve this profound conflict either through wishful thinking or by seeking some form of escape from a situation that focuses this conflict for them. One attempt to escape this dilemma was that of the northern Negro boy who insisted that he had a "sun-tan."

The finding that these fundamental conflicts about the meaning of race appear at such an early age is significant. Another important discovery is that these young children begin to develop techniques for self-protection in an effort to cope with developing racial conflicts and threats to the personality.

As children grow older, they become more sensitive to larger aspects of the environment. The pattern of their responses and accommodations to these larger social pressures becomes increas-

---

[4] The conclusion that the future personality adjustment of the northern Negro is healthier than that of the southern Negro may be supported by an examination of the statistics of admissions of Negroes to a northern state hospital for the mentally ill. These figures show that the annual rate of admission of northern-born Negroes is 40 per 100,000, compared to 186 per 100,000 for those Negroes who were born and lived in the south. These figures, striking in themselves, become even more significant when they are compared with the annual rate of admission of 45 for northern-born whites. See B. Malzberg, "Mental Disease among American Negroes," in *Characteristics of the American Negro*, edited by O. Klineberg.

ingly complex, subtle, and sometimes obscure. Although the effects of prejudice, discrimination, and segregation on the personality of adolescents and adults reflect the accumulation of childhood experiences, the later reactions are more indirect and complicated than the concrete effects observed in children. The discovery that very young children develop techniques for protecting themselves against negative racial status must be balanced by the observation that it takes time before these children learn all of the many subtle and complex ways of disguising the symptoms of personality damage. In studying this problem among adolescent and adult members of a minority group, therefore, one must not only look for the direct signs and symptoms of personality distortion such as are clearly observable in children, but also realize that these symptoms at the older age levels may express themselves in forms apparently unrelated to the racial problem. The consequences of prejudice and segregation for the personality continue with increasing complexity from childhood through adolescence as part of the development of the total personality.

Racial discrimination and segregation result in adverse social situations. It must be expected therefore that individuals who develop and are required to function within a segregated society will be affected adversely. The relationship between the emerging personality pattern and the social stresses is not of course a simple and direct one. Furthermore, students of personality are forced to recognize that the complexity of personality and society makes it difficult to isolate any one factor of a complex society and demonstrate unequivocally the effect of this single factor upon the whole personality of an individual. Nevertheless, the evidence from social-science research, from general observations, from clinical material, and from theoretical analyses consistently indicates that the personality pattern of minority-group individuals is influenced by the fact of their minority status.

Studies of the skin-color preference of older Negro children and adolescents demonstrate a continuation of the conflict concerning racial status. One investigator who studied Negro children between the ages of nine and twelve in a segregated school found that they generally preferred light skin color. The significance of this preference may be seen in the fact that these children (like the younger Negro children tested by other investigators) tended to judge their own skin color as lighter than adults would have judged it. The nine- and ten-year-olds were more definitely committed to the assumption that light skin color was of superior value than the eleven- and twelve-year-olds. One wonders whether these older children were actually learning to accept themselves without apology or whether they were merely developing better techniques for protecting their self-esteem. This study also found that eleven- and twelve-year-olds attending a non-segregated school were more likely to prefer light skin color than children of the same age attending an all-Negro school; this suggests the possibility that the greater social pressures inherent in a segregated setting demand an earlier development of self-defense. Similar conclusions from a study of younger children also suggested that the need for self-protection is not lessened by racial segregation, because there are still some contacts with the outside world, and conflicts in self-esteem are thus inevitable.

A study of older adolescents (by Eli Marks) revealed a tendency among Negro college students attending a southern Negro college to express a preference for light-brown skin color, and to ascribe unfavorable characteristics both to white skin color and to black or very dark-brown skin color.

From these and similar studies the following general conclusions may be drawn: Negro children from three through six tend to have an uncritical preference for white skin color; from seven through ten this choice diminishes somewhat; eleven- and twelve-year-old children, particularly those in a segregated group, tend to say they prefer brown skin color; and the preference for a light-brown skin color persists through adolescence. It appears that this spoken preference for an intermediate skin color may resolve for the Negro the basic conflict between his need for self-esteem and his awareness that a darker skin color is a basis for rejection by society. Negro children and adolescents generally rate their own skin color lighter than it actually is.

Even though older children are more likely to say they prefer their own color, does this represent a fundamental change in their feelings? Observation of the behavior of many Negro adults seems to indicate that this indication of preference is a form of self-protection rather than a fundamental change in the ability of the individual to accept himself without apology. The often-observed tendency of successful Negro men to marry very light Negro women — and the less conspicuous tendency of successful or famous Negroes to make interracial marriages — are pertinent here. For the adult Negro the association of higher status with lighter skin color tends to persist, regardless of what he says.

Clinical studies support these general observations. General studies of a thousand Negro psychiatric patients in a mental hospital and detailed case histories of eight of them revealed that Negro patients frequently had delusions involving the denial of their skin color and racial ancestry. Some of these patients insisted that they were white in spite of clear evidence to the contrary.

As the Negro observes the society in which he lives, he associates whiteness with superior advantage, achievement, progress, and power, all of which are essential to successful competition in the American culture. The degree of whiteness that the individual Negro prefers may be considered an indication of the intensity of his anxiety and of his need to compensate for what he considers the deficiencies of his own skin color. The various terms prevalent among Negroes to describe different shades of skin color indicate the degree of emotionality involved in the skin-color conflict.[5] Warner, Junker, and Adams contend that various physical characteristics of the Negro have been given an exaggerated importance in American society, "and consequently

---

[5] These terms include "pink" and "ofay" for whites; "high yaller" for very fair Negroes; "durk" and "blue" for very dark Negroes.

are bound to have far-reaching consequences on the formation of personality."

These various studies and interpretations contribute to an understanding of the problem of self-hatred among Negroes. As has been shown, self-rejection begins to occur at an early age and becomes embedded in the personality. This self-rejection is a part of the total pattern of ideas and attitudes that American Negro children learn from the larger society. It demonstrates the power of the prevailing attitudes, and their influence on the individual even when these attitudes run counter to his need for self-esteem. Self-hatred is found among individuals who belong to any group that is rejected or relegated to an inferior status by the larger society. Kurt Lewin has systematically described this pattern among Jews. Other students have observed and discussed patterns of self-hatred among the children of voluntarily isolated religious sects and among children of first-generation immigrant groups.

An extensive study of two thousand children of Italian-born parents in New York City revealed that these children, between eleven and fifteen years of age, suffered from feelings of inferiority and self-hatred which showed they knew that they and their parents occupied an inferior social, economic, and educational status. Although group self-hatred is not restricted to Negroes, it is clear that the problem may be a more difficult one for Negro children. Disadvantaged white groups have a greater chance of increasing their economic status and being assimilated into the dominant culture. The barriers against such assimilation are more formidable for the Negro child and are further complicated by the fact that everyone can see what his color is.

Younger children, as we have seen, tend to express their self-hatred by concrete and direct rejection of brown skin color. Older Negro children and adolescents express their self-hatred in more devious forms. J. A. Bayton found that Negro college students were not unlike white college students in the pattern of their negative stereotypes about the "typical Negro." These students tended to mask their self-hatred by referring contemptuously to the "typical Negro" — a category from which they excluded themselves. In interpreting his findings, Bayton concluded that the stereotype of the "typical Negro" as held by other Negroes is indicative of low morale within the group, and that this pattern of self-hatred among Negroes must be seen as a part of the total pattern of negative feelings toward whites as well as other Negroes. In the deep south, for example, Negro students reveal a basic pattern of distrust and suspicion of white Americans. Other studies of this problem suggest that Negro adolescents are basically antagonistic to white people (whom they see as fundamentally hostile) and that they develop a virtually impenetrable wall to protect themselves from meaningful contacts with whites.

The problem of self-hatred among Negroes must be understood as one aspect of the total pattern of feelings and attitudes of minority-group members toward all other members of the society which relegates them to an inferior and humiliating status. Self-hatred is not an isolated phenomenon. It cannot be understood in terms only of the minority-group member's reactions to other members of his group. It is in fact a reflection of the Negro's reaction to all of the negative pressures that bombard him. It is a symptom of a social disease and must be seen in the context of the Negro's relationship with whites and as a result of his hostility toward whites. As he learns from the whites the stereotypes about himself which form the substance of his self-hatred, he begins at the same time to resent the whites for imposing this stigma upon him. If there are to be significant changes in the Negro's attitude toward himself, these changes can come only from positive and fundamental changes in the way in which the larger society views and treats the Negro.

Hostile and aggressive reactions to the inferior status imposed upon the Negro have sometimes received over-dramatic description in the public press and in novels. Richard Wright's *Native Son* — as well as other descriptions of Negroes who react to racial frustrations by blind expressions of hostility and aggressions toward any convenient person in the environment — may stimulate the interests of the laymen and make him aware of the high human costs of racial prejudice. At the same time dramatic and sensational descriptions of violence and other negative responses to racial frustration are often cited as proof of the inferiority and barbarity of the Negro race, and used to justify and reinforce existing patterns of prejudice, discrimination, and segregation. Regardless of how they are interpreted, these patterns of reaction to racial frustration exist; they are a part of the high human and social costs of racial oppression.

Statistics show a disproportionately high rate of crime and delinquency among persons of oppressed minorities, whether based on racial, economic, or nationality factors. The meaning of hostile, aggressive, and anti-social behavior among Negroes should be considered in the light of the following question: Are Negroes as a group subject to a more general condition of social isolation, rejection, and frustration than other groups in America? Although the condition of the Negro in American life has been steadily improving during recent years, this question unfortunately must still be answered in the affirmative. To the extent that Negroes as a group are still bombarded with negative social pressures, to this extent a relatively large minority of them will be driven to express their humiliation and defiance in self-destructive and anti-social behavior. The importance of race as a factor is that this is the basis upon which Negroes are oppressed.

The case of an adolescent Negro boy who participated in the 1943 Harlem riot shows some of the complicated personality problems involved in an aggressive reaction to racial frustration. This eighteen-year-old Negro male, who had always lived in New York City, was a product of a broken home and lived alone in a furnished room, although he occasionally visited his mother. He attended a vocational high school irregularly. His clothing, speech, and manner fitted into the basic requirements of the "zoot suit" styles. After the Harlem riot he talked freely and with some pleasure about his part in it. He showed no guilt feelings as a result of his participation in the riot, which involved destruction of property, looting, and random physical violence. In his speech he showed an habitual and seemingly deliberate disregard of the most basic rules of grammar. In his ordinary conversation he used profanity excessively; the frequency of profane words suggested that they had become emotionally meaningless to him, and were being used merely as a symptom of social defiance and cynicism. He showed no evidence of sympathy, sorrow, or concern for other human beings, regardless of race, as he almost gleefully reported acts of brutality he had seen inflicted upon them. He was without apparent feeling even when describing brutality directed toward himself. In general he tended to engage in exhibitionistic exaggeration of his role or his observations; these exaggerations at times were indistinguishable from fantasy. There was clear evidence of his rejection and defiance of the larger society — a repudiation of prestige figures, public authorities, Negro leaders, and the police. This rejection of the larger society seemed to be a reaction, fundamentally unconscious and inarticulate, against society for its isolation, rejection, and chronic humiliation of himself.

Generally accepted social values have significance for accepted individuals, but little meaning for those who are rejected and involuntarily isolated from society's benefits. The rejected individual must either construct for himself or acquire from his narrow environment new values appropriate to his restricted and inferior status. These new values may be anti-social. But they strengthen his ego. They tend to give him some security, prestige, and status within the caste to which he has been relegated. It is possible that his disregard for property rights stems from a basic desire for revenge and aggression against something considered so important by the society which has humiliated him.

It is important not to oversimplify the reactions of the Negro to racial frustrations. Because of the dramatic impact of aggressive and violent reactions, it is all too easy to lose sight of the fact that only a small proportion of Negro adolescents react in these ways. One study of the attitudes of Negroes toward the 1943 Harlem riot revealed that a very high proportion of younger Negroes rejected violence as a method for improving the condition of the Negro in America. The younger Negroes for the most part reacted to this display of mass racial frustration with a revulsion which reflected their acceptance of the middle-class values of the larger society. They expressed the belief that violence and other indications of bad manners were not likely to help the Negro in his struggle for racial advance. In short, they recognized the self-defeating nature of open aggressive behavior.

One study suggested that a large number of Negro youths engage in boxing as a form of racial compensatory behavior; it was implied that boxing is an activity that symbolizes mastery and also offers few barriers to the Negro. The same explanation could also be used for the success of Negroes in other sports from which they have not been excluded. However, one should realize that the field of boxing is one in which a majority of the contestants come from underprivileged socio-economic strata of society; since a high proportion of Negroes are found in these lower levels of society, one would expect a high proportion of Negroes to be aspiring prize fighters. In addition to the compensatory factor involved, the minority status of the Negro makes it easier for him to be exploited by white managers and promoters. In this regard, sports like golf and tennis, which do not have mass appeal, continue to exclude Negroes.

It cannot be denied that the outstanding success of some Negro professional fighters and baseball players offers the mass of Negro people a basis for identification. The intensity of this identification partly reflects generalized racial frustration, feelings of hostility toward whites, and the need to compensate. For the oppressed Negro the exploits of Joe Louis, Jackie Robinson, and (more recently) Willie Mays have become the symbols of the breaking of racial barriers and demonstrations of the equality of Negroes.

In his need for racial heroes the Negro in America today is not likely to accept uncritically any Negro who catches the fancy of the white public. The modern Negro hero must be generally free of the usual stereotyped behavior and personality; he must not present himself to the white public as meek, subservient, unreliable, or comic. His personal behavior must be such as to demand respect from even reluctant and prejudiced whites. He must carry himself with dignity as an individual and accept the role of racial ambassador. When these conditions are met, these individuals are acclaimed by their group; they are able to serve as rather complex symbols of compensation for the Negro people and as leaders in the continuous cold war for status.

The various compensatory mechanisms of the Negro are not always clearly conscious or articulate; but they are almost always present. Sometimes the Negro compensates by exaggerated dominant behavior in his relations with whites, particularly under conditions where he is not dependent upon them. At other times his compensatory reactions take the form of an exploitation of the racial guilt feelings of a given white or group of whites, in demanding constant demonstrations of lack of prejudice. More recently, as the economic status of the Negro has been improving, his compensatory techniques have taken the form of the traditionally American demonstrations of conspicuous consumption, such as large and expensive cars, houses, and other materialistic symbols of success. These are his demands for the attention and recognition which he has been denied because of his race and which he believes he deserves as a human being.

Hortense Powdermaker, a social anthropologist, has studied the factors involved in the Negro's handling of his aggressive impulses. She maintains that, in view of the social reality in which whites have superior power and generally are in control of political and law-enforcement agencies of the community, Negroes are rarely able to express their hostility and aggressive impulses directly against them. In his relations with whites, therefore, the Negro is required to adopt substitute or indirect forms of aggression. The larger culture frequently encourages — or certainly does not discourage — the substitution of other Negroes as victims of the repressed aggressions against whites. The relatively large incidence of violence within the Negro group itself tends to support this observation. Other ways in which the Negro may disguise his aggressions are: a retreat to an ivory tower; an identification with his white employer, particularly if the latter has great prestige; a diversion of his aggression into witty and humorous observations on his racial status or on the behavior of whites; or an assumption of the role of the meek, humble, and unaggressive Negro who makes a point of being deferential to whites. He learns what role is expected of him by observing and participating in the larger culture.

However, the culture changes — and the behavior of the Negro alters accordingly. Among the most significant changes is the tendency of the younger Negro to refuse to assume the role of the meek, unaggressive, and ingratiating individual in his relations with whites. These younger individuals have accepted the same goals as whites, and are demanding the attainment of these goals now rather than in the future. The methods by which they seek to attain these goals are the methods characteristic of the American culture — mainly competition and aggressive assertion of individual worth rather than meekness and subservience. Hortense Powdermaker made these observations more than twelve years ago; yet they still provide a sound basis for understanding the role of the Negro in stimulating much of the progress in race relations that has since occurred.

Is it possible to discover what types of individuals are most likely to react anti-socially to their minority status? F. D. Watts studied whether it was possible to differentiate between delinquent and non-delinquent Negro boys in terms of their academic potentialities, emotional stability, social maturity, or differences in habits, interests, and attitudes. He measured all of these factors by standardized tests. He found that it was not possible to distinguish between delinquent and non-delinquent boys, nor was it possible, on the basis of these factors, to predict which boys were likely to become delinquent. When age and intelligence were the same for both groups, Watts found that the essential difference was the fact that the delinquent group seemed to be subject to less parental or adult control than the non-delinquent group. This observation points up need for further study of the role of the immediate home environment of the individual child or adolescent in determining whether his reactions to minority status will result in anti-social behavior. It is possible that a stable family pattern, parental love, and adequate control are particularly necessary for the Negro child if he is to be kept from displaying the more violent and anti-social symptoms.

Allison Davis and his colleagues have made important contributions to an understanding of how differences in social class influence the way in which a given minority-group child adjusts to the larger society. These social scientists maintain that in order to understand how the individual reacts to the larger social forces it is important to understand specific social and economic class pressures, because the child is trained primarily by his family, by his family's social clique, and later by his own peer-group clique. Much of the behavior of children and adolescents is influenced by factors of social class. Deviant sexual, educational, and aggressive behavior by some Negro adolescents may therefore be understood as a reflection not of racial but of class factors.

A comprehension of the effects of minority status upon the personality of Negro children and youth, according to these observers, requires an understanding of the fact that the majority of Negro families belong to the lower social and economic classes. Lower-class Negro children are taught by their families and by contacts with the white society that they must not display open aggression toward white people. Because of this fact and because their inferior status leads to frustration and a need for the expression of aggression, they are required to adopt defensive methods of aggression toward whites, which are acceptable within the bounds of the racially established role or caste. Examples of these defensive aggressions characteristic of lower-class Negro individuals are exaggerated patterns of slowness, clumsiness, simulated ignorance, and general apathy and indifference in contacts with whites. Although the lower-class child is generally taught that he must be subservient to whites because he must work for them, when pushed beyond the accustomed or accepted limits of deference he is more likely than the middle- or upper-class Negro to become openly aggressive toward white people.

It has been observed that lower-class children are more likely to react with violence and anti-social behavior, since they are generally taught to defend themselves by striking first. Aggressive patterns of behavior are a part of the struggle for survival within the lower-class pattern of living. The self-destructive implications of overt aggression and violence in reaction to minority status are less threatening to lower-class Negro adolescents and adults, because they have less to lose than middle- or upper-class Negroes.

The middle-class Negro parent in preparing his child for life teaches him — at least in words — that in spite of racial restrictions and taboos he is in fact equal to whites. Children of this class are trained to control their impulses, to adhere strictly to the demands of respectability, to avoid negative contacts with whites — in short, to keep out of trouble. This parent-child relationship would not be consistent with direct expressions of aggression, overt violence, or anti-social behavior.

The major parental pressure upon the middle-class or upper-class Negro child is the demand that he be a living refutation of the stereotyped picture of the primitive and inferior Negro. Parents sometimes attempt to conceal from their children the lower status of the Negro people in American society. They believe that they thus protect their children from the deep psychological scars resulting from an awareness of belonging to a rejected minority group. However, this tendency is not without its high human costs. These parents often require that their children behave with unrealistic virtues; that they be compulsively clean; that they repress normal aggressive impulses or sexual curiosity; that they assert racial equality by over-compensatory academic, artistic, or athletic achievements. Sometimes this results in exceptional achievement. At other times, when the particular child is not endowed with the necessary intelligence or talent, it results in a psychological casualty.

Margaret Brenman made an intensive study of a small group of Negro girls in order to determine the effects of social class on their personal adjustment; her findings confirm those reported by Davis and his collaborators. Lower-class Negro girls give more open expression to aggressive feelings in their relationships with whites. Among their characteristics are acceptance of the assumption that the Negro is inferior; acceptance of the usual stereotypes of the Negro, which are rejected, at least verbally, by middle-class Negro girls; and rejection of the usual middle-class standards that regulate sexual behavior. The fact that the lower-class Negro girl is not likely to win approval by accepting middle-class standards in restraining her impulsive behavior makes it possible for her to behave with a greater degree of personal freedom.

Middle-class and upper-class Negro girls, on the other hand, closely resemble white middle-class girls in that they accept the same restraints and social demands which they believe will aid them in the attainment of a higher social status. Margaret Brenman noted that these girls not only observed the conventions of the dominant middle-class society in respect to speech, clothes, and general etiquette, but also reacted against the stereotyped concept of the Negro by rigidly controlling their own behavior and at times maintaining almost unrealistically high standards of personal and sexual conduct. A specific manifestation is sexual rigidity in the middle-class Negro girl, which Margaret Brenman believes results from the pressures of well-meaning Negro mothers who demand that their daughters refute the stereotype of sexual promiscuity among Negroes.

There is, then, convincing evidence of the significance of social and economic class status as important factors in the personality adjustment of Negro children and adolescents to their minority status. However, one must be cautious about accepting these interpretations too literally. Class lines among Negroes, although in many ways distinct, are not static, absolute, or rigidly drawn. The process of upward social and economic mobility among Negroes is probably greater than among whites. More and more working-class Negro families are making progress through the usual American techniques of upward class mobility. More of them are sending their children to college; are entering occupations from which they had been previously excluded; are buying houses outside of the Negro ghetto; are becoming a part of the American middle-class pattern. This increasing number of Negroes in the middle class may in itself speed up further positive changes in race relations in America.

As the number of middle-class Negroes increases, the more overtly negative, aggressive, and anti-social reactions to racial frustration will necessarily decrease. One may expect that racial feelings and anxieties in the aspiring middle-class Negro will take different forms. He may seek to cope with his racial conflicts not through self-destructive and anti-social patterns of behavior but by concentrating his energies on overcoming the remaining barriers of his acceptance by the larger society. As he does so, he necessarily identifies himself with the values, methods, and goals of the larger society and seeks to function within its framework. He rejects anything that is contrary to his identification as an American. He tries to attain success and status in ways that are acceptable to the dominant society. In the pursuit of these goals and in their successful achievement, he hopes to demonstrate his equality and his acceptability as an American. Political movements that seek to exploit the grievances of the Negro tend to fail because they do not understand the desire of the Negro to be accepted as an American, rather than to place himself in the role of an antagonistic outsider. The conspicuous failure of the Communist party in its attempt to enlist mass support from Negroes in America indicates this lack of understanding. The Communists' most specific blunder was their promise to provide Negroes with a "separate but equal" nation in the south. All classes of Negroes revolted against this policy of "self-determination" as the ultimate expression of racial segregation.

The extraordinary achievement of individual Negroes in various aspects of American life must be understood not only in terms of their exceptional ability, but also as manifestations of racial compensatory behavior. The pride that Negroes feel not only in sports figures but in such leaders as Ralph Bunche and Marian Anderson is related to the profound currents of racial frustration and aspirations of the masses of Negro people. The psychological value of these individuals is their demonstration that racial oppression need not result in a distortion or dehumanization of human personality. Racial oppression may under certain circumstances stimulate individuals to an extraordinary success unusual for individuals of any group. The fact that such achievement cannot be accepted or understood in purely personal terms demonstrates the degree to which minority racial status involves almost every aspect and every level of personal adjustment. These individuals achieved success because of superior intellect, talent, or abilities; but as they made their contributions to the larger society, their racial status was always a factor in describing or evaluating them.

The recognized achievements of some Negroes, despite rigid racial barriers, indicate that society by its prejudices may be depriving itself of valuable contributions from many others. It is now doubtful whether America can afford the luxury of such a waste of human resources.

It is a mistake to believe that personality patterns found among Negroes indicate inherent racial tendencies. Whenever a group is placed in a position involving disadvantages or stigma, the individuals within the group express comparable symptoms of personality conflicts. This is true of many other groups besides Negroes. One study of the adjustment of Amish children found that these children tended to feel that they were being persecuted. They also betrayed feelings of inferiority as reflected in the belief that they were not as smart as other children, and that other children were stronger and did things better. This study is significant in showing that even the *voluntary* segregation of a group has negative effects on the personality development of its children. The feelings of these Amish children were similar to the feelings observed in Negro children subjected to involuntary segregation.

J. W. Tait in his study of children of Italian-born parents found through personality tests and personal interviews that prejudice and rejection resulted in such character defects as feelings of inferiority, awareness of rejection, poor social adjustment, introversion, and emotional instability.

Guy V. Johnson made an extensive field study of the personal adjustment of the Croatan Indians of Robeson County, North Carolina, in order to determine the nature of their accommodation to the dominant white and Negro world. The Croatans are not accepted by the whites as equals, and at the same time they desire to escape the stigma of being classified with Negroes. Johnson maintains:

> The Indian, then, is forever on the defensive. His wish to escape the stigma of Negro kinship, and thus be identified with the white man is uppermost in his mind. . . . The child learns that the ultimate insult that anyone can give an Indian is to intimate that he has Negro blood. . . . So intense is the feeling on this subject that one can conclude that there is present in many persons a certain "sense of guilt" which arrives from the observed reality (Negroid physical traits) and which calls for constant denial of the reality.

In seeking to resolve this basic conflict, these Indians withdraw among themselves and have as little contact as possible with whites and Negroes. Under the constant pressure of frustration and tension, they develop patterns of aggressive behavior often directed against themselves. Some display displaced hostility and self-hatred. Most violent crimes are committed against fellow Indians.

Similar examples can probably be found among the Mexicans in the southwest portion of the United States, and among the more recent Puerto Rican immigrants in New York City.

When one examines the theoretical discussions and systematic studies of the effects of rejected minority status upon the personality development of children, and when one tries to organize all of this material into a total pattern, certain conclusions and suggestions clearly emerge. Rejected minority status has an unquestioned detrimental effect upon the personality of children. No systematic study or theoretical article dealing with this problem suggests that a human being subjected to prejudice, discrimination, or segregation benefits thereby. There is convincing evidence that the personality damage associated with these social pressures is found among all children subject to them, without regard to racial, nationality, or religious background. The resulting personality distortions therefore must be understood as the consequences of social pressures rather than as reflections of any inherent group characteristics.

As minority-group children learn the inferior status to which they are assigned and observe that they are usually segregated and isolated from the more privileged members of their society, they react with deep feelings of inferiority and with a sense of personal humiliation. Many of them become confused about their own personal worth. Like all other human beings, they require a sense of personal dignity and social support for positive self-esteem. Almost nowhere in the larger society, however, do they find their own dignity as human beings respected or protected. Under these conditions, minority-group children develop conflicts with regard to their feelings about themselves and about the value of the group with which they are identified. Understandably they begin to question whether they themselves and their group are worthy of no more respect from the larger society than they receive. These conflicts, confusions, and doubts give rise under certain circumstances to self-hatred and rejection of their own group.

These children are forced at an early age to develop ways of coping with these fundamental conflicts. Not every child reacts with the same patterns of self-protection. A particular pattern depends upon many interrelated factors, such as the stability and quality of his family relations; the amount of genuine love, support, and guidance he receives from his parents and other important adults in his environment; the social and economic class to which he and his family belong, and the values, attitudes, and aspirations of his friends and associates; the cultural and educational background of his parents; the traditions and patterns of adjustment of the particular minority group to which he belongs; and, finally, his own personal characteristics — his intelligence, his special talents, his unique personality.

Some children, usually of the lower socio-economic classes, may react by overt aggressions and hostility directed toward their own group or less frequently toward members of the dominant group. Anti-social and delinquent behavior may often be interpreted as this kind of reaction to racial frustrations. These anti-social reactions are self-destructive in that the larger society not only punishes the individuals involved, but often interprets aggressive and delinquent behavior in minority-group members as justification for continued prejudice and segregation. The higher proportion of delinquency among minority-group members must be explained in terms of the psychological burdens inherent in racial restrictions.

Middle-class and upper-class children of a minority group are more likely either to react to their racial conflicts by withdrawal and submissive behavior, or to seek a resolution of their racial problems by over-compensatory methods and the attainment of personal success. These children and their families may seek to mold their lives in rigid conformity to the prevailing middle-class values and standards, in order to offer themselves as living refutations of unjust racial stereotypes. They channel their aggressive energy toward this goal with a strong determination to attain personal success in spite of the handicaps of their minority status. While some children in this group have the intelligence and other characteristics to achieve this kind of success, others do not. And all of them are required to pay a high price in emotional tension.

Minority-group children of all social and economic classes often react to their group conflicts by the adoption of a generally defeatist attitude and a lowering of personal ambition. Many of these children also tend to be hypersensitive and anxious about their relations with the larger society, and to see racial hostility and rejection even where they may not actually exist. Although the range of individual differences among members of rejected minority groups is as wide as among other peoples, and although a large proportion of these children develop into constructive and socially useful adults, the evidence suggests that all of these children are unnecessarily burdened by arbitrary racial prejudices.

4. The White Child and Race Prejudice

A normal American parent would resent a description of his child as having the following characteristics — characteristics that a group of University of California social scientists have ascribed to what they call the "authoritarian personality":

He worships the strong and despises the weak.

He has strong impulses toward cruelty toward others and sometimes toward himself.

He is incapable of genuine feelings of love.

He is rigid, compulsive, and punitive in his ideas and behavior.

He is constantly striving for superficial social status; he is willing to grovel before those whom he believes to be his superiors while he is contemptuous of those whom he considers his inferiors.

Even his feelings toward his parents and others in authority are not without deep conflicts; on the one hand he subjugates his own desires to their demands while on the other hand he hates them.

Because he cannot face his negative feelings toward parents and other authorities, he takes out his frustration by aggressions against those whom he considers weak and acceptable as victims.

This description is based on studies of the personality patterns of a group of prejudiced individuals — children, adolescents, and adults.

Because a compulsive strain of cruelty runs through the total pattern of the personality of individuals who view human beings in terms of rigid categories, and who have an intense need to identify themselves with members of their group and to reject members of other groups, it is inevitable that the "authoritarian person" should be prejudiced. He views his own group as superior in every way; any demands for equality on the part of other groups he sees as a threat to his own security.

One of these social scientists, Else Frenkel-Brunswik, described the development of the intensely prejudiced authoritarian personalities in terms of certain factors in childhood experience. These included harsh and threatening discipline at home, distant and severe parents, the suppression of impulses unacceptable to the parents, and the child's fearful subservience to parental demands. The parents tended to be conventional in their goals, anxious about status, and rigid in their social conformity and in their quest for acceptability. They discouraged genuine and spontaneous expressions of feelings. Their children became afraid of their parents and yet dependent on them, eventually surrendering to all parental demands. These children repress negative and hostile feelings toward their parents and consciously accept only an exaggerated idealization of them. These mixed feelings are later expressed in the worship of strong and powerful people and a contempt for weak or "inferior" people.

Non-prejudiced individuals report that their parents demanded less arbitrary obedience, were less preoccupied with status, were less conventional, and showed less anxiety in their demands for conformity. These parents were less punishing and condemning, more constructive, and more spontaneous in demonstrations of affection and emotions.

These unprejudiced individuals, however, are not "ideal" personalities. As adolescents and young adults they searched unrealistically for affection and love in their attempt to re-create the type of relationship which they enjoyed as children in the family. When these cravings were not satisfied, they sometimes resorted to rebellion against society. Because they were basically more secure in their family relationship they could express their disagreements with their parents without fear of retaliation or the loss of love. This did not leave them without some anxieties, conflicts, and feelings of guilt.

Unprejudiced or non-authoritarian persons are more likely to be openly rebellious against other authorities, since they do not need to fear the expression of their opinions about their parents. But unprejudiced individuals are more likely to express their aggressions against relevant and appropriate objects or persons. Unlike prejudiced individuals, they do not feel compelled to find a scapegoat and to vent their repressed hostility and aggression on weak and convenient individuals or groups in society. Dr. Frenkel-Brunswik concluded that in our culture unprejudiced individuals are generally more creative and imaginative than prejudiced individuals. Children growing up in a situation that encouraged the development of intense prejudices were found to be less popular with their classmates, less frequently mentioned as best friends, more talkative and demanding of attention, more concerned with being the boss, more frustrated and complaining, less trustworthy and less helpful.

These findings, however, do not support the view that unprejudiced children are necessarily well adjusted socially and personally. In fact, such children were found to have "more open anxieties," "more conflicts," and "more directly faced insecurities." This observation touches on some of the problems involved in this kind of approach to the understanding of prejudices in children and adults. In a society where prejudice, discrimination, and segregation are the normal social behavior, it is questionable whether an individual who does not conform to this pattern can be wholly adjusted to that society. Nonconformity associated with social sensitivity and creativity may be maintained only at a high personal cost.

The studies of the "authoritarian personality" contribute to an understanding of the childhood and adolescence of intensely prejudiced persons. These individuals are seen within a family setting in which parental attitudes, striving for status, anxieties, conflicts, and rigidities of the parents are transmitted to their children and thus influence the manner in which they see and react to other individuals. These findings would be more meaningful if they showed how the problems reflected in this type of family setting stem from the many and complex pressures of the larger society. The studies of the "authoritarian personality" have not produced adequate explanations either for what determines prejudice or for the consequences of prejudice on the personality. They do show that there is a certain type of personality (with similar childhood experiences) common to some intensely prejudiced individuals. It is still important to discover why one individual reacts to this type of family pressure by the development of intense prejudices, while another individual reacts with less prejudice or even by identification with the victims of prejudice. Another problem raised rather than solved by these studies is whether the "authoritarian personality" always expresses itself in prejudice, or whether intense prejudice is merely one facet which may or may not be present. As we have seen, each individual who develops in a culture in which racial discrimination plays a crucial role necessarily develops some degree of racial prejudice as a normal part of social learning.

The novelist Lillian Smith has written extensively on the problem of racial prejudices in American life. She contends that they result from the same pattern of social forces that influence children's attitudes in such areas as religion, sex, and social status. She has arrived at conclusions strikingly similar to those of the social psychologists who have studied the problem more systematically. She contends that the major forces responsible for the development of prejudices in American children are the anxieties and pressures that parents impose on their children in order to foster the values of respectability and conformity. Conflicts and anxieties in the areas of religion, sex, and social values are part of the context within which the child develops conflicts and anxieties about race.

Some psychologists have approached the problem of the nature of racial prejudice by conducting experiments of the laboratory type. They have concluded that the more prejudiced the individual the less he will be able to modify his behavior when objective conditions require it; that prejudiced individuals have a more constricted range of general interests; that they show less interest and originality in their thinking; that they demonstrate a lower capacity to understand the problems of others; that they have a smaller range of emotional response; that they show less insight into themselves; and that they are generally more inhibited.

There have been a number of psychoanalytic explanations of the origin and nature of intense racial prejudices: that they result from the continuation of infantile patterns of repressed resentment and hostility toward a younger brother or sister; that they are the manifestations of unrealistic and irrational thinking which reflects deep frustrations and repressed hostilities; that they reflect the tendencies of human beings to protect their own self-esteem by ascribing to others the negative characteristics that might apply to themselves. This view explains the stereotyped view of Negroes as an attempt on the part of whites to idealize their own egos by projecting onto Negroes all of the undesirable and negative characteristics that might be found in any group of human beings.

These interpretations offer a fascinating basis for further speculation and research. However, in view of the fact that most of these observations have come from the study of emotionally disturbed individuals, it is a question whether they can be considered as proven. J. F. Brown advises caution in the evaluation of the various psychoanalytic explanations of racial prejudice. He maintains that, because racial prejudices are pervasive and latent throughout the American culture, one should question the value of a search for distinct characteristics in the individual personality that may lead to the development of prejudice. A culture that predisposes the individual to develop some form of prejudice would exert its influence to a certain degree on all individuals — with little regard to their traits of personality or their infantile experiences. It is now widely recognized that human behavior is influenced by repressed and unconscious motives, and that one of the ways in which these motives express themselves is in hostility toward other races and religions. It is equally true that this applies to all types of personalities. Therefore, racial prejudice in the American culture should probably be examined in terms of the problems of the larger society rather than in terms of the difficulties of the individual personality.

Allport and Kramer maintain that approximately 80 per cent of the American population have some appreciable degree of racial prejudice. This estimate raises serious questions about the approach to racial prejudice in terms of the individual personality. It is not reasonable to maintain that four-fifths of the American population have disturbed personalities — unless one assumes that the total culture is unstable. It must be emphasized, however, that the studies attempting to demonstrate an association between prejudice and the personality pattern have dealt primarily with extremely prejudiced individuals. Furthermore, the type of prejudice measured was necessarily based on verbal expression rather than observed behavior. It is not clear whether intense verbal prejudices are necessarily associated with such intense negative racial behavior as incitement to violence. Individuals who take an active role in opposition to the granting of rights to minority people — for instance, leaders in anti-Negro activities — may thereby reveal a fundamental emotional instability. But these individuals, who are a minority in the total population, have not yet been studied.

The individuals who have the normal, respectable, genteel, and acceptable forms of prejudice constitute another large group that has not yet been studied. These individuals cannot be understood simply by classifying them as unstable personalities. They are considered respectable members of society and would understandably be outraged at the spectacle of overt and violent expressions of the racial prejudices of the small number of extreme bigots. If these individuals saw injustices of a non-racial variety perpetrated against other human beings — or even against animals — their concept of their own respectability would be so outraged as to demand vigorous expressions of disapproval. However, studies of racial tensions reveal that these individuals rarely take an active role in discouraging or demanding punishment for the excesses of the bigots. Usually they stand by passively and in effect lend encouragement to the fanatical racists by remaining silent. It does not add to our understanding to explain this type of passive form of racial prejudice in terms of a disturbance of personality.

The college official who tacitly accepts racial and religious quotas for the admission of an individual student to a graduate or professional school; the school superintendent who condones a pattern of gerrymandering of school districts that leads to segregated schools and who closes his eyes to inferior educational standards in the schools attended by underprivileged children; the church official who preaches the virtues of brotherhood while he bows to his congregation's coldness to Negroes or exclusion of them from his church — these people are in general respected members of their community. They are often admired and their opinions sought on important social issues; they may even be active on the boards of interracial and intergroup agencies. Nevertheless they contribute to the entrenchment of racial and religious prejudices by their acceptance of — and at times involvement in — the existing patterns of discrimination. The personality approach to the understanding of this type of passive prejudice is necessarily an oversimplification. It is an academic abstraction of a difficult practical problem.

It is important to know more about the motivation and role of these respectable, non-violent supporters of the racial *status quo.* On the whole, such individuals have more influence on the developing attitudes of children than the small group of emotionally unstable bigots who openly spout vulgar anti-Semitic and anti-Negro remarks. Whatever influence the fanatical racist exerts in a given community, he wields it only through the tolerance and passive support he receives from the more respectable members of the community. The bigot can easily be curbed by existing laws and police power. When he is not so curbed it is because the government authorities, the police, and the respectable members of the community express their own latent conflicts and prejudices by refusing to deal with him as a criminal. They thus deny to members of minority groups the protection against criminal assault and conspiracy that are guaranteed to more privileged citizens. Unfortunately there is no evidence that this "normal" expression of racial prejudice, this ability to tolerate and function in terms of a double standard of social decency, is peculiar to any particular type of personality in American society.

A realistic understanding of the problem of prejudice and personality concerns itself with the larger social climate within which children develop and within which their families seek status and security. Children who are taught the basic, conventional middle-class values of the American culture are at the same time required to learn the appropriate attitudes and patterns of behavior expected of them in their relations with the various groups at different levels of the social hierarchy. While American children of respectable parents are being taught to pursue the symbols of status and success, they are at the same time being taught to compete with others — and to exclude from the area of meaningful competition those who are "obviously inferior." These attitudes are subtly and effectively taught to children from before the time they are required to compete with their classmates for the highest marks, through the inevitable status competition of the adolescent period, up to the time when they are taught the essentials for successful social and economic mobility which should end in a "good marriage" with the "right person."

This total pattern of striving for status and success which characterizes American middle-class life provides the context in which one should seek for an understanding of the origin and nature of hostile attitudes toward other groups of individuals. Anxieties about success and status seem necessarily associated with the need for conformity and the need to deal with those anxieties either through personal achievement or through finding some scapegoat. In a society that provides convenient and socially approved groups as scapegoats, many members of that society uncritically direct their hostility toward these groups. It is, therefore, important to determine under what conditions it is possible for an individual to avoid having some form and degree of racial prejudice in such a culture.

A number of social psychologists have emphasized not the instabilities of the personality but the psychological advantages that prejudices confer on the individual who has them. For instance, Bohdan Zawadski sees a danger in the assumption that prejudice is the result of a neurotic personality structure, or that prejudice may be understood in terms of the simple "scapegoat" theory. He emphasizes that prejudiced individuals gain economic, sexual, and political status. Although he does not deny that some forms of racial prejudice reflect frustrations of members of the dominant group (for frustrations are found among all human beings), he contends that it is necessary to realize that some prejudices are maintained because they appear to be advantageous to those who hold them.

One of the most satisfying advantages derived from prejudice is the feeling that the minority group provides an "excuse" for one's own shortcomings and failings. Prejudiced individuals may substitute wishful ideas of racial grandeur for the realities of personal mediocrity. They may feed their own personal vanities at the expense of members of the rejected minority group, without regard to reality. In order to do this, they must see in their own racial group chiefly virtues and desirable characteristics, while they see in the minority group chiefly vices and infantile characteristics. The feeling that they can identify themselves with the "superior" group and look down upon the "inferior" group provides them with the rationalization for their own wishes for personal superiority. All of this may be done without running the risk of being considered paranoid — provided the delusions are restricted to the area of race. For example, a white shopgirl may with social impunity and sanction play the role of a duchess or privileged debutante in her contacts with a Negro artist or intellectual; a Negro of superior intelligence, talents, and achievements is expected under such circumstances to be deferential in his associations with a mediocre white person merely because of color differences. A white gentile of average intellectual attainments is privileged to behave in a condescending and patronizing manner toward an outstanding Jewish scientist.

These are illustrations of the pattern of relationship between members of a minority and a majority group, which must be satisfying to the egos of the latter. Without such convenient objects for gratification of the ego, the mediocre member of the dominant group would be left in the intolerable predicament of being required to satisfy his vanity by realistic achievement. To fail in this would be to face the stark reality of his own personal inadequacy. Under these conditions, his attitude toward the minority group provides him with the possibility of evading what might otherwise be the devastating realization of his own social, economic, sexual, or intellectual inadequacies.

The evidence of the effects of prejudice on the personality of white children is not so conclusive as that dealing with the effects on Negro children. There are many reasons for this. One is that white children have been less thoroughly studied. Systematic investigations of the personality of the prejudiced individual have only recently been attempted. In addition, it is more difficult to extract the factor of prejudice from the total complex of social pressures and forces which influence white children and to which they react. However, it is possible to use the available findings as a basis for further research into the likely effects of discrimination on the personality of members of the dominant or privileged group.

There appears to be a complex relationship between the total personality structure of an individual and the quality and intensity of his racial feelings. Although this relationship has not yet been stated in precise and definite terms — and might not be any greater than the relationship between total personality structure and attitudes toward sex, religion, war, or politics — it is axiomatic that such a relationship exists. All of the individual's ideas, feelings, and behavior are a part of his total personality and in some ways reflect it. There are some individuals who are extremely prejudiced and at the same time show symptoms of personality disturbances; this would suggest that there is a certain relationship between extreme expressions of prejudice and personality problems. On the other hand, some individuals who show symptoms of extreme personality disturbance are *not* extreme in their racial or religious prejudices. Furthermore, there are no indications of a relationship between average amounts of prejudice and personality disturbances.

There are indications that certain neurotic symptoms may be used by a prejudiced individual to support or express his prejudices. Conversely, some neurotic individuals may express their neuroticism through the absence of racial prejudices — which may reflect a deeper need to rebel against the prevailing norms of their society.

For the present we must be satisfied to see prejudices as the product of many related factors. A prejudiced individual may be expressing, through his prejudice, displaced hostility stemming from some unrelated source of frustration. He may be using his prejudice as a means of expressing unresolved guilt feelings, anxieties, sexual or other conflicts which arise from sources related or unrelated to the objects of his prejudices.

Like other aspects of the personality, racial prejudices reflect basic motives that differ in intensity, quality, and method of satisfaction among human beings. Among the more significant of the complex motives that might be related to prejudices are the need for adequate social status; the need to identify oneself with those who have high status, power, and prestige and to feel a sense of "belonging with" these individuals; the need to conform to the norms, values, attitudes, and behavior patterns that prevail in the society in which acceptance and approval are sought; the need to disassociate oneself from those who are seen as lacking power, prestige, and status; and the need to express hostile and aggressive impulses particularly on a socially approved and convenient object or group. These needs are found in normal and apparently stable individuals as well as in neurotic individuals. The mere existence of them in a person is not enough, at least in American society, to justify diagnosing him as unstable. The intensity of those needs, the factor of whether they can be satisfied in a socially approved manner, and the anxiety and guilt associated with the method of satisfying them might be the basis for distinguishing the neurotic from the normal personality. It has not been clearly demonstrated that individuals with the normal range of prejudices are therefore neurotic.

In observing normal forms of expressions of prejudice among average Americans, one observes certain types of reactions which, if demonstrated in relations with other members of an individual's own race, would be considered symptoms of emotional disturbance. Anti-Negro prejudices are usually associated with unrealistic and irrational fears and hatreds of Negroes. A child who developed unrealistic and irrational fears and hatreds in other areas would be recognized as emotionally disturbed. Anything in an environment that contributed to the development of such symptoms would necessarily be considered detrimental to the child.

The social influences responsible for the development of racial prejudices in American children at the same time develop deep patterns of moral conflict, guilt, anxiety, and distortion of reality in these children. In order to understand the basic and probably inevitable personality problem which the learning of racial prejudice imposes upon the child of the dominant group — who ironically enough is supposed to be the beneficiary of the segregation and discrimination imposed upon children of the minority group — one must understand that such a child is faced with a social situation containing inherent contradictions. The same institutions that teach children the democratic and religious doctrines of the brotherhood of man and the equality of all human beings — institutions such as the church and the school — also teach them to violate these concepts through racial prejudice and undemocratic behavior toward others. It is difficult for the young child to resolve the contradictions when he is taught the importance of justice and fair play by the same persons and institutions who punish him for playing with a child of a different color, or who hold up other children to ridicule or humiliation.

For the white child this poses a fundamental moral conflict, which becomes as much an aspect of his personality as the feeling of inferiority is an aspect of the personality of the Negro child. Just as the Negro child is required to use and adjust to various techniques for the protection of his self-esteem, so must the white child fall back on various techniques of adjustment in his attempt to cope with his profound moral conflict, which soon becomes a personal one. Some children react by a rigid repression or a refusal to recognize the contradiction of the democratic creed inherent in racial prejudice. Others fall back upon partial or temporary repression of one or more of the contradictory ideas. Others begin to accept the rationalizations or excuses that their parents or other adults offer in the attempt to resolve this moral conflict. The uncritical acceptance of the "superiority" of one's own group and the related assumption of the "inferiority" of the rejected group may be considered one way of dealing with this basic problem. Some of these children may develop intense guilt feelings; others may become more hostile and more rigid in their stereotyped ideas in order to protect themselves from recognizing the moral confusion in which they are placed.

It is conceivable that this basic moral conflict imposed upon children of the dominant group influences their adjustment in other areas of society. It is possible that this confusion may express itself in a confusion of the moral and ethical aspects of social and interpersonal relations in general. Moral cynicism and a disrespect for authority may arise in the child of the dominant group as he observes what he may consider the hypocrisy and deceit of his parents and other respected adults in their handling of the racial problem. As alternatives to a repudiation of the parents and other figures of authority, the individual child may seek to resolve his moral conflict by the development of the morally convenient ideology reflected in such assumptions as: "Everyone should look out for himself." "The strong should dominate the weak." "Get what you can while you can get it." "The end justifies the means."

Such manifestations of moral expediency might eventually be expressed in such social problems as political corruption; unethical manipulation in business, sports, and government; a high incidence of criminality and delinquency; and other indications of a general moral breakdown. The uncritical idealization of parents — and then of strong and powerful political and economic leaders — which was described in the studies of the "authoritarian personality" may be seen as an attempt on the part of some children to erect strong defenses against surrendering to the more negative manifestations of the fundamental moral conflict which has been imposed upon them. As we have seen, these individuals, at the same time that they despised the weak, obsequiously conformed to the demands of the strong whom they turned to for moral guidance by fiat — and whom they also hated subconsciously.

The moral quandary and inner stress that racial prejudices impose upon members of the dominant group in a democratic society may express themselves in devious and peculiar forms. Some individuals may express their conflict and guilt by becoming converted to the cause of racial justice. Many such individuals have made valuable contributions to progress in race relations. Others bring to this crusade an intensity and complexity of personal problems and confusions that make it difficult for them to be effective. It is not uncommon for some of these individuals to seek a resolution of their basic racial conflict and guilt by self-conscious attempts at friendliness with members of a minority group — repeating over and over again, as if needing to convince themselves, their protestations that they are free of all racial and religious prejudices. It is difficult to predict how reliable such individuals would be if an issue of human rights were to present itself in their community and if they were required to take an unpopular stand. It is questionable whether such individuals would be able to run the personal risk inherent in taking a strong stand against the prevailing mores.

Undoubtedly the particular way in which a white person reacts to the conflicts aroused by racial discrimination depends upon many factors. Middle- and upper-class whites do not react in precisely the same way to Negroes — nor do they have the same threats and anxieties — as working-class whites. Variations in intelligence, personal stability, integrity, social sensitivity, and experience with different types of human beings are all factors that would influence the particular way in which a given individual handled his attitudes and reactions to Negroes. However, it seems clear that, under conditions of pervasive racialistic thinking in a society, all of the individuals within that society are in some ways influenced by racial considerations.

Although there is no conclusive and systematic evidence that white children are damaged by racial prejudice and segregation to the same extent as Negro children, there is suggestive evidence that they are insidiously and negatively disturbed by these contradictions in the American democratic creed. Children who are taught prejudices are being taught the prevailing racial attitudes, methods, policies, and superstitions of their society. To the extent that they learn these and other social values, they must be considered normal within the framework of the society. On the other hand, children who are being taught prejudices are being given a distorted perspective of reality and of themselves, and are being taught to gain personal status in unrealistic ways. They are learning to establish their own identity as persons and as members of a group through hatred and rejection of others, and they are encouraged and rewarded if the persons they reject happen to be members of the minority group.

One must recognize that children, adolescents, and adults who are struggling for security and positive self-esteem may often take the easy way out by finding someone to look down upon. The encouragement of this tendency discourages the more difficult task of having the individual seek to build his self-esteem by solid and realistic personal achievements.

If parents are to be convinced that it is desirable to eliminate prejudices in their children, they must be convinced in terms of realistic arguments. They must be shown that these prejudices inhibit social progress — that they are signs of primitive tendencies which express themselves in man's inhumanity to man and in his tendency to depress, humiliate, and dehumanize his fellows. They must come to see that prejudices are related to destructive social tensions and conflicts; that they threaten the stability of the democratic foundations of our nation by draining energy from the attempts at constructive solution of our many and vast social problems; and, finally, that they block the full creativity inherent in the personalities of white as well as Negro children. It is for these reasons that one must seek to prevent in American children the continuation of this social disease.

PART TWO

A PROGRAM FOR ACTION

5. What Can Schools Do?

In its decision of May 17, 1954, the United States Supreme Court ruled that state laws requiring or permitting racially segregated schools violate the Fourteenth Amendment of the United States Constitution. The Court reminded all Americans of some of the fundamental principles of democratic education when it discussed the traditional role of our public schools:

Today education is perhaps the most important function of state and local governments. Compulsory school attendance laws and the great expenditures for education both demonstrate our recognition of the importance of education to our democratic society. It is required in the performance of our most basic public responsibility, even service in the armed forces. It is the very fundamental of good citizenship. Today it is a principal instrument in awakening the child to cultural values, in preparing him for later professional training, and in helping him to adjust normally to his environment. In these days, it is doubtful that any child may reasonably be expected to succeed in life if he is denied the opportunity to an education. Such an opportunity, where the state has undertaken to provide it, is a right which must be made available to all children on equal terms.

The Court maintained that to segregate children in public schools solely on the basis of race deprives children of the minority group of equal educational opportunities. According to the Court, "to separate them from others of similar age and qualifications solely because of their race generates a feeling of inferiority as to their status in the community that may affect their hearts and minds in a way unlikely ever to be undone."

For these reasons, the Supreme Court concluded that the doctrine of "separate but equal" — which since 1896 had been the basis of racial segregation in public schools and other areas of life in seventeen states and the District of Columbia — has no place in public education.

Although this decision deals only with the constitutionality of certain laws, its clear and eloquent language calls attention to the problem of the responsibility of the schools for the development of social and racial democratic attitudes in all children.

Long before this historic decision, many Americans believed that in segregated schools it was difficult, if not impossible, to strengthen democracy through sound public education. It is an educational axiom that democracy cannot be taught effectively in an undemocratic setting. Segregated schools are concretely and perceivably undemocratic. White and Negro children who must attend segregated schools are being effectively taught that democracy is, at best, an abstraction that need not influence the individual in daily life. A segregated school gives children an indelible impression of the inferiority of a whole group of people — an impression that cannot be neutralized by any amount of classroom indoctrination in the ideals of democracy; nor by the most effective intergroup-relations programs and assemblies; nor by the best teacher-training methods in human relations; nor by the most sensitive and objective textbooks that present the contributions of different races to the growth of American civilization. Democratic ideals taught only through words are abstract; segregated schools are concrete. Children are less likely to learn from abstract teachings than from the concrete realities of their daily experience.

Segregated schools are symbols of discrimination and a mockery of our democratic ideals. The schools set aside for Negroes are almost always inferior both physically and esthetically. The educational standards in these schools are almost always inferior. Both white and Negro children soon learn that the white school is considered superior, and that the Negro children are sent to separate schools because the society in general considers them unworthy of association with other children. Even if the Negro schools were made equal or superior to the white schools, they would remain concrete monuments to the stigma of the alleged inferiority of the Negro; they would in fact be gilded educational ghettos, reflecting undemocratic and unscientific attitudes that are incompatible with the goals of education.

Segregated schools perpetuate feelings of inferiority in Negro children and unrealistic feelings of superiority in white children. They debase and distort human beings. They impair the ability of children to profit from democratic education. Indeed, they make it practically impossible to educate children in the ideals of democracy. Before the schools of America can play an effective role in improving the level of our democracy — before they can prepare children for life in terms broader than mere academic subject matter — the system of segregated schools must be eliminated.

It would be a serious mistake to maintain that the May 1954 decision of the United States Supreme Court poses a challenge only to the southern and border states where laws require or permit racially segregated schools. With the migration of large numbers of Negroes to northern cities, segregated schools have also developed in the north. This form of segregation is supported not by law but by established custom or by public apathy or by lack of understanding of the general social dangers inherent in segregated residential areas and schools. School segregation arising from these causes is no less damaging to human personality than school segregation based on laws. In the Supreme Court decision, Chief Justice Warren did not contend that segregated schools result in detrimental personality effects only where the segregation is legal. The Supreme Court quoted a decision of the Kansas court holding that the unfavorable impact of segregation in public schools upon colored children "is *greater*[1] when it has the sanction of the law." Even the Kansas decision

[1] Italics added.

made the unqualified statement that "segregation of white and colored children in public schools has a detrimental effect upon the colored children." This language of the Kansas court and the more general language of the United States Supreme Court reflect a recognition of the negative consequences of segregation in education, whether by law or by custom.

Where segregation is based on law, desegregation must be achieved through litigation in the Federal courts. This method has been effective in southern and border states, in a few communities in southern Illinois, and in one community in Ohio. In northern urban communities, however, it is necessary to develop effective methods of community action in order to break down the pattern of segregated schools.

In response to pressure from private citizens, the Board of Education of New York City has taken steps to put the Supreme Court decision into effect. Starting from the proposition that education in a racially homogeneous school is inconsistent with effective democratic education, the Board of Education set up a commission to devise a plan that would prevent the further development of segregated schools and would integrate the existing segregated schools. In December 1954 this commission was also asked to consider the closely related problem of raising the educational standards and vocational aspirations of talented students from economically and socially depressed groups.

Educators must face not only the immediate problems of an effective transition from segregated to non-segregated schools but also the equally important — though less dramatic — problems of subtle discrimination in non-segregated schools. It would be reasonable to expect that these subtle racial problems would be particularly troublesome in schools that have recently changed from a segregated to a non-segregated pattern. If these problems are not understood and dealt with, they may give rise to the mistaken belief that non-segregated education arouses more problems than it solves. It is therefore necessary to examine some of the types of racial problems that may arise in a non-segregated school.

Perhaps the most important of these subtle problems concerns the racial attitudes of Negro and white teachers and administrators, and the various direct and indirect manifestations of these attitudes. One must expect that white teachers and administrators who themselves have been influenced by patterns of segregation will bring to their initial contacts with Negro students feelings, attitudes, and stereotypes reflecting their lack of previous contact with Negroes. It is not uncommon for such whites to believe that Negro children are intellectually and psychologically different from white children, and that these differences will result in inferior academic performance. As a result of these fundamental assumptions, they believe that when a significant number of Negro students are admitted to their school the educational standards will be lowered, and that they must provide specialized counseling to conform to their stereotyped notion of the Negro's inferior abilities and job opportunities. This results in the development of an actual inferiority in the Negro children which appears to justify the original assumption of their inferiority. The burdens on Negro children in an educational situation where they are regarded as peculiar, exotic, or inferior is intensified if they are rejected or ignored by their teachers and classmates. To be regarded and treated as a problem tends almost inevitably to make a human being a problem.

Sometimes teachers in a non-segregated school engage in educational procedures that intensify the racial and social burdens of their students, like the teacher in the New York City public school who segregated her white, Negro, and Puerto Rican pupils according to her estimate of their reading ability. She maintained that this was a wise educational procedure designed to encourage her students to do better work, and that it just happened that her white students were the best readers. This type of psychological insensitivity can be devastating to children in a racially mixed school.

If a school is to be truly interracial, it must include Negroes and whites not only as students but also as administrators and teachers. If a child observes that in his school all the adults with prestige and authority are of one skin color, while all those in menial positions are of another, naturally he begins to believe that skin color is an aspect of status. This belief is all the more likely to arise if reinforced by his observations of his community. A school can therefore contribute to the democratic education of its students by selecting and assigning personnel on the basis of training, skill, competence, and personality, without regard for skin color.

Some Negro teachers who are placed in a non-segregated setting for the first time may bring their own anxieties and stereotyped thinking to the new situation by being self-conscious and over-critical of themselves. Others may be hypersensitive or defensive in their relations with white parents and colleagues. Still others may be either aggressive or retiring. The ability of a competent Negro teacher to play a constructive role in the non-segregated school environment will be largely determined by the degree to which he feels that he is accepted as a human being — that he is judged by the same standards of professional skill and performance as other teachers. When administrators manage to provide this climate, then the initial manifestations of awkwardness can be expected to disappear in a surprisingly short time.

Some private schools have developed the practice of recruiting at least one Negro for each class, either as a demonstration of democracy or to provide an educational experience for their other students. (Since relatively few Negroes can afford the fees of such schools, these Negro children are often given substantial tuition allowances.) Occasionally the Negro child in these circumstances is intellectually inferior to his average white classmate. When this difference is conspicuous, the children may tend to associate the child's inferiority with his skin color. Rather than learning "democracy," these children are learning racial discrimination in a very concrete way. Furthermore, no child should be required to bear the burden of being a mere symbol — and certainly not a racial symbol. Any child with special talents may develop disturbing personality symptoms if his parents or teachers react to him primarily in terms of his talents rather than as a complete person. Similarly, a Negro child who is accepted, not for himself, but merely because he is Negro might be expected to react by symptoms of aggressiveness, exhibitionism, or submissiveness.

A Negro mother discussed with a psychologist her daughter's difficulties with a social-studies teacher. The girl was the only Negro in the class. The teacher, probably with the best intentions, always chose this child to give reports on topics dealing with the Negro. The child, who bitterly resented being thus singled out, showed her resentment. The teacher asked the parents to a conference. She told them that the child's behavior reflected an unrealistic desire on the part of middle-class Negroes to deny their racial heritage. This interpretation increased the hostility of the parents toward the teacher; and this parental hostility was communicated to the child.

What the teacher did not take into account was the fact that a child who is the only Negro in a class is almost certain to be hypersensitive about racial matters. Any child, in his almost unceasing struggle for status in the eyes of his classmates, resents being singled out — unless the respect in which he is being given special attention is clearly one of high status. Even these, if repeated, may disturb the delicate balance of his relations with his peers.

Some teachers in a non-segregated school may bend over backward in their desire to be fair to their Negro students. These teachers, probably motivated by over-solicitous feelings that reflect deep feelings of guilt, may react by not holding Negro students to the same standards of achievement and conduct as prevail for the white children. Conceivably this might be necessary, in some communities, in the initial stages of transition from a segregated to a non-segregated school, in order to help the

Negro child make up for the handicaps of his previous inferior schooling. However, it would be unfortunate if this pattern persisted and became a fixed practice. Certainly under these conditions the Negro child would not be helped to develop his full potentialities. Furthermore, the white children would understandably resent demonstrations of preferential treatment for the Negro children. The teacher's pet has always been resented. There is no reason to believe that the "pet" will be less resented if he is set apart on racial grounds.

Another type of problem in a newly non-segregated school may reflect the difficulty posed for some whites by having to deal with unusually intelligent or competent Negroes. An exceptional student of any race poses significant psychological threats for some teachers; this general problem may be intensified when the intelligent child is a Negro. If the teacher does not react to him in terms of his needs as an individual, he may become a serious behavior problem. If the teacher treats such a child as a freak, or if she resents him not only because of his exceptional intelligence but also because of his race, he will understandably react with deep resentment. He may express his feelings by boastful and exhibitionistic behavior designed to call attention to his brilliance; or he may use devious means to express his hostility toward the teacher. By virtue of this confusion in his school relationships, such a child may become unable to use his intelligence constructively.

In the early stages of the transition from segregated to non-segregated schools, many teachers and administrators will be anxious about the role of the Negro parent and the kind of relationship they can establish with these parents. Many Negro parents, understandably, will bring to the new situation certain anxieties, perhaps reflected in self-conscious, aggressive, or oversubmissive behavior. If teachers and administrators realize that these symptoms arise from natural awkwardness in a new social situation, and if they avoid giving the symptoms a racial interpretation or more significance than they warrant, the awkwardness will tend to disappear as the Negro parents and their children become accepted as an integral part of the life of the school. Condescension or rejection by teachers and administrators, or over-aggressive and hypersensitive behavior by parents, will prolong this period of adjustment.

A non-segregated school should re-examine its textbooks in order to see that no race or nationality is held up to ridicule, intentionally or unintentionally. Standard textbooks in American schools almost never deliberately attack or humiliate any of the groups that comprise the American population. However, the overwhelming majority of textbooks fail to deal positively with the basic problems of good human relations; generally they do not describe the contributions made by various races to the growth and development of America as a great nation. The average child may well assume that the greatness of America is solely the result of a Northern European or even an Anglo-Saxon heritage. This conception deprives many children of their share in the pride that comes from being an integral part of America.

The normal concern for insuring an effective transition from segregated to non-segregated schools may lead to an exaggeration of the anticipated problems. Actually, successful interracial activity in public schools may be achieved by relatively simple procedures. If teachers and administrators see children as human beings with the ability to learn — rather than as Negro children or white children, who will necessarily present certain racial and educational problems — then there should be little difficulty in meeting their educational needs. The basic principles of fair play and justice, important in any group of children, are even more important in a classroom where there are children of different races, religions, and nationalities.

Negro children should be neither preferred nor rejected because of their skin color. All children are sensitive to unjust or preferential treatment on the part of adults in authority. Children recognize injustice and — at least when they are young

— seem deeply resentful, even if some other child is the immediate victim. It is only later that they become calloused to the subtle injustices of the adult world. Classroom practices should not violate the child's sense of his own worth and integrity — or his sense of the worth and integrity of others. The humiliation of any single child in a very real sense robs every other child of some of his humanity.

If teachers and administrators recognize their responsibilities in the area of racial practices and procedures, including a concern for the control of prejudiced behavior on the part of those in authority; if they refuse to exaggerate "racial" incidents or differences; if they are concerned with the constructive role of textbooks and class discussions; if they are sensitive to the many subtle human problems that may be expected in the transitional stages; if they realize that the over-all atmosphere of the school, including the assignment of personnel, inevitably communicates either democratic or undemocratic racial patterns — then one can expect that in a surprisingly short time Negro and white children will gain a respect for one another based on the intelligence and personality of each individual. Such an atmosphere will produce a setting where it will be possible to provide all children with the foundations of democratic education.

In such a school, there will be no need for the self-conscious and often ineffectual procedure of an isolated "intergroup relations" program, with a specified duration of a day or a week. In such a school, children will not be required to attend an assembly program on a given day of the year when it is emphasized that Negroes too are considered to be Americans — thus implying that on other days they may be considered less "American" than other children. Concern for all children, every day of the school year, means that an "intergroup relations" program is an integral part of the atmosphere. This is the achievement of the truly non-segregated school.

6. What Can Social Agencies Do?

Many Americans have long recognized that racial prejudice, discrimination, and segregation are not only violations of our democratic creed but also symptoms of a dangerous social situation. For both ethical and practical reasons, a large number of organizations and agencies have been established in America for the improvement of race relations. A recent survey showed that there were nearly four hundred public and private race-relations agencies, with at least 750 local branches. Some of these agencies concentrate on the problem of a given minority group, some on specific areas of discrimination (in housing, employment, or education), while others attempt to deal with the total problem of racial and religious injustice. The time, money, and attention now being devoted to the attainment of a more democratic America are truly impressive. This is not only a testament to the average American's willingness to join or support organizations, but an indication of the strong belief in the validity of the American democratic creed. (One could also consider these agencies as in part a reflection of the basic guilt that many Americans feel in the area of race. Sometimes it is easier to appease one's conscience about a disturbing problem by supporting and working with an organization than exposing oneself to the risk of unpopular individual action.)

In spite of the imposing array of these race-relations agencies, there is none with a specific and systematic program designed to prevent the detrimental effects of prejudice, discrimination, and segregation on the personalities of children. The increasing recognition of the human consequences of these forms of social injustice demands the attention of educators, religious and social-welfare workers, politicians, and parents. No society can afford the luxury of having a sizable proportion of its children distorted and crippled in their social and personal functioning. It is clear that practically no American child fully escapes some of the impact and burden imposed by racial discrimination. The absence of agencies with the specific purpose of protecting children from racial tensions is a serious gap in the chain of child-welfare and race-relations activities; a general program designed to develop positive personality characteristics in children does not necessarily help children cope with racial problems. Certainly, even if this were true for children of the dominant group, it would not be so true for children of the minority group. Children of a rejected minority group do not generally obtain equal benefits from the constructive programs, institutions, and services provided for more privileged children. Not infrequently the minority-group child is either excluded, segregated, or in some way treated differently. This is observed by the other children and inevitably creates moral and ethical confusion in them, thereby negating the intended benefits for all.

As the importance of the personality consequences of racial discrimination becomes more generally recognized, social agencies will have to re-examine their own racial policies and practices. Social and child-welfare agencies contribute to the stability of our society through strengthening the personality of individuals. Their ability to make a contribution to the improvement of race relations depends upon the degree to which they themselves are not influenced by racial thinking and practices. It is too much to expect that all of the individuals who control and execute the policies would themselves be free of the personal and social manifestations of racial prejudices. It is a paradox that some social-service agencies continue to exclude members of minority groups who are most in need of their help. Others accept a token number of such people in order to appease their feelings of guilt and in an attempt to satisfy some part of their social conscience. Still others have strict quotas as to the number of minority-group members whom they will serve.

Another sign of discrimination is the existence of agencies dealing exclusively with a given minority group. Many such agencies — with, for instance, only Negro clients — reflect the general pattern of community segregation. What is even more serious, they tend to perpetuate segregation and thereby reinforce rather than ease the detrimental effects on the personality.

A social agency that demonstrates through its own structure a pattern of genuine interracial activity will be most effective in helping members of minority groups. At present it is difficult to find a truly interracial agency that works effectively in reducing the economic and psychological racial pressures upon the Negro. Such an agency cannot be imposed upon the Negro community by detached, impersonal whites, no matter how great their good intentions and intellectual motives. The agency must be careful not to strengthen the barriers of segregation but must help individuals attain dignity and acceptance as human beings. A genuinely successful interracial agency will be the result of the co-operative efforts of truly mature individuals sensitive to the fundamental human needs of the people whom they seek to help. It cannot select its personnel through the transparent maneuver of having a token number of individuals of one or the other group. Nor can a strong and effective interracial agency be built by selecting staff members of different races primarily in terms of their race, with little regard for their qualifications and the degree to which these are appropriate to the job at hand. To have an unqualified Negro in a job in order to demonstrate that an agency is democratic helps neither the agency, the society, nor Negroes. There are a number of qualified Negroes who can be evaluated by the same standards used for professional evaluation of whites. Either a positive or a negative use of a "double standard" of judgment is an indication of racial prejudice

— and an increasing number of intelligent Negroes see it as such.

The same is true for an effective unsegregated school or other social institution such as a church. (Effective racial policies and programs for schools, churches, and other community institutions are discussed in other chapters.)

Child-guidance clinics and other mental-hygiene agencies are even more inadequate for Negro children than for the general population. It is true that many children with behavior problems so severe as to require specialized psychiatric services are reacting not primarily to racial difficulties but to more general social and family maladjustments. Nevertheless, some of these children reveal in their approach to life, and often in their symptoms, the important role that racial feelings play in the total pattern of their personalities.

The following case offers an extreme example of the effects of the confusion of racial problems in the total pattern of personality difficulties of an intelligent Negro boy of twelve. One of a few Negroes in a school for exceptional children, he was referred to a child-guidance center because he was unable to concentrate on his school work. His role in the classroom seemed intentionally disruptive. Instead of doing his assignments or answering the teacher's questions, he would embark on long, esoteric discussions of theoretical physics or obscure and confused mathematical problems. While his classmates were sometimes amused, sometimes irritated, and sometimes awed by him, his teachers understandably interpreted his attention-getting behavior as a symptom of deep maladjustment. The teachers recommended that he be given psychiatric help. He was accepted by a child-guidance clinic and assigned to a white psychiatrist, who was soon able to win the boy's respect and encouraged him to talk out his basic anxieties and conflicts. The psychiatrist reported that it was not long before the child began to express directly and indirectly many feelings and frustrations about race and his racial identity. His preoccupation with racial stereotypes and frustrations was indicated in a fantastic play he wrote.

The play is called *Morlow, King of Blacks, of the NiggIlses* and its characters are divided into "Niggers," "Kikes," and "whites." The Negroes come to the king of the Jews, and a messenger reports their arrival:

> There await without
> Two niggers of rank,
> One black as the tar
> That roofs this place,
> The other brown as mahogany.

The Jew addresses them as follows:

> Oh, pagan Blacks,
> As homage, you
> Are commanded to
> Set your lips
> Upon my foot.

And the Negro king replies:

> Hold, Jew!
> If this I pay you,
> In turn I expect the same.

Then the young playwright reports: "They kiss each other's feet." The reason why the Negroes have come, he continues, is this:

> Those of the whites are here.
> I fear that they would take
> The NiggIlses
> And kill my black race . . .

The Jewish leader answers in the play's most bitter speech:

> O damned niggers,
> O bastards of thy pagan race,
> I am like all of Jews
> (Mercenary, rich) . . .
> I spit upon your face.[1]

For this boy, symbols of racial and religious inferiority, conflict, and ambivalence have been deeply imbedded in his feelings.

---

[1] In these passages, the boy's erratic spelling has been corrected.

However, not all Negro children seen in child-guidance clinics display such intense racial conflicts. It is not uncommon for seriously disturbed children to go through an entire period of treatment and be discharged as significantly improved without once expressing any serious racial anxieties. Many of these children, like other children, are preoccupied with immediate family or community problems that obscure or displace any concern with racial problems. However, even some of these children may under certain circumstances reveal their sensitivity and awareness to racial pressures by indirect ways. The following case has been described in a psychiatric journal:

Jane was an attractive seven and one-half year old Negro girl who was brought to the child guidance clinic because of nervousness, forgetfulness, and confusion about family relationships. She tended to be domineering with playmates, but with adults was talkative and friendly in an indiscriminate fashion. She came from a broken home, and had lived in two different foster homes. The first foster parents complained that she was aggressive and unmanageable. The confusion about family relationships was very understandable. Not only had she lived in three different homes, but she and her sister, who lived a block away, used the different surnames of their respective foster parents. Also Jane's foster parents from time to time cared for other temporary foster children, and during their residence in the household these children were called sisters and brother.

In play therapy she showed compulsively neat activity with each toy, but disorganized, disconnected and confused play with an inability to sustain any one theme, and easy distractability by outside stimuli. Her verbalizations were facile and the psychiatrist felt that Jane made only a superficial relationship to her.

The differential diagnosis was between neurotic personality with confusion as to identity, and psychopathic personality. After two months of weekly play therapy sessions, she began to show silly, buffoonish and irritating behavior, alternating with ingratiation. The therapist's questions were either ignored, mimicked or ridiculed. This behavior continued for the next three months, and the therapist finally considered her inaccessible to therapy, with the diagnosis of psychopathic personality. The therapist recommended that therapy be discontinued. However, at this time, a report of the child's outside living relationship gave an entirely different perspective on the results of treatment. The report indicated that the child had improved dramatically and markedly in every area of functioning. It was clear that the therapist's evaluation had been incorrect; and discussion of the case revealed that the therapist, a white woman, was judging the child's reactions to her, without giving adequate consideration to the fact that the child was Negro and that this would profoundly influence her reactions to any white person. In terms of the hostile, unbridgeable gap that this Negro child felt between her and any white woman, the development of this buffoonish behavior actually represented a movement toward the therapist. Her "carrying on" in this flippant manner was her manner of establishing an initial relationship with this hitherto awesome, threatening figure, rather than an inability to establish a relationship.[2]

In the same article, the discussion of another child reveals still another way in which racial problems may become involved in the serious adjustment problems of children:

Edward was an eight year old Negro boy, referred to the clinic with a variety of symptoms and fears in his school situation. He wet himself in school, didn't play with the other children, would not read, and was afraid of his teacher. At home, he manifested none of this behavior.

His symptoms were intense, and ordinarily would have been considered evidence of serious emotional disturbance. However, evaluation in terms of social setting shed a different light on them. His family had recently come from the south, where they had been sharecroppers and had lived on a marginal income. They had had a number of fear-inspiring experiences with white people, in which they were cheated, threatened, intimidated and terrorized. Edward, like the rest of the family, had been taught not to fight back with white people, and to exercise the greatest care not even to express his thoughts and feelings to them. In New York he found himself in a strange, bewildering school set-up, and had a white teacher for the first time. In terms of his experiences and conditioning with white authority figures, it was normal for him to be fearful, afraid to ask questions, and even afraid to ask permission to go to the toilet. It is not strange that he could neither learn or hold his own with the other children in such a setting.

The final diagnosis was a situational reaction in an essentially normal boy. This diagnosis was confirmed by the rapid strides he made in treatment, which included active work with the school.

There is a need for specialized psychiatric services for these children, whose racial and social maladjustments impair their

---

[2] From S. Chess, K. B. Clark, and A. Thomas, "The Importance of Cultural Evaluation in Psychiatric Diagnosis and Treatment."

functioning in the home, school, or community. This need has not been met. This lack reflects not only the general inadequacy of child-guidance facilities but also public indifference to the need of some children for psychiatric help in order to cope with intense racial burdens.

Unfortunately many of the existing child-guidance clinics may not be able to provide the specialized kinds of services which might be needed by these children. Private psychiatric services cost more than most Negro families and many white families can afford to pay. Moreover, child-guidance clinics are scarce even in the more advanced communities, and completely absent in most American communities. In addition, most existing child-guidance facilities are neither sensitive to nor equipped to deal with the manifestations of racial pressures in the behavior of children. In order to meet this problem effectively, professional personnel would have to be trained.to recognize the many forms, direct and indirect, obvious and subtle, that racial preoccupation can take in children. The staff of these child-guidance clinics should be individuals who are themselves relatively free of racial stereotyped notions and racial rationalizations. They should recognize that differences in cultural and educational background may be reflected in differences in personality, and they must be sensitive to the essential humanity common to all people.

A professional worker who sees children primarily in stereotyped terms of their minority status, or who is subtly condescending and patronizing in his relations with them, cannot help them with their fundamental racial problems. The essential task of the representatives of these agencies should be that of providing for these children at least one haven within which they may obtain respect, dignity, and acceptance as human beings. As the child begins to understand that is so, as he takes this for granted in his visits to the center and in his relations with the professionals whom he sees, he may be able to understand that the world in which he lives need not always be hostile and rejecting. He may come to learn that it is possible for him to be respected and, in learning this, feel more adequate and therefore more capable of respecting others.

It must be clearly understood that a psychiatric service for children whose personalities have been severely disturbed by racial oppression must not attempt to have these children accept and submit to prevailing racial injustices. Instead, an effective and socially meaningful goal of psychiatry for these emotionally disturbed children must be to strengthen their personalities. When this is done, they can then contribute their energies to an effective and intelligent change of those conditions which distort and cripple the personalities of other children.

The goals of a child-guidance center must therefore be an integral part of the goals of all social agencies and other organizations working for social progress. Improvements in economic and living conditions, in health, housing, and nutrition; the elimination of various forms of segregation; the encouragement of all children to prepare themselves for increased vocational opportunities so that they can make the best possible contribution to the progress and stability of society — all of these will help to provide the climate within which no child will be required to bear an arbitrary and excessive burden. This, after all, is the promise of American democracy. The primary responsibility for guaranteeing the fulfillment of this promise for the benefit of all children must be borne by vigilant parents.

7. What Can the Churches Do?

A majority of American children have some contact with churches, Sunday schools, or other religious institutions. These religious organizations can play a decisive role in the development of more positive racial attitudes in children. In fact, this would seem to be one of the responsibilities of religious institutions in our society, since they are primarily responsible for the perpetuation of the moral and ethical heritage of our civilization. To what extent has the church taken the initiative in providing moral guidance for children in the area of their racial attitudes and behavior?

There is no simple and direct answer to this question. During the past decade, many Protestant denominations have issued statements and passed resolutions in favor of better race relations in America. As early as 1946 the Department of Racial and Cultural Relations of what is now the National Council of Churches of Christ in the U.S.A. made the following pronouncement:

> The Federal Council of Churches of Christ in America hereby recognizes the pattern of segregation in race relations as unnecessary and undesirable and a violation of the gospel of love and human brotherhood. Having taken this action, the Federal Council requests its constituent communions to do likewise. As proof of their sincerity in this renunciation they will work for non-segregated church and a non-segregated society.

In spite of this and similar pronouncements and resolutions calling for an end of segregation in the Christian churches, and in society as a whole, the Christian Protestant churches represent one of the most entrenched areas of racial segregation still existing in American society. Of the nearly 7,000,000 Negroes who are members of Protestant denominations, only about 500,000 are affiliated with denominations that have Negro as well as white churches; of these 500,000, only 50,000 are in denominations that are predominantly white. Practically all of these 50,000 worship in segregated congregations and have only infrequent contacts with white church members of their denominations. The stark fact is that less than one-half of 1 per cent of Negro Protestant Christians in the United States worship regularly in non-segregated churches.

The bulk of white and Negro children therefore may well view their churches as cloistered islands of racial exclusion. These children inevitably observe that their churches not only reflect, but appear to intensify, the pattern of racial segregation that exists in the larger community. Under these circumstances the church focuses for the child the moral dilemma inherent in preaching the ideals of brotherhood while practicing racial segregation. This discrepancy between ideals and practice is all the more conspicuous in churches and religious institutions, since their reason for existence is their moral and ethical role.

Just a few years ago, the research staff of the Mid-Century White House Conference on Children and Youth asked major church organizations to furnish information concerning their racial policies and specific programs designed to combat racial prejudices in their parishes. The answers suggested the following conclusions:

A majority of these church organizations had no specific programs in the area of improving race relations. Some replies stated that such programs were unnecessary, because the principle of Christian brotherhood was implicit in their religion.

There was evidence, sometimes explicit, that some of the social-welfare agencies affiliated with religious organizations and denominations practiced racial discrimination and religious sectarianism in the selection of the individuals whom they would serve.

Many of the pronouncements and programs described by these organizations seemed vague and tentative; there was little evidence that the fight for interracial justice was being waged in a definite, systematic, vigorous manner and as a sustained aspect of their over-all religious program.

No one of these groups described a concrete program designed specifically to help children develop more positive attitudes and patterns of behavior in their relations with individuals of other racial and religious groups.

The closest approach to such a systematic program was found in a study outline developed by the Board of Christian Education of the Presbyterian Church, and published by the Westminster Press in the form of one of the units in a Youth Fellowship Kit. The material included an article by Frank S. Loescher entitled "The Protestant and the Negro." In this article Mr. Loescher stated:

Protestantism, by its policies and practices, far from helping to integrate the Negro in American life, is actually contributing to the segregation of the Negro American. . . . The Negroes are largely Protestant, but are not associated with white Protestants. Most of them are separated from Caucasians by being in different denominations; there are separate local churches or even racially separate synods, districts, jurisdictions, etc.

This Fellowship Kit did not encourage its readers to deal with the problem only in verbal and abstract terms. It raised provocative questions, and outlined the following concrete program for action:

YOU DECIDE:
As you and the group read through these suggestions for action and discuss them, remember that this topic will be used by thousands of young people all over the country. We have tried to include some suggestions that will illustrate every situation. You must decide which

suggestions fit your situation. But be sure you decide as a *Christian*, not as a person who wants above all else to be popular, or to avoid criticism. Be sure you are looking for the right way, not the easy one.

1. Through prayer and Bible study, seek the grace of God in overcoming any "strange feelings" you may have toward any group and in developing a sincere feeling of kinship with all your fellowmen.

2. As a beginning, find ways to become acquainted with at least one person or family of each racial and cultural group in your community.

3. Extend common courtesies and titles of address to persons of all groups, regardless of sinful community customs, regardless of their position, and however strange it may seem at first.

4. Learn the difference between paternalism (that is, loving down, loving in "their place") and true Christian respect of one human being for another.

5. Keep a close check on your thought and feelings. Watch out for any tendency to blame whole groups of people for what individuals do.

6. When you hear rumors that reflect on any group, demand proof. Do not repeat lies.

7. Never use hateful terms that slur any group. Show disapproval when others use them.

8. Do not tell stories, however funny, that reflect on any group. Do not laugh at them.

9. As a present or future employee, welcome new workers without regard to race or creed. Make very sure the boss does not refuse to hire people of some group because he imagines you would resent it. If you are seeking a new job, inquire among organizations where no such distinctions are made.

10. Request a policy of non-discrimination where you spend your money. (Remember, business firms may discriminate in employment and in serving customers because they imagine this pleases *you*. Make sure they know that it *does not.*)

11. Where there is a choice, take your patronage where there is the most democracy in every way. And let the proprietor know why.

12. In the North, when going with interracial groups to public places, always assume that you will be served. Many places will say "no" if you ask in advance, but will serve you when you come. It is good education for them to know you assume that they will serve you.

13. When informed by summer resorts and hotels that they serve "Christians only," be sure you are one Christian they will not serve. Cancel reservations and tell why.

14. Watch out for the term "restricted." It generally means discrimination against someone.

15. When the first families of a new racial or cultural group move into the neighborhood, take the lead in extending a cordial welcome.

16. Refuse to be a member of any social club or fraternity or sorority if other people are barred because of race or creed. A "general understanding" may be a most effective and vicious bar. (How many of us Christians are members of clubs to which Jesus the Jew would be ineligible?)

An evaluation of this excellent guide to concrete and positive racial behavior leaves unanswered the following question: To what extent have these excellent suggestions influenced the day-to-day behavior of the individuals who were exposed to them?

Probably American churches, like American schools and colleges, have generally failed to offer moral guidance in terms of concrete action programs for the improvement of race relations because the church, like secular institutions, feels compelled to conform to the existing patterns of social attitudes, values, and norms found in the larger society. If the church permits itself to become a captive of the more practical and materialistic pressures of the larger society, then it will be unable to provide for our children the example of positive race relations which they need.

A refusal to take the initiative in this regard can only intensify the conflict and dilemma of church officials. They might be fearful that a vigorous action program designed to break down segregation and improve race relations would lead to a loss of power and status for themselves. In fact, however, a refusal to take the initiative must inevitably result in loss of effective moral leadership and an inability to exert a positive influence on the racial attitudes of American children.

It is significant that the Federal courts, and particularly the United States Supreme Court, have taken the moral leadership and initiative in the area of improving race relations in America. Before the Supreme Court's decision of May 17, 1954, the Roman Catholic Church had provided important demonstrations of methods that might be applied in the desegregation of the public schools, by the desegregation of their parochial schools in border communities. The effect of this action on the Supreme Court's decision is not definitely known; but it may have had some influence on the opinion of the Court that desegregation of the public schools could be accomplished. If this is true, then the Catholic Church has made a major contribution to the improvement of race relations in America.

Since the May 17 decision, many national church organizations, including many of the southern church bodies, have passed resolutions supporting the decision and indicating their willingness to work for its implementation. The May 17 decision may well provide the necessary stimulus and encouragement for the Christian churches of America to develop vigorous programs in race relations.

A survey of the role of the church in American race relations from 1900 to the present seems to indicate that the reiteration of formal resolutions is not in itself effective. Resolutions and pronouncements cannot in themselves determine the kinds of experiences that children must have in order to develop more positive racial attitudes and behavior. The church cannot expect to be taken seriously in this area of moral guidance as long as it continues to talk against segregation while maintaining rigid patterns of racial segregation within its own walls. The concrete fact of segregation within the church is more likely to influence the racial attitudes of children than abstract pronouncements and resolutions, no matter how strongly worded. Isolated examples of interracial parishes, or an occasional visit to a Negro church, or the extension of an invitation to a "nice" Negro family — these cannot be considered meaningful racial experiences for children. While these activities are not in themselves detrimental, the church can be effective in the improvement of race relations only when it demonstrates in a concrete and dramatic way that it is willing to abolish racial segregation in a major social institution in America. In many communities in northern and southern states the Roman Catholic Church has demonstrated that a systematic program of desegregation within the church can be accomplished without social chaos in the church or in the community.

While it must be recognized that an individual church is generally considered to be an intimate family social institution, it must also be recognized that the church has the responsibility of developing moral sensitivity in the children and the families associated with it. The Negro church historically developed as a protest against the racial discrimination of the white church, either in the segregation or in the exclusion of Negroes. The Negro faced this paradox of Christianity by developing his own religious denominations where he could worship God without being humiliated. With the progress in race relations in other areas of life, Negro and white Christians must modify existing racial patterns within the Church itself.

The claim that Negroes themselves desire segregation may be more true in their attitudes toward the church than toward any other institution. Middle-aged Negroes may see their church not only as a source of religious inspiration but also as a social center where they obtain personal gratifications denied them elsewhere in the larger community. For this and other reasons they may be reluctant to accept the dissolution of the Negro church. But younger Negroes may well see segregation in the church as part and parcel of other patterns of social segregation.

Recently the Colored Methodist Episcopal Church passed a resolution in its national convention to change its name to the "Christian Methodist Episcopal Church." The change, while conveniently maintaining the same initials, officially indicates that this church body is no longer restricted to Negroes. Effective action, of course, requires not only changes of name among Negro and white denominations but also positive programs that will result in congregations composed of individuals with similar religious interests without regard to skin color.

While this change is developing, Negro and white parents concerned with the effects of segregation on their children will wish to give them the opportunity to attend racially mixed churches wherever this is possible. This might seem strange at first to the children and to other members of the congregation; but with fundamental good-will and a basic appreciation of the meaning of religion on the part of all concerned, there should be no reason for this strangeness to continue for long. Furthermore, this type of experience should contribute to the strengthening of religious conviction of the white and Negro members of the congregation — provided the church neither restricts the number of Negro members, nor acts over-solicitous in its treatment of the Negroes. If the Negro family is accepted in the church and the Negro child accepted in the Sunday school on the same basis as other new members of the congregation, there should be no reason for problems to develop or continue.

At the time when the church is first moving toward racial inclusiveness, it should find some opportunity to make this fact perfectly clear to all members of the community. By being either apologetic and defensive or self-righteous in its proclamations, the church would defeat its own purpose. It might be advisable to make a public announcement of the new racially inclusive policy. Such a forthright announcement by a given church would encourage other churches to take a similar stand. In this way, individuals concerned with problems of racial injustice in America will feel that they have support and backing for their personal behavior from a respected social institution.

While acknowledging the important role the church can play in the formation of positive racial attitudes in children, one must also recognize the realistic limitations of the influence that any single social institution can exercise in a given community. This is particularly true when the ideas communicated by the given social institution are different from, or in conflict with, the patterns that the child observes in the larger community in which he lives. Schools and churches cannot in themselves significantly improve the community's attitudes and behavior merely by the development of isolated programs that are not part of the total pattern of daily life. The maintenance of rigid patterns of racial segregation within the community makes difficult, if not impossible, significant changes in the racial attitudes of children. More and more attention must be paid to such urgent community problems as the abolition of residential segregation, equality of opportunity for employment, and the breaking down of all arbitrary racial restrictions that interfere with the general and political freedom of individuals.

8. What Can Parents Do?

A Negro mother confided to a white friend that she had tried to protect her children by "lying" to them. She had told her children that white people really love Negroes. She did not believe this herself; but she did not know how to tell her children that they were going to be disliked merely because of their color. She had also made severe economic sacrifices in order to send her children to a private school where the majority of the children were white. Expecting love rather than hate, her children easily made friends with a number of their classmates. It was not long before they were visiting the homes of their classmates and in turn were entertaining them in their own home. The mother felt anxious and fearful; she dreaded the day when the racial problem would arise and her children would be hurt. But as time went on and these friendships seemed to strengthen rather than weaken, the mother confessed to her white friend: "Those children taught me that what I believed to be a lie can be the truth."

Undoubtedly many Negro parents are torn with conflict and anxiety as they anticipate the racial problems that their children will have to face. Some parents, like the mother just mentioned, understandably attempt to postpone as long as possible a discussion of racial problems with their children. Middle-class

Negro parents often handle problems of race in the same way as many middle-class parents handle problems of sex with their children: they either deny that the problem exists or deal with it in an embarrassed and apologetic manner.

Some Negro parents of the upper middle class interpret racial problems to their children in terms of class differences. They tell their children, either directly or indirectly, that the undesirable personality traits found in some Negroes reflect their lower-class backgrounds or demonstrate personal deficiencies. These parents demand that their children behave in an exemplary manner in order to refute the contention that all Negroes are "inferior." This type of parental pressure, as we have seen, may result in exceptional achievement by some Negro children — provided they have the intellectual potentialities to meet such demands. If they do not, these pressures may only increase their frustrations.

A working-class Negro parent may have a similar desire to protect his children. But economic pressures and the immediate demands of daily life may prevent him from expressing his concern by demands that his children reach a high level of achievement and behavior. In their attempts to demonstrate their own adequacy, such children may try to conform to the standards of their peers. Acceptance by friends from their own economic and social group proves to them that they are worthwhile. The importance of adolescent gangs in underprivileged neighborhoods may reflect the tendency among adolescents from minority groups to turn to their peers in the quest for self-esteem. The control of delinquency and other anti-social behavior in these youngsters requires that their parents, teachers, and church leaders understand the need of these children for socially acceptable ways of obtaining recognition and attention. This clearly cannot be done by ignoring the social realities which at present prevent these children from getting the type of attention and stimulation which they — like all human beings — must obtain.

The desegregation of public schools poses a challenge for

Negro parents in providing for their children socially constructive opportunities for competition and achievement. Parents from minority groups in general have an even greater responsibility to their children than other parents. They must be sensitive to the necessity of counteracting the social forces that ordinarily tend to rob their children of self-esteem. When the children must face an unfamiliar situation in a recently desegregated school (or similar social setting), their parents have the additional responsibility of providing the kind of support and guidance that the children will need, at least at first.

Parents of Negro children can help them develop healthy reactions to these new pressures by providing them with the basic warmth, love, understanding, and guidance that have been found necessary for the healthy growth of *all* children. In spite of the important and rapid steps toward better race relations in the larger society, the Negro parent is still faced with the responsibility of providing his children with the basic foundations of a healthy personality. It is difficult for these children to feel that they are of value unless they are given such indications within the intimate family unit. Negro children need special assurance that their parents love them and want them. These children need to know that this love is unconditional — that they are loved because they are human beings worthy of love and respect from other human beings.

Paradoxically, the social forces that necessitate this relationship in the Negro family may interfere with the ability of these parents, particularly of the working classes, to express warmth, love, and acceptance for their children — for the Negro parent is himself the product of racial pressures and frustrations. It is imperative, however, that this cycle be broken. Because it cannot be broken by the child, it must be broken by parents and by the larger society. The present pressure toward the desegregation of public schools may well provide an impetus in this direction.

Realistic self-esteem in the Negro child can be built only upon the foundation of a frank and honest appraisal of the child's abilities and of the situation within which he will live and work and play. In the sympathetic guidance of the Negro child, it is essential to help him achieve a sense of personal worth based upon his actual accomplishments. A child who is held to high standards of achievement appropriate for his own abilities develops a realistic basis for self-confidence as he learns that it is possible for him to meet and solve the challenges of life. Parents who seek to help their children by over-protecting them and by isolating them from disturbing social realities are robbing them of the experiences necessary if they are to achieve a solid sense of their own integrity and worth.

Parents of Negro children, like all other parents, must be sure that their aspirations for their children are realistic as well as challenging. The standards by which the child is evaluated should be geared to the child's level of development, to his intelligence, and to his abilities. If a child is presented with premature or too difficult goals, he will necessarily fail in his efforts; he may then develop a sense of personal inadequacy, particularly if he believes his failure is associated with his race. This feeling may reinforce his sense of inferiority until it becomes imbedded in his personality. Negro children, like other children, sometimes react to unrealistic pressures from parents or teachers by withdrawal, resignation, submissiveness, lack of ambitions, or even open rebellion.

On the other hand, if the goals set for these children are not challenging enough or if they receive extravagant praise for normal or mediocre achievement, they may develop grandiose ideas of their personal worth, tendencies toward over-evaluation of themselves, or exhibitionistic attempts to gain attention. These patterns may seriously interfere with the child's adjustment outside of his home and can lead to his rejection by his peers. If the child believes that this rejection is associated with his color, it adds to his racial burdens and frustrations. Such an interpretation of rejection makes the child feel even more inadequate; it may make him increasingly hypersensitive and aggressive as he struggles desperately for a social acceptance that his own behavior continues to deny him.

Responsible parents do not evade, minimize, or exaggerate a child's questions or conflicts about race. A child old enough to ask questions about problems of race, religion, or nationality is old enough to receive honest and appropriate answers. If a child is different from the majority of other children in his community in religion, skin color, or cultural background, nothing is gained by telling him that he is not different, or that all people are alike. Parents may find it difficult, especially at first, to discuss these problems; but if the questions are not faced, they will form the basis of festering anxieties and self-doubts.

Psychologically speaking, it is probably more economic in the long run to discuss realistically the problems of differences among human beings when the child first raises them. Human beings differ in their appearance, in the ways they worship God, in their dress, in their dances, songs, and language. These differences are natural and in a very real sense desirable. In a just society, no human being need apologize for the fact that he is different, unless his difference expresses itself in cruel or anti-social behavior. These ideas should be reassuring to a sensitive and intelligent child.

When a child asks questions about the inferior status assigned to his group because of its color or religion, these questions require an honest, even if painful, answer from the parents. Nothing can be gained from denying that in an imperfect society these forms of injustice exist. A parent might explain to his child: "People are treated differently, and often for unimportant reasons. It may be because their skin is a different color, or because they do not have as much money as other people, or because they go to a different church, or because they speak with a different accent. This is known as prejudice and discrimination. Prejudice and discrimination are wrong and unfair. Many people are working hard to eliminate them, and in many ways are succeeding."

A direct statement of an elementary truth can be one of the child's first lessons in social ethics. Similar statements, geared to the level of the child's understanding, can help him to realize that he is not to blame when people hate or reject him for personal characteristics over which he has no control. He can be helped to understand that prejudice against him is not a sign of his own inferiority. With sympathetic understanding and guidance, the child can come to realize that prejudice is primarily a symptom of the inadequacy of those who hold the prejudice.

When a child is struggling for self-esteem, he may sometimes be helped by identification with one of his parents. For example, when the parents of a nine-year-old Negro boy moved to one of the suburbs of New York City, he was transferred from a school in which he was well known and liked to a new school, where he was the only Negro in his class. Because he was normally outgoing and sociable, he made friends easily. However, he resented the fact that his new classmates wanted to feel his hair and asked him questions about the difference between his hair texture and that of the other children. The difference was particularly noticeable because his skin color was as light as that of the white children. As his classmates showed more interest in his hair texture, he became increasingly aware of this characteristic as something that set him apart from the other children. He complained to his parents that he did not like to have the other children feel his hair. His unhappiness became so great that he asked to be sent back to the school in the city.

His parents were quite disturbed, as they recognized how important this problem was becoming for the boy. One evening, when the child was tearfully telling his parents of his unhappiness, the father said: "The next time people say anything about your hair, tell them that your hair is just like your father's. Come here. Feel my hair. Now feel your own hair. Aren't they the same?" The boy's face lighted up. He smiled and said, "That's right, isn't it? My hair is just like yours." From that point on, there were no more tearful discussions of this problem.

Whenever it was raised it was dismissed casually. The youngster has since become an accepted leader of his group and seems to need no apology for himself.

In spite of the need for love, acceptance, and warmth in the family group, it must be emphasized that a Negro child should never be permitted to use his minority status as an excuse for inferior achievement or for undesirable personal characteristics. The tendency to hide behind the injustice of prejudice and discrimination in order to avoid recognition of personal inadequacy is unfortunately as common among members of a minority group as the parallel pattern of a prejudiced person who uses his prejudices to avoid facing his own personal inferiority. This tendency has its beginning in late childhood or adolescence; it will increase if encouraged or tolerated by the child's parents or by well-meaning and guilt-ridden white adults. It must be dealt with by openly recognizing these excuses as alibis, and by helping the child to face his problems realistically and thereby solve them through constructive personal achievement. The contention that the existence of prejudice excuses all indications of incompetence or mediocrity in the victims provides support for the racists. Children of a minority group must learn early in life that some types of behavior resulting from social rejection are self-destructive and will lead to further rejection. These children must learn that aggressive, anti-social, exhibitionistic, or delinquent behavior will not result in personal effectiveness and social acceptability. Although such behavior is understandable as a reaction to a pathological social situation, the child can be helped to direct his energies into channels that are realistic and constructive both for himself and for society.

To be personally effective in the face of racial pressures, the child should be taught tolerance and compassion for other human beings — even for those who are prejudiced toward him. It is difficult to understand that the person who hates is a victim of his own ignorance and distortions; but if a child understands this, he has an antidote for the venom and bitterness that frequently develop in the victims of discrimination. Parents should explain to their children that not all members of the dominant group are necessarily prejudiced. If a child is permitted to think that everyone who is not a member of his own group feels hostile toward him, he may come to believe that prejudices are inevitable. This can lead to feelings of hopelessness and despair that may block his creativity. The group that society considers "superior" includes some kind, mature, and unprejudiced individuals, and others who are struggling to overcome the more disturbing manifestations of their prejudice. It is important that such individuals be brought to the attention of the minority-group child. An effective way is for his parents to have friends and acquaintances among different racial, religious, and nationality groups.

Parents may also help their children to cope successfully with the problem of minority status through discussions of the achievements of outstanding members of various minority groups. When kept in perspective, such discussions help the child to understand that minority status need not be a permanent shackle. When exaggerated, such discussions create the impression that the successful individuals are exceptions whose achievements stand in contrast to the general inadequacy of the group. A positive use of the socially acceptable achievements of members of the minority group may reinforce the self-esteem and raise the aspirations of children. A negative use reflects an empty and pathetic minority-group chauvinism.

The minority-group father and mother can help their child most by showing him that his family does not itself apologize for its own minority status. It is not enough for the parents to use words to express this self-acceptance; they must also behave in a way that reflects self-esteem. A child who sees his parents actively engaged in democratic social action, a child who sees his parents working for racial progress without apology, a child who sees in his parents' actions a respect for the dignity of human beings — this child is learning in a most concrete and fundamental sense the way to respect himself.

In the normal course of events, parents communicate to their children the values, attitudes, and aspirations that were communicated to them when they were children. For the most part children become like their parents either through the processes of love or through the fear of loss of love. When some children reach an age when they begin to rebel against parental influences, the very fact of rebellion is a reflection of parental influence. Some parents are more active and direct than others in influencing their children's racial attitudes; but every parent has some degree of influence on the social attitudes of his children. Parents who do not take a conscious stand may still exert an influence on their children by their passive acceptance of the prevailing racial myths and customs.

The present generation of white parents grew up in a world where their racial prejudices were not obviously destructive, personally or socially. But the world in which their children will become parents can no longer afford the luxury of these prejudices. Narrow nationalistic and racialistic attitudes are inconsistent with the realities of the present interdependent world. The peoples of Asia and Africa have been strongly influenced and stimulated by Western European and American democratic ideals. Since the First World War these peoples have been increasingly successful in freeing themselves from the bonds of imperialism and in eliminating the various evidences of European racial condescension. In short, these people have been demanding and obtaining full equality as human beings.

The Communist ideology has attempted to exploit the grievances associated with colonialism and imperialism. Communists have appealed to these peoples by pretending to offer full racial and economic equality. This seductive lure can be counteracted by the democratic nations only if they grant to these peoples, not merely the propaganda of democracy, but the fact of genuine acceptance as equals in the struggle for freedom and against Communism. These peoples have made it clear that they will not accept a partnership with the American and Western European nations on any other basis. If America persists in the old negative racial prejudices, it must expect to lose this ideological contest. Even the tremendous military might of America, while an important deterrent to aggression, cannot win the minds of the peoples of the world.

The May 17, 1954, decision of the United States Supreme Court, which has stimulated extensive desegregation of the public schools and other social institutions, is an important contribution in this area. There is no doubt that this decision is a significant step in the history of race relations in America. This decision may well have provided America with another opportunity to bring its racial practices in line with its democratic ideals — and thereby persuade the peoples of the world of the validity of our democracy.

The responsibility for translating the words of this decision into action — the responsibility for genuine changes in race relations — rests upon individual citizens in local communities. The churches, social-welfare groups, race-relations agencies, and other responsible organizations must play active roles in implementing the Supreme Court decision. But they can succeed only in so far as parents and other individual citizens lend their energies to helping rather than blocking racial progress.

Understandably, white parents will have doubts and anxieties about whether a non-segregated school is good for their children. The few instances of open resistance to desegregation of public schools reflect these fears. All major social changes have been accompanied by such doubts and anxieties and in extreme cases by intense resistance. The fear of change in race relations has been exploited by unscrupulous demagogues or political opportunists, who use the doubts and conflicts of the public in their own quest for power. The history of race relations in America makes it easy to exploit racial changes in these ways.

Most parents were brought up in a segregated society where the social, economic, and educational status of Negroes was clearly inferior. These parents tend to judge what is good for their children in terms of their own experiences. They may feel more secure when their children function in a segregated setting. They may see desegregation in terms of loss of their own social status, or at least as a threat to the social aspirations of the family. Generally they feel that what was "good" for them is necessarily good for their children — or even that their children must be provided with "better" opportunities.

Many white American parents do not clearly understand that the world has changed considerably since their own childhood. While there might be a question as to whether a racially segregated America was ever good, there is no question that it is no longer tolerable in today's world. It is now known that racial segregation, by distorting their perspective, impairs the ability of all children to live creatively. It blocks communication among groups, increasing unrealistic fears and hatreds; and it generally interferes with an individual's ability to understand and work constructively with people who are different. In the past, the average middle-class white American might not have been required to have contacts with Negroes except those in menial positions; but the advances of the Negro people and the increasing number of Negroes who have attained middle-class status for themselves make it unlikely that whites will be able to avoid contacts with some Negroes on an equal level. Furthermore, as America promotes her ideological and economic interests throughout different regions of the world, American whites will be required to adjust to, and function with, other colored peoples. Provincial and chauvinistic Americans can only be liabilities in our struggle for attainment of a democratic world.

An average parent may recognize the need for a change in his own racial attitudes and may wish to exert a positive influence on the racial attitudes of his children; but he may still be bothered by some disturbing questions. He may wonder:

Will my child and my family lose status by attending a non-segregated school, church, or recreational institution?

Will academic standards of the school be lowered by the admission of Negro children, and will my child's academic achievement suffer?

What about the moral standards of a school when Negro children are admitted? Won't white children become delinquent from their associations with Negro children in the school?

Will my child be more likely to catch communicable diseases in a non-segregated school?

A white child does not lose status by attending a non-segregated school unless the other schools in his community are racially restricted. It is understandable that a child and his family would resent being used as guinea pigs in timid, apologetic, and partial experiments in race relations. Under these circumstances the child and his family might get the impression that there is something peculiar about an interracial situation; those involved would normally resent being singled out. A white family that volunteered for this role would need courage to risk being considered "strange" or having its motives questioned and misunderstood by more conventional neighbors. It is a question whether parents have the right to subject their children to this type of experience without full and frank discussion.

Status problems associated with attendance in a non-segregated school can be resolved by not allowing such attendance to be a matter of personal decision and personal risk. This can be achieved by desegregating *all* of the schools of a given community. If all of the schools are non-segregated, no child has a special advantage or handicap in this regard.

The anxiety about whether academic standards will be lowered when Negroes are admitted to a previously all-white school arises from the fact that the academic standards of segregated Negro schools are generally lower. At one time it was believed that this was because the native intelligence of Negro children was inferior to that of white children. Psychologists have since determined that the apparent differences in intellectual levels were due not to inherent racial differences but primarily to differences in educational opportunity and general social environment. Segregation itself retarded the academic achievement of Negro children. Otto Klineberg, the eminent social psychologist, demonstrated that, as Negro children moved from southern segregated schools to northern non-segregated schools, their level of achievement rose. After about three or four years in the new environment, they reached the average level of achievement of children who had had all of their schooling under more favorable circumstances. It would seem likely, therefore, that the desegregation of schools will improve the intellectual level of these children. White children will not suffer from the admission of Negro children unless school administrators permit overcrowding, poor teaching, or other educational handicaps at the time when Negro children are enrolled. All parents must be vigilant in seeing that the desegregated schools maintain academic standards at least as high as prevailed in the previous all-white schools. Under these conditions all children will gain and no child will be handicapped.

Similar considerations apply to an understanding of whether a desegregated school will have increasing problems of delinquency. Juvenile delinquency is not primarily related to race; it reflects a complex pattern of social, economic, and community forces influencing the adjustment of the given child. The higher rate of delinquency among Negro children reflects not only the factors that influence other children but the low economic status, overcrowding, and psychological complications induced by racial segregation in housing and schools. As the economic condition of the Negro improves, and as racial segregation decreases, the rate of delinquency among Negro adolescents will also decrease. White children will not become delinquent merely through attendance at a school with Negro children; and the tendency for some Negro children to express anti-social behavior may decrease as they realize they are accepted as human beings in a non-segregated school, rather than segregated and rejected because of their race.

The problem of communicable disease is also related to socio-economic status, overcrowded housing, and other social problems aggravated by ghetto living. Advances in medicine and public health — and specifically a well-organized school-health program — should provide protection for all children from most dangerous diseases. Non-segregated schools will necessarily have to main-tain the same health facilities and safeguards that are now maintained in any well-run school — and unfortunately not found in the majority of segregated Negro schools. Again it is clear that, as the economic and social conditions of the Negro improve, the incidence of certain diseases among Negroes will decrease.

Probably the most disturbing problem in the minds of well-intentioned white parents is anxiety about interracial marriage. This question may have kept many unprejudiced parents from becoming involved in the struggle for racial justice. These parents have been told — and many of them believe — that the granting of economic, political, and educational equality to the Negro will necessarily lead to increased demands for social and sexual equality. Although this is an understandable anxiety in a segregated society, the fear of social intermingling among races does not justify the denial of full rights of citizenship to any group of individuals. Furthermore, in regions of this country where there has never been appreciable segregation in schools and cer-tain other social institutions, interracial marriages are rare. Social relations and marriage are always a matter of personal choice and decision. Even individuals of the same race cannot force an unwilling person into friendship, romance, or marriage with another person. The fears associated with interracial marriages appear to stem primarily from the recognition that the Negro, up to the present time, has been relegated to an inferior status in American life. As he improves his status and overcomes many of the consequences of his past inferior status, anxieties concerning the dangers of interracial marriages may decrease. The opportunity to know and understand other individuals as human beings rather than as stereotypes will in all probability increase the frequency of social relationships without regard to race. Friendships based upon individual preferences and interests will become more common as the artificial barriers that prevent them are removed. Laws or judicial decisions compelling such friendships would be intolerable and unthinkable in a democracy; both Negroes and whites would rightly rebel against them.

What, then, can white parents do specifically to help their children develop more positive racial attitudes and make a more effective adjustment to the present rapid changes in race relations? The first requirement for a well-intentioned parent is that he exercise control over expressions of his own racial feelings. A parent who makes disparaging racial remarks or who refers to members of other races and religions by vulgar epithets (such as "Nigger," "kike," and "wop") in the presence of his children is not helping these children to function effectively in the modern world.

But it would be hypocritical for many parents to set themselves up before their children as paragons of racial tolerance. So a second important step is for parents to face their own prejudice and recognize its manifestations. A parent cannot deal constructively with this problem through ignoring or attempting to evade it. As long as his prejudice exists but is not understood, he will display it in ways that add to the child's confusion. It would be beneficial for the parent to discuss the origins and complexities of his own prejudice with his children in an appropriate situation — thus showing an honest desire to eliminate the more disturbing manifestations. Since it is the responsibility of parents to provide basic moral and ethical guidance for their children, white parents are almost obliged to deal with the moral, ethical, and religious implications of racial prejudice.

A parent who believes in the religious principle of the brotherhood of man and the fatherhood of God, a parent who accepts the American democratic creed, should under no circumstances punish his child for favorable expressions of racial democracy. It is both tragic and pathetic to hear a white adult recall the shock of recognizing the hypocrisy of his parents when he invited a Negro child to his home. The modern world demands that such friendships be encouraged rather than discouraged.

White parents should not establish different standards for their children's Negro friends than for their children's white friends. They should set up neither special requirements nor special allowances in intelligence, behavior, or cleanliness for the Negro friend if they would not do the same for other children.

A well-intentioned white parent can set an example for his children by the nature and quality of his own relationships with individuals of other groups. Genuine interracial friendships among adults — as among children — can be based only on common interests, compatibility of personality, and other criteria that are also relevant to friendships with members of the same race. There is, of course, a possibility that some whites, in the first stages of their contacts with members of other races, will bend over backward in their acceptance of Negroes, without regard to the personality or character of the individual. The oversentimentalized approach to individuals of a minority group not only is a symptom of latent guilt feelings but also reflects a type of "reverse prejudice." A white person has reached a high level of maturity in the area of race relations when he is able not only to recognize but also to behave in terms of the fact that there is as wide a range of individual differences among Negroes as there is among other people. Under the most ideal social and racial conditions, any individual will encounter some Negroes, as well as some whites, who will be personally unacceptable to him. It would be a distortion of perspective to teach a child that in the quest for racial justice he must love everybody who is different from himself.

White parents, then, can make a major contribution to America. They can strengthen the democratic foundations of our nation by helping their children to be free of the distortions inherent in racial thinking, and thus helping them to attain strong and creative personalities. In doing this they will help not only their own children but all children.

9. American Children and the Future

American children can be saved from the corrosive effects of racial prejudice. These prejudices are not inevitable; they reflect the types of experiences that children are forced to have. Such prejudices can be prevented — and those already existing can be changed — by altering the social conditions under which children learn about and live with others. When human intelligence and creativity tackle the problem and bring about the necessary changes in the society, then these prejudices and their detrimental effects will be eliminated. This conclusion is supported by the systematic investigations of social scientists, and by the dramatic improvements in race relations that have taken place during the past ten years.

The American people are not generally aware that there have been extensive improvements in the relationships between Negroes and whites — changes tantamount to a major social revolution. It is paradoxical (and probably characteristic of the ability of Americans to take social progress for granted) that the significance of these changes has not been generally recognized. Extensive desegregation has taken place in the armed forces, in interstate transportation, in public accommodation, in hospital and health services, in some churches and some parochial schools, in organized sports, in industrial employment, in politics and government, in higher education, and most recently in public elementary and secondary education. While specific instances have occurred mainly in northern, midwestern, southwestern, and border states, successful desegregation has also taken place in some states of the deep south — particularly in the armed forces and in Catholic churches.

Probably the next major problem that must be solved in order to continue progress in American race relations is the problem of segregation in housing. Residential segregation spawns not only segregated public education but also such other symptoms of social disorganization as overcrowded and substandard housing, public-health problems, juvenile delinquency, and crime. Racial ghettos are generally recognized as a major social and political problem. In order to eliminate this last significant obstacle to the attainment of racial democracy, it will be necessary to mobilize the highest level of intelligence, understanding, and realistic social planning.

Some experts have pointed out that the problem of racial segregation in housing is not isolated and does not arise only from racial prejudice. Among the factors other than race influencing the perpetuation of residential segregation are: (a) a strong trend toward economic segregation, which has developed in modern cities during the past century; (b) a trend toward class segregation, which has been accelerated by the tendency on the part of public and private agencies to build housing in a given section for groups of low, medium, or high income, or to restrict the tenants to special groups, such as veterans; (c) the standardization of types of dwellings, which promotes the segregation of families according to size, type, and age groups.

According to one expert (C. Bauer), this tendency toward standardization of American housing, so that everyone fits "in his place" and housing developments tend to become homogeneous in terms of "class, age group, and color of the residents," is not a result of any conscious over-all plan or of any public decision to encourage racial segregation. He believes the tendency arose more or less by accident, or as a by-product of pressures and policies being employed at the time for progressive or even idealistic purposes. The development of rigid patterns of segregation and other forms of homogeneity in housing reflects the absence of any conscious planning in this area, or of a willingness to anticipate or assume responsibility for the social consequences of this pattern. Now that it is clear that racial segregation in housing brings detrimental consequences both to society and to the growth and development of our children, it becomes necessary to develop a program to eliminate existing patterns of residential segregation as soon as practicable.

In many northern and border cities, there have been significant experiments in the elimination of segregation in public-housing projects. Some of these examples of interracial public housing have been extensively studied by social scientists. The general conclusion of these studies is that increased interracial contacts in housing projects result in an improvement in the racial attitudes of whites. As one group of investigators pointed out, there appears to be overwhelming evidence that the integrated projects are characterized by an increase in friendliness and more cohesive social atmosphere among the individuals of the different races. Such changes on the part of many of the whites seem to extend to their attitude toward Negroes in general — not merely to the Negroes with whom they associate within the project. Some of the whites limit their positive feelings to the Negroes whom they knew; in general, however, a more wholesome pattern of interracial attitudes and behavior has developed as a consequence of the experiences in non-segregated living.

These investigations clearly indicate that racial attitudes and behavior are not rigid, fixed, and unchangeable attributes of human nature. It is also clear that the attitudes of our children may become more positive if we provide them with positive types of interracial experiences. We cannot expect significant changes in children's attitudes toward people of other races as long as their experiences merely reinforce past attitudes. If we change the patterns of racial segregation — if we provide opportunities for constructive and positive experiences with members of different races — then we can expect significant positive changes in racial attitudes, feelings, and behavior. The answer to the problem of how we can develop more favorable attitudes in our children must be found in the total pattern of community experiences that we provide for them.

In the past, specific instances of desegregation have resulted from various origins, according to the region, community, institution, or situation. Determining factors have included decisions of the Federal courts, personal decisions by persons in authority, moral arguments, population changes, the pressure of public opinion, votes by the electorate, non-judicial government action, and legislation.

Any given incident of desegregation may have been the result of one or more of the above factors. Desegregation resulting from litigation, judicial decision, or legislation has proved just as effective as desegregation resulting from other causes.

In this regard, it should be pointed out that the extensive desegregation of the graduate and professional schools of southern states was a direct consequence of a series of decisions by the United States Supreme Court. Such court decisions seem to facilitate rather than restrict progress in race relations. For example, when the Supreme Court established the principle that a state could not use public funds to provide education for some of its citizens without providing the same education for all, many of the private colleges and universities in southern states, though not directly affected, voluntarily began to admit Negro students. Apparently the Court's decision provided many individuals with the moral and legal support to express their resentment against racial segregation by putting their private beliefs into action.

A systematic study of many recent instances of desegregation provides a basis for at least tentative answers to some of the questions that will be asked by individuals of good-will as they seek to cope with similar problems in their own communities.[1]

---

[1] For an analysis of actual instances of desegregation in many institutions during the last ten years, see Kenneth Clark, "Desegregation: An Appraisal of the Evidence." For additional data, see *The Negro and the Schools* by Harry S. Ashmore.

(1) *Is it wiser to desegregate a school or other social institution immediately or gradually?*

A systematic study of actual cases reveals that the length of
time involved is not the major factor in whether desegregation will be effective or not. Some forms of rapid desegregation
have been successful, whereas there have been some social difficulties associated with different types of gradual desegregation.
Gradual desegregation may provide an opportunity for those
who are opposed or anxious about the consequences to mobilize
their opposition; this may increase the likelihood of prolonged
social disruption. More rapid desegregation, on the other hand,
not only shortens the period of anxiety and stress, but also is
often accepted by the general community in a shorter period of
time and with a minimum of overt resistance or controversy.

(2) *In desegregating schools, would it be wiser to take in a
few Negroes at a time (or some Negroes in certain grades or certain schools) and then, as the white children become more accustomed to the presence of Negroes, introduce them throughout
the school or the school system?*

Attempts to solve the problem by introducing a limited number
of Negroes in certain segments of the school or other social institutions have generally increased the likelihood of difficulties and
resentments. This segmental approach to desegregation has prolonged the period of opposition and open resentment on the part
of the whites immediately involved in the desegregation. These
individuals understandably resented the role of guinea pigs —
of being singled out to bear the brunt of this "affliction." As the
whites not immediately involved observed the anxiety and resistance behavior of the first group, their own opposition became
reinforced and intensified.

(3) *What should one do when those who are opposed to desegregation organize active and outspoken resistance?*

There is always some degree of opposition to desegregation.
The existence of opposition does not in itself mean that the de-

segregation will necessarily be unsuccessful. Before the successful desegregation of the armed services, many white soldiers were personally opposed to it and expressed prejudices against Negroes. But this fact did not affect the speed or effectiveness of desegregation. One of the important findings in this area is that desegregation has been successfully accomplished in many instances even where the initial opposition was strong. In many cases such opposition ceases when the alternative for the prejudiced whites is the loss of a desired public facility, the imposition of a direct economic burden, or some other important stigma. The opposition may be eliminated and desegregation may proceed successfully if the following conditions are met:

(a) A clear and unequivocal statement of the new policy by leaders with prestige and by other acknowledged authorities.

(b) A firm enforcement of the new policy by these authorities and persistence in the execution of this policy even in the face of continued resistance.

(c) A willingness to deal with violations, attempted violations, and incitements to violence by the use of the law and strong enforcement action.

(d) A refusal on the part of responsible local authorities to initiate, engage in, or tolerate subterfuge, gerrymandering, or other devices for evading desegregation.

(e) Appeals to the individuals immediately involved in terms of their religious principles of brotherhood and their acceptance of the American traditions of fair play and equal justice.

(4) *What about the likelihood of violence as a consequence of the attempts to desegregate?*

Incidents of overt violence as a reaction to desegregation have been quite rare. Unfortunately these incidents, probably because of their rarity, have been considered newsworthy, and therefore have been dramatized far beyond their importance. In the few instances of violent resistance to desegregation, the following conditions have invariably been present: ambiguous or inconsistent policy on the part of responsible officials or agencies; ineffective police action; conflict between competing governmental authorities or officials. There is some evidence that overt violence is more likely to occur when the situation involves lower-class or lower-middle-class whites who see themselves threatened socially and economically by contact with Negroes, or who are in fact competing with Negroes for limited and inadequate facilities.

An intensive study of one situation revealed that violence is more likely to be associated with desegregation where there already exists a pattern of serious community disorganization and a general background of lawlessness. Violence and lawlessness associated with race relations, therefore, may reflect a general pattern of civic and political corruption inherent in a community with a tradition of disrespect for law and order. Certainly a child required to grow up in this type of environment is harmed as much by this general community disorganization as he is by the existing racial pattern.

(5) *What are the short-run and long-run consequences of desegregation?*

Where desegregation has been put into effect, it has generally been evaluated as successful and socially desirable. Even army officers who had had doubts of the desirability of changing the racial pattern, after observing the fact of desegregation in the army, were forced to conclude that there was no loss in efficiency — that desegregation could and did work.

While there is some evidence that effective desegregation in one institution of the community or in one area of American life tends to facilitate desegregation in other institutions, there is also evidence that it is possible to have effective desegregation restricted to a given institution of a community. In other words, the desegregation of a church, a school, or a hospital does not necessarily in itself bring about desegregation in other areas of community life.

In the initial stages of the desegregation of a school or other social institution, there may be some problems reflecting attitudes and reactions developed in the earlier, segregated way of life. If individuals are allowed to behave in terms of feelings and attitudes consistent with social conditions of the past, they will understandably resist change. When they are required by moral, political, or practical circumstances to change their behavior, there will understandably be a continuation of the effect of their past attitudes and feelings in the new situation. However, these past attitudes and feelings must not be permitted to determine their behavior in the changed situation. It is the responsibility of democratic government to exercise controls over personal behavior when they are necessary for the welfare and stability of all individuals.

The exercise of this control has been generally accepted in many spheres of life. The most notable examples are in the field of public health. The government, in spite of initially strong resistance from large groups of individuals against vaccination or other hygienic regulations, insisted that the responsibility could not be left up to the attitudes of the individual or group. For the health and welfare of all, it was essential that the full force of government authority demand individual compliance. It is now recognized that the mental health, personality stability, and social effectiveness of children are as important as their physical health. It is therefore necessary to provide children with the same safeguards and protections in this sphere that has been provided for them in the sphere of public health.

A democratic society must not deny civic rights to some of its citizens because of the attitudes, feelings, or whims of others. Indeed protection of the individual and of minorities against the power and prejudices of the majority is the crucial responsibility of the democratic society — the responsibility that differentiates democracy from anarchy or totalitarianism.

Moreover, it has been demonstrated that changes in the social situation and required changes in the behavior of individuals bring about compatible changes in their social attitudes. We can, therefore, develop positive racial attitudes in our children and free them from the personality burdens of racial prejudice by controlling the nature of the society in which they live. We can decide that they will learn positive rather than negative attitudes toward others. This is the most effective form of education.

There are still some fundamental problems to be solved. How do children develop a sense of empathy, justice, and fair play, and become sensitive to the welfare of others? How can one translate a verbal acceptance of these values into actual behavior toward others? In what specific ways can the church and the school contribute to the development and strengthening of these characteristics which are essential for an effective personality and a stable society? Answers to these questions may in the long run provide us with answers to the bedeviling questions of the nature of racial prejudices and what can be done about them.

While we await the findings of basic research into these fundamental problems, there are many things that can be done on the basis of available knowledge to save our children from the corroding effects of racial prejudices. As has already been pointed out, our schools, churches, and other social institutions will have to play a constructive role during this transition period, when American children will still be suffering from existing patterns of prejudice, discrimination, and segregation. It is small comfort to reassure human beings that conditions will eventually be better. The point of maximum vulnerability for the individual human being is the present. Every day that a child is subjected to the unnecessary bombardment of racial prejudices, every day that a child is forced to be an accessory to an injustice inflicted upon another child, every day that a child is forced to bear the brunt of the stigma inherent in being rejected and humiliated because of his race, is a day when our society is failing to fulfill its responsibility to these children and is contributing to their distortion and debasement. A nation that, in the 1940's, won a successful war for human dignity with barely a year of preparation is a nation that can prepare itself within a short time to wage a successful battle for the conservation of our children.

We already have enough systematic knowledge and technical know-how to begin an all-out program for the benefit of our children. No single agency or institution in our society can in itself free the minds of our children from the consequences of racial prejudice. While court decisions are important goads to the conscience of our nation, the translation of these decisions into beneficial social changes finally depends upon the clear thinking and democratic understanding of many people on the local community level. People must be helped toward this understanding through the forceful and democratic actions of their leaders and through continuous interpretations of the fundamental meaning of democracy. The job of providing such interpretations must be shared by all the instruments of communication (including the press, magazines, radio, television, and moving pictures) and by all of our social institutions — the churches, schools, social agencies, and political organizations.

Our society can mobilize itself to wage a dramatic and successful war against racial prejudice and its effects upon human beings. In doing so it will eliminate the situation where the prejudiced individuals are the ones who have higher status, and where they compel others to conform to their prejudices. A mobilization of the total society against prejudice will be successful to the extent that it gives moral, legal, and social status to unprejudiced individuals, making them unafraid to express their belief in decency and justice and to behave in accordance with their belief. The day when Americans need no longer be surreptitiously in favor of equality among human beings — the day when they may proudly proclaim their belief in complete democracy — is the day when our children will be free to develop genuine health, strength, and stability of personality.

PART THREE

APPENDICES 1-5

Appendix 1. The Legal Background of the School Segregation Cases

by Philip Kurland

Dr. Clark's study[1] was utilized by the Supreme Court to provide a factual base on which to rest its conclusion that segregation of white and Negro school children was a deprivation of the equal protection of the laws commanded by the Fourteenth Amendment. That decision has been condemned and challenged by many. So far as I know, however, no adequate evidence has been adduced to contradict the factual propositions offered by Dr. Clark. The reader may assay for himself the validity of the data set forth in *Prejudice and Your Child*. He can reach only one conclusion, the conclusion reached by the Supreme Court in the *Brown* case, and there is nothing that a lawyer can add to this social science presentation.

Any contribution I can make to this new edition of *Prejudice and Your Child* must lie in a description of the *School Segregation Cases* in their legal setting, including a consideration of the criticisms of the judgment that have been made and the answers that these criticisms necessarily call forth.

Because people tend to think of the great principles of our constitutional jurisprudence in abstract rather than real terms,

---

[1] *Prejudice and Your Child* is a summary and revision of the manuscript "Effect of Prejudice and Discrimination on Personality Development" which Dr. Clark prepared for the Midcentury White House Conference on Children and Youth, 1950. It was this manuscript which was cited in footnote 11 of the *Brown* decision.

it might be well to recall, too, that the cases which resulted in the *Brown v. Education* opinion involved real controversies between actual parties. And it was in the course of deciding four such flesh-and-blood contests that the Court, through Mr. Chief Justice Warren, rendered its famous and unanimous opinion. The cases involved state segregation laws in Kansas, South Carolina, Virginia and Delaware. They bear the name of Oliver Brown, who was the father of an eight-year-old girl who had been prohibited from attending an elementary school within five blocks of her home in Topeka, because it was reserved for white students. Instead she was compelled to walk through railroad yards to take a bus to a Negro school twenty-one blocks away. Brown and the parents of other Negro children were responsible for these cases. They asked the courts to enjoin the states from maintaining this segregation. The United States District Court for Kansas refused relief because, it said, "the physical facilities, the curricula, courses of study, qualifications of and quality of teachers, as well as other educational facilities in the two sets of schools are comparable." The federal court in South Carolina found that the Negro school facilities were grossly inferior to those available to the whites, but refused to grant the injunction when, on the order of the court, the state made appropriate efforts to equalize them in the county in question. So, too, with the federal court in Virginia. The Delaware courts, however, found that the inequality of school facilities required that the injunction be issued.

The cases were first argued at length before the Court early in its 1952-1953 term. At the end of that term, the Court set the cases down for re-argument in the 1953-1954 term and asked the counsel to prepare briefs in response to five questions. Earl Warren came to the Court at this point in the development of the desegregation cases. Early in the 1953 term, the Court again heard oral argument. In addition, it received about 2,000 pages of written argument. On May 17, 1954, the Court handed down its unanimous opinion. But it did not frame its decree, which ultimately required the states to comply with its judgment "with all deliberate speed," until May 31, 1955. That the Court gave its fullest consideration to these cases cannot be gainsaid even by its most rabid critics. It concluded that laws, state or federal, requiring racial segregation in public schools were in violation of the Constitution.

What were the legal factors that properly affected the Court's judgment? First, of course, was the Fourteenth Amendment, one of the three Constitutional amendments enacted after the Civil War, primarily for the purpose of protecting the newly freed slaves from the tyrannies of their former masters. It is not surprising that the conquered South has never displayed any great affection for the Thirteenth, Fourteenth and Fifteenth Amendments.

The pertinent section of the Fourteenth Amendment provides that "No State shall make or enforce any law which shall abridge the privileges or immunities of citizens of the United States, nor shall any State deprive any person of life, liberty, or property, without due process of law; nor deny to any person within its jurisdiction the equal protection of the laws." If it is asked as the Court did in one of the questions it put to counsel, whether the framers of the Fourteenth Amendment intended by the phrase "equal protection of the laws" to prevent the states from segregation in terms of race, two answers are offered. "The discussion and our own investigation," said Mr. Chief Justice Warren, "convince us that, although the sources cast some light, it is not enough to resolve the problem with which we are faced. At best they are inconclusive." A more forthright answer about the intent of the framers has been provided by Professor Bickel of the Yale Law School: "The obvious conclusion to which the evidence . . . easily leads is that section 1 of the Fourteenth Amendment . . . was meant to apply neither to jury service, nor suffrage, nor anti-miscegenation statutes, nor segregation. . . . If the Fourteenth Amendment were a statute, a court might very well hold . . . that it was foreclosed from applying it to segregation in the public schools." But because it is a Constitutional provision, the second question asked by the Court had to be answered: Is the Court confined to the exact and immediate intent of the framers in interpreting provisions with such vague contours as "privileges and immunities," "due process of law," and "equal protection of the laws"? In short, is the Constitution a document of rigid and unchanging meaning or is it to be treated as a vital, living organism? It is the argument of Professor Bickel and the observation of Dean Leflar and Professor Davis of the Arkansas Law School that the framers of the Fourteenth Amendment knew and understood that, whatever its immediate effect, its appropriate interpretation would vary with the demands of the future and that the job of giving meaning to the words was assigned, in our system of government, to the Supreme Court.

This is the answer that Mr. Chief Justice Warren gave on behalf of the Court in the *Brown* case. It is the answer that the Court itself has long given to the question of the rigidity of meaning of the grand phrases in the Constitution. It may be put in the words of Mr. Justice Holmes:

> When we are dealing with words that also are a constituent act, like the Constitution of the United States, we must realize that they have called into life a being the development of which could not have been foreseen completely by the most gifted of its begetters. It was enough for them to realize or to hope that they had created an organism; it has taken a century and has cost their successors much sweat and blood to prove that they created a nation. The case before us must be considered in the light of our whole experience and not merely in that of what was said a hundred years ago.

Or, in the language of Mr. Chief Justice Hughes, a judge whom the State of Georgia never sought to impeach:

> If by the statement that what the Constitution meant at the time of its adoption it means today, it is intended to say that the great clauses of the Constitution must be confined to the interpretation which the framers, with the condition and outlook of their time, would have placed upon them, the statement contains its own refutation. It was to guard against such a narrow conception that Chief Justice Marshall

uttered the memorable warning — "we must never forget that it is a constitution we are expounding — a constitution intended to endure for ages to come, and consequently, to be adapted to the various crises of human affairs."

No serious student of the Court can deny that throughout its history it has interpreted the Constitution as a living and not a moribund document. Indeed, if a static meaning were to be given to the Constitution, the States' Righters might find, as Professor Crosskey of the Law School of the University of Chicago has asserted, that the appropriate function of the States in the American body politic approximates the function of the appendix in the human body: a source of trouble but otherwise a vestigial remainder.

In addition to the language of the Constitution, of course, the Court was called upon to consider the gloss that it had, through its decisions and opinions, put upon the Equal Protection Clause as it related to the Negroes it was framed to protect. The main pillar of the Southern argument is the case of *Plessy v. Ferguson.* Plessy, who numbered one Negro grandparent among his forebears, was arrested in Louisiana for refusing to ride in the colored coach of a railroad train. He brought an action to enjoin the enforcement of the Louisiana segregation law. The Supreme Court refused to interpret the Fourteenth Amendment as barring Louisiana from requiring separation of the races in transportation facilities. There are four points to be noted in this case. First, it did not involve educational facilities at all and the rationale proffered by Warren in *Brown,* resting on Dr. Clark's study, that there cannot be separate equal educational facilities, would not be inconsistent with the result in *Plessy,* though it would be inconsistent with the reading later given *Plessy* by the lower courts. Second, although *Plessy* has been repeatedly cited as a basis for the "separate but equal" doctrine, the opinion will be searched in vain for any language suggesting that segregation is permissible under the Equal Protection Clause where equal facilities are provided. Third, Mr. Justice Harlan, the grandfather of the present Justice, dissenting, stated: "Our Constitution is color blind, and neither knows nor tolerates classes among citizens. . . . In my opinion, the judgment rendered this day will, in time, prove to be quite as pernicious as the decision made by this tribunal in the *Dred Scott* case." Fourth, the vitality of the *Plessy* case was sapped almost a decade before the *School Segregation Cases,* when the Supreme Court held, in *Morgan v. Virginia,* that State segregation laws imposed an invalid burden on interstate commerce.

Three years after *Plessy v. Ferguson,* in 1899, the Court refused to close the white schools in Richmond County, Georgia, until a separate school was provided for Negroes. The question whether separate but equal schools violated the Constitution was not opportunely timed and the Court did not consider the question. The issue was again avoided in the *Berea College* case in 1908. In 1928 came the high-water mark of the separate but equal doctrine and strangely enough it involved not a Negro but a Chinese, who was attacking not the separate but equal rule but the classification by Mississippi that prohibited her attendance at white schools and, therefore, compelled her attendance at a Negro school. The Supreme Court, which then included Holmes and Brandeis, speaking through Mr. Chief Justice Taft, approved the classification of the Chinese girl with Negroes rather than whites, and gave its blessing in dicta to lower court cases approving the separate but equal doctrine in education. After this the tide of educational segregation as constitutionally approved behavior began to ebb.

In 1938, Lloyd Gaines, who had been denied admission to the University of Missouri Law School because of his color, brought his case before the Supreme Court. The state had offered to pay his way to any law school that would have him. But the Supreme Court said that this was not enough; that the state must afford him the opportunity to attend law school within the state if it gave that opportunity to others; and that the white law school, the only one that the state maintained, must be opened to him.

In this instance, the Supreme Court reached a result that the Maryland courts had reached on their own some two years earlier.

Herman Sweatt's case came to the Supreme Court in 1950. Texas had established a Negro law school in addition to its white law school. Sweatt, a Negro, applied for and was denied admission to the white school. But the Supreme Court granted him the relief he sought. In effect, the Supreme Court held that there was no such thing as separate but equal law schools. On the same day, the Court decided *McLaurin v. Oklahoma State Regents,* holding that the segregation within a graduate school at the University of Oklahoma, *i.e.,* segregation by classroom seat, by library table, and by cafeteria section, was in violation of the Equal Protection Clause. The separate but equal doctrine as applied to education was nearly done to death on this day in June 1950, when the *McLaurin* and *Sweatt* cases were decided. This is not to suggest that the Court was ready to say in 1950 what it said in 1954, nor that the rationale in these cases provided a basis for the *Brown* decision. But long before *Brown* there were signs other than these school cases pointing to the early demise of that notion. The states, which had been barred from segregating by zoning since 1917, despite the separate but equal argument, were held to be impotent to enforce racial restrictive covenants in 1948. Protection to the Negroes in their voting rights — to the extent that such protection could be extended by a court — was afforded Negroes despite the subterfuges used by the states, and the Fourteenth Amendment was held to mean that Negroes could not be excluded from jury service.

These were the legal factors that were involved in the opinion that the Chief Justice wrote for the Court, but they obviously were not the only relevant factors. In the interpretation of the Constitution, as in lesser matters, the Court, from its inception, has looked not only to the intent of the framers, to the lessons of history, to legal precedent and to logic; it has always weighed the potential consequences of its decisions. No one can catalogue these in the same fashion that one can list the legal authorities. In addition to those set out by Dr. Clark, however, two are apparent.

The first was the fact that to millions of Americans, segregation had long been a cardinal principle in their way of life. In the words of President Truman's Committee on Civil Rights:

> Legally enforced segregation has been followed throughout the South since the close of the Reconstruction era. In these States it is generally illegal for Negroes to attend the same schools as whites; attend theaters patronized by whites; visit parks where whites relax; eat, sleep or meet in hotels, restaurants or public halls frequented by whites. This is only a partial enumeration — legally imposed separation of races has become highly refined. In the eyes of the law, it is also an offense for whites to attend "Negro" schools, theaters and similar places. The result has been the familiar system of racial segregation in both public and private institutions which cuts across the daily lives of southern citizens from the cradle to the grave.

The Justices were not unaware of the profound changes in the Southern way of life that would be required by a desegregation decree. At least three of them had grown up and lived in the kind of community described in the quotation from the President's Civil Rights Commission: Hugo Black in Alabama, Stanley Reed in Kentucky and Tom Clark in Texas. All of the Justices had lived, for greater or lesser periods, in the District of Columbia or its environs, which is not an untypical Southern community. It is hardly possible to believe that all eagerly sought after so fundamental a change. Evidence of the concern of the Court over this problem is revealed by the length and care of its deliberations and by the unusual form of its decree. The decree did not command immediate compliance, nor even compliance within a fixed period of time which was requested by the plaintiffs and by the Department of Justice. It required only compliance "with all deliberate speed," a novel form of decree so far as the Supreme Court is concerned. The form was chosen to allow a gradual rather than a precipitous change. That the choice might have been a desirable one is attested by those jurisdictions that have, in good faith, utilized the grace period for working out plans for compliance. It has proved worse than useless, positively harmful, in those jurisdictions where the "razorback" or "cracker" influences have used the time to destroy the possibilities of a calm and peaceful transition.

The second of the non-technical factors was the recognition by the Court that the separate but equal doctrine had always resulted in separation but never in equality. Dr. Clark has demonstrated the impossibility of separate but equal educational facilities. In the only Supreme Court cases on the subject of segregation of educational facilities, either there has been no question as to the equality of the facilities, as in the case of the Chinese girl required by Mississippi to attend Negro schools, or, where the question had been presented, as in *Sweatt* and *Mc-Laurin,* the Court had found that the facilities did not satisfy the demands of equality — not even when the segregation took place within the same school. Thus, there never had been any direct Supreme Court sanction of the notion that separate but equal educational facilities can actually exist.

To cut further toward reality, it must be recognized that the Court would have to assume the roles of two of the three monkeys, seeing and hearing no evil, in order to fail to recognize the want of good faith on the part of the states urging the retention of the separate but equal doctrine. From 1868 to 1954, this doctrine purportedly governed their actions. No person visiting the states of Georgia or Mississippi — the states which have produced the most vehement supporters of the separate but equal doctrine — prior to the *School Segregation Cases,* would have found any evidence of a good faith attempt to afford equal educational opportunities to their Negro citizens. Unless the Court was to make a monkey of itself, it had to face the fact proved by Dr. Clark: that the separate but equal doctrine was a mere excuse for the continued subordination of the Negro people, for a two-class system with the whites dominant; that the maintenance of an inferior educational system for Negroes would inhibit their capacity to secure the equality of status that the Fourteenth Amendment was designed to afford them.

Given the fact, then, that the function of segregation was a two-class system of citizenship, the Court had to decide whether the result that had been attained under the separate but equal flag was really consonant with the principles of democracy, freedom and equality that are both explicit and implicit in the language of the Constitution; whether it was consonant with the principles of morality that underlie our American jurisprudence; whether it was consonant with our role as leader in the cold war fight of the free world against the spread of totalitarian doctrine. Chief Justice Warren, speaking for the Court, gave the only answer possible. As Professor Paul Freund of Harvard has said: "It is proving very hard indeed in some quarters to live physically with the Court's decisions; would it not have proved even harder to live intellectually and morally with a contrary decision?"

The critics of Warren's opinion in these cases have shouted that it is a rejection of our principles of *stare decisis*. Two of the principal goals of our legal system are certainty and equality and the doctrine of *stare decisis* is essential to both. It contributes to certainty by giving a lawyer a reasonable basis for anticipating the rules that will be applied to his legal problem. It contributes to equality by requiring that the rules applied to one set of litigants will also be applied to a later set of litigants. It is a worthy and desirable principle, but like most basic principles of law is not inflexible. It has not reached the stage which was described by Jonathan Swift in *Gulliver's Travels:*

It is a maxim among these men, that whatever has been done before may legally be done again; and therefore they take special care to record all the decisions formerly made, even those which have through ignorance or corruption contradicted the rule of common justice and the general reason of mankind. These under the name of precedents, they produce as authorities and thereby endeavor to justify the most iniquitous opinions. . . .

" 'There is no virtue in sinning against light or in persisting in palpable error, for nothing is settled until it is settled right.' " Thus spake, not Zarathustra the god of light, but Senator Ervin when he was Mr. Justice Ervin of the Supreme Court of North Carolina. So, too, spoke James F. Byrnes, not when he was Governor of South Carolina or counsel to that State in the *School Segregation Cases*, but when he was a Justice of the Supreme Court of the United States. He was then called upon to write the opinion in a case in which the constitutionality of a California statute making it a crime to bring indigent persons into that State was at issue. He rejected earlier decisions which would have justified the California statute in this language:

[w]e do not consider ourselves bound by the language referred to. *City of New York v. Miln* was decided in 1837. Whatever may have been the notion then prevailing, we do not think it will now be seriously contended that because a person is without employment and without funds he constitutes a "moral pestilence."

It must be appreciated that a rigid doctrine of *stare decisis* would be inconsistent with the notion of a dynamic, vital constitution. The appropriate principle was perhaps best stated in 1891 by Lord Bryce, a totally impartial but astute observer:

[The Supreme Court] has not always followed its own former decisions. This is natural in a court whose errors cannot be cured by the intervention of the legislature. . . . as nothing less than a constitutional amendment can alter the law contained in the Federal Constitution, the Supreme Court must choose between the evil of unsettling the law by reversing, and the evil of perpetuating bad law by following, a former decision. It may reasonably, in extreme cases, deem the latter evil the greater.

History as well as reason will exonerate the Court of the charges leveled against it because of the *School Segregation* opinions. The task was not an easy one. As Justice Frankfurter has reported:

It may be that responsibility for decision dulls the capacity of discernment. The fact is that one sometimes envies the certitude of outsiders regarding the compulsions to be drawn from the vague and admonitory constitutional provisions. Only for those who do not have the responsibility for decisions can it be easy to decide the grave and complex problems they raise especially in controversies that excite public interest.

Certainly Frankfurter and his brethren displayed courage as well as wisdom in this opinion. They may take pride in the fact that it revealed a courage and wisdom that the Congress has never shown on this issue; a courage and wisdom that no President has yet shown on this issue.

It is ordinarily true that the courts are behind the people in the formulation of guiding principles of law. In this instance, however, the Supreme Court, following the lead of scientists such as Dr. Clark, has advanced faster than the public has yet been willing to follow. This is true not only in the area of discrimination against the Negro because of his race, it is equally true, as the recent *Regents' Prayer* case has shown, where the prejudice involved is not race prejudice but religious prejudice. The failure of the people to provide the support to which the Court is entitled, a failure demonstrated in the newspapers each and every day, underlines the importance of Dr. Clark's book and this new edition of it, which includes the Supreme Court's own convincing language in the *Brown* decision.

Not only does the public lag behind the Court in these areas, but the public fails to accept and live the democratic ideal itself. In this age of anxiety, it is perhaps appropriate that the major ill of the American body politic is suggestive of a schizophrenic psychosis. The image is totally separated from reality. The incompatibility between the American creed, as it is termed by Myrdal and Dr. Clark, and American practices of racial and religious prejudice is at the center of many of this nation's most crucial problems. What makes a people dedicated to reason and justice behave in a manner totally contradictory of its intellectual and moral standards? Essentially this is the problem with which Dr.

Clark deals in this excellent study of the causes of and cures for the invidious discrimination in which this country indulges. In terms that can be understood by all, he has demonstrated the exorbitant price that these practices extort both from the dominant and dominated groups. Equally clear are the suggested practices that will help to eliminate the evils.

The problems created by and resulting from racial and religious prejudices are not likely to be eliminated by judicial fiat. Prejudices like these will diminish only to the extent that people are made to realize that the price of retaining them will necessarily be the destruction of our society. In short, the elimination of the evil can come only through education. It is just such education that Dr. Clark offers the reader of this volume.

Appendix 2. Text of the Supreme Court Opinions May 17, 1954

Mr. Chief Justice Warren delivered the opinion of the Court.

These cases come to us from the States of Kansas, South Carolina, Virginia, and Delaware. They are premised on different facts and different local conditions, but a common legal question justifies their consideration together in this consolidated opinion.

In each of the cases, minors of the Negro race, through their legal representatives, seek the aid of the courts in obtaining admission to the public schools of their community on a non-segregated basis. In each instance, they had been denied admission to schools attended by white children under laws requiring or permitting segregation according to race. This segregation was alleged to deprive the plaintiffs of the equal protection of the laws under the Fourteenth Amendment. In each of the cases other than the Delaware case, a three-judge federal district court denied relief to the plaintiffs on the so-called "separate but equal" doctrine announced by this Court in *Plessy* v. *Ferguson*, 163 U. S. 537. Under that doctrine, equality of treatment is accorded when the races are provided substantially equal facilities, even though these facilities be separate. In the Delaware case, the Supreme Court of Delaware adhered to that doctrine, but ordered that the plaintiffs be admitted to the white schools because of their superiority to the Negro schools.

The plaintiffs contend that segregated public schools are not "equal" and cannot be made "equal," and that hence they are deprived of the equal protection of the laws. Because of the obvious importance of the question presented, the Court took jurisdiction.[2] Argument was heard in the 1952 Term and reargument was heard this Term on certain questions propounded by the Court.[3]

Reargument was largely devoted to the circumstances surrounding the adoption of the Fourteenth Amendment in 1868. It covered exhaustively consideration of the Amendment in Congress, ratification by the states, then existing practices in racial segregation, and the views of proponents and opponents of the Amendment. This discussion and our own investigation convince us that, although these sources cast some light, it is not enough to resolve the problem with which we are faced. At best, they are inconclusive. The most avid proponents of the post-War Amendments undoubtedly intended them to remove all legal distinctions among "all persons born or naturalized in the United States." Their opponents, just as certainly, were antagonistic to both the letter and the spirit of the Amendments and wished them to have the most limited effect. What others in Congress and the state legislatures had in mind cannot be determined with any degree of certainty.

An additional reason for the inconclusive nature of the Amendment's history, with respect to segregated schools, is the status of public education at that time.[4] In the South, the movement toward free common schools, supported by general taxation, had not yet taken hold. Education of white children was largely in the hands of private groups. Education of Negroes was almost nonexistent, and practically all of the race were illiterate. In fact, any education of Negroes was forbidden by law in some states. Today, in contrast, many Negroes have achieved outstanding success in the arts and sciences as well as in the business and professional world. It is true that public education had already advanced further in the North, but the effect of the Amendment on Northern States was generally ignored in the congressional debates. Even in the North, the conditions of public education did not approximate those existing today. The curriculum was usually rudimentary; ungraded schools were common in rural areas; the school term was but three months a year in many states; and compulsory school attendance was virtually unknown. As a consequence, it is not surprising that there should be so little in the history of the Fourteenth Amendment relating to its intended effect on public education.

In the first cases in this Court construing the Fourteenth Amendment, decided shortly after its adoption, the Court interpreted it as proscribing all state-imposed discriminations against the Negro race.[5] The doctrine of "separate but equal" did not make its appearance in this Court until 1896 in the case of *Plessy* v. *Ferguson supra,* involving not education but transportation.[6] American courts have since labored with the doctrine for half a century. In this Court there have been six cases involving the "separate but equal" doctrine in the field of public education.[7] In *Cumming* v. *County Board of Education,* 175 U. S. 528, and *Gong Lum* v. *Rice,* 275 U. S. 78, the validity of the doctrine itself was not challenged.[8] In more recent cases, all on the graduate school level, inequality was found in that specific benefits enjoyed by white students were denied to Negro students of the same educational qualifications. *Missouri ex rel. Gaines* v. *Canada,* 305 U. S. 337; *Sipuel* v. *Oklahoma,* 332 U. S. 631; *Sweatt* v. *Painter,* 339

U. S. 629; *McLaurin* v. *Oklahoma State Regents*, 339 U. S. 637. In none of these cases was it necessary to re-examine the doctrine to grant relief to the Negro plaintiff. And in *Sweatt* v. *Painter, supra,* the Court expressly reserved decision on the question whether *Plessy* v. *Ferguson* should be held inapplicable to public education.

In the instant cases, that question is directly presented. Here, unlike *Sweatt* v. *Painter,* there are findings below that the Negro and white schools involved have been equalized, or are being equalized with respect to buildings, curricula, qualifications and salaries of teachers, and other "tangible" factors.[9] Our decision, therefore cannot turn on merely a comparison of these tangible factors in the Negro and white schools involved in each of the cases. We must look instead to the effect of segregation itself on public education.

In approaching this problem, we cannot turn the clock back to 1868 when the Amendment was adopted, or even to 1896 when *Plessy* v. *Ferguson* was written. We must consider public education in the light of its full development and its present place in American life throughout the Nation. Only in this way can it be determined if segregation in public schools deprives these plaintiffs of the equal protection of the laws.

Today, education is perhaps the most important function of state and local governments. Compulsory school attendance laws and the great expenditures for education both demonstrate our recognition of the importance of education to our democratic society. It is required in the performance of our most basic public responsibilities, even service in the armed forces. It is the very foundation of good citizenship. Today it is a principal instrument in awakening the child to cultural values, in preparing him for later professional training, and in helping him to adjust normally to his environment. In these days, it is doubtful that any child may reasonably be expected to succeed in life if he is denied the opportunity of an education. Such an opportunity, where the state has undertaken to provide it, is a right which must be made available to all on equal terms.

We come then to the question presented: Does segregation of children in public schools solely on the basis of race, even though the physical facilities and other "tangible" factors may be equal, deprive the children of the minority group of equal educational opportunities? We believe that it does.

In *Sweatt* v. *Painter, supra,* in finding that a segregated law school for Negroes could not provide them equal educational opportunities, this Court relied in large part on "those qualities which are incapable of objective measurement but which make for greatness in a law school." In *McLaurin* v. *Oklahoma State Regents, supra,* the Court, in requiring that a Negro admitted to a white graduate school be treated like all other students, again resorted to intangible considerations: ". . . his ability to study, to engage in discussions and exchange views with other students, and, in general, to learn his profession." Such considerations apply with added force to children in grade and high schools. To separate them from others of similar age and qualifications solely because of their race generates a feeling of inferiority as to their status in the community that may effect their hearts and minds in a way unlikely ever to be undone. The effect of this separation on their educational opportunities was well stated by a finding in the Kansas case by a court which nevertheless felt compelled to rule against the Negro plaintiffs:

> Segregation of white and colored children in public schools has a detrimental effect upon the colored children. The impact is greater when it has the sanction of the law; for the policy of separating the races is usually interpreted as denoting the inferiority of the Negro group. A sense of inferiority affects the motivation of a child to learn. Segregation with the sanction of law, therefore, has a tendency to retard the educational and mental development of Negro children and to deprive them of some of the benefits they would receive in a racially integrated school system.[10]

Whatever may have been the extent of psychological knowledge at the time of *Plessy* v. *Ferguson,* this finding is amply supported by modern authority.[11] Any language in *Plessy* v. *Ferguson* contrary to this finding is rejected.

We conclude that in the field of public education the doctrine of "separate but equal" has no place. Separate educational facilities are inherently unequal. Therefore, we hold that the plaintiffs and others similarly situated for whom the actions have been brought are, by reason of the segregation complained of, deprived of the equal protection of the laws guaranteed by the Fourteenth Amendment. This disposition makes unnecessary any discussion whether such segregation also violates the Due Process Clause of the Fourteenth Amendment.[12]

Because these are class actions, because of the wide applicability of this decision, and because of the great variety of local conditions, the formulation of decrees in these cases presents problems of considerable complexity. On reargument, the consideration of appropriate relief was necessarily subordinated to the primary question — the constitutionality of segregation in public education. We have now announced that such segregation is a denial of the equal protection of the laws. In order that we may have the full assistance of the parties in formulating decrees, the cases will be restored to the docket, and the parties are requested to present further argument on Questions 4 and 5 previously propounded by the Court for the reargument this Term.[13] The Attorney General of the United States is again invited to participate. The Attorneys General of the states requiring or permitting segregation in public education will also be permitted to appear as *amici curiae* upon request to do so by September 15, 1954, and submission of briefs by October 1, 1954.[14]

It is so ordered.

DISTRICT OF COLUMBIA DECISION

Mr. Chief Justice Warren delivered the opinion of the Court.

This case (*Bolling* v. *Sharpe*) challenges the validity of segregation in the public schools of the District of Columbia. The petitioners, minors of the Negro race, allege that such segregation deprives them of due process of law under the Fifth Amendment. They were refused admission to a public school attended by white children solely because of their race. They sought the aid of the District Court for the District of Columbia in obtaining admission. That court dismissed their complaint. We granted a writ of certiorari before judgment in the Court of Appeals because of the importance of the constitutional question presented. 344 U. S. 873.

We have this day held that the Equal Protection clause of the Fourteenth Amendment prohibits the states from maintaining racially segregated public schools.[15] The legal problem in the District of Columbia is somewhat different, however. The Fifth Amendment, which is applicable in the District of Columbia, does not contain an equal protection clause as does the Fourteenth Amendment which applies only to the states. But the concepts of equal protection and due process, both stemming from our American ideal of fairness, are not mutually exclusive. The "equal protection of the laws" is a more explicit safeguard of prohibited unfairness than "due process of law," and, therefore, we do not imply that the two are always interchangeable phrases. But, as this Court has recognized, discrimination may be so unjustifiable as to be violative of due process.[16]

Classifications based solely upon race must be scrutinized with particular care since they are contrary to our traditions and hence constitutionally suspect.[17] As long ago as 1896, this Court declared the principle "that the Constitution of the United States, in its present form, forbids, so far as civil and political rights are concerned, discrimination by the General Government, or by the States, against any citizen because of his race."[18] And in *Buchanan* v. *Warley*, 245 U. S. 60, the Court held that a statute which limited the right of a property owner to convey his property to a person of another race was, as an unreasonable discrimination, a denial of due process of law.

Although the Court has not assumed to define "liberty" with any great precision, that term is not confined to mere freedom from bodily restraint. Liberty under law extends to the full range of conduct which the individual is free to pursue, and it cannot be restricted except for a proper governmental objective. Segregation in public education is not reasonably related to any proper governmental objective, and thus imposes on Negro children of the District of Columbia a burden that constitutes an arbitrary deprivation on their liberty in violation of the Due Process Clause.

In view of our decision that the Constitution prohibits the states from maintaining racially segregated public schools, it would be unthinkable that the same Constitution would impose a lesser duty on the Federal Government.[19] We hold that racial segregation in the public schools of the District of Columbia is a denial of the due process of law guaranteed by the Fifth Amendment to the Constitution.

For the reasons set out in *Brown* v. *Board of Education*, this case will be restored to the docket for reargument on Questions 4 and 5 previously propounded by the Court. 345 U. S. 972.

It is so ordered.

THE SUPREME COURT'S FOOTNOTES

[1] In the Kansas case, *Brown* v. *Board of Education*, the plaintiffs are Negro children of elementary school age residing in Topeka. They brought this action in the United States District Court for the District of Kansas to enjoin enforcement of a Kansas statute which permits, but does not require, cities of more than 15,000 population to maintain separate school facilities for Negro and white students. Kan. Gen. Stat. (Sec.) 72-1724 (1949). Pursuant to that authority, the Topeka Board of Education elected to establish segregated elementary schools. Other public schools in the community, however, are operated on a non-segregated basis. The three-judge District Court, convened under 28 U. S. C. (Secs.) 2281 and 2284, found that segregation in public education has a detrimental effect upon Negro children, but denied relief on the ground that the Negro and white schools were substantially equal with respect to buildings, transportation, curricula, and educational qualifications of teachers. 98 F. Supp. 797. The case is here on direct appeal upon 28 U. S. C. (Sec.) 1253.

In the South Carolina case, *Briggs* v. *Elliott*, the plaintiffs are Negro children of both elementary and high school age residing in Clarendon County. They brought this action in the United States District Court for the Eastern District of South Carolina to enjoin enforcement of provisions in the state constitution and statutory code which require the segregation of Negroes and whites in public schools. S. C. Const., Art. XI, (Sec.) 7; S. C. Code (Sec.) 5377 (1942). The three-judge District Court, convened under 28 U. S. C. (Secs.) 2281 and 2284, denied the requested relief. The court found that the Negro schools were inferior to the white schools and ordered the defendants to begin immediately to equalize the facilities. But the court sustained the validity of the contested provisions and denied the plaintiffs admission to the white schools during the equalization program. 98 F. Supp. 529. This Court vacated the District Court's judgment and remanded the case for the purpose of obtaining the court's views on a report filed by the defendants concerning the progress made in the equalization program. 342 U. S. 350. On remand, the District Court found that substantial equality had been achieved except for buildings and that the defendants were proceeding to rectify this inequality as well. 103 F. Supp. 920. The case is again here on direct appeal under 28 U. S. C. (Sec.) 1253.

In the Virginia case, *Davis* v. *County School Board,* the plaintiffs are Negro children of high school age residing in Prince Edward County. They brought this action in the United States District Court for the Eastern District of Virginia to enjoin enforcement of provisions in the state constitution and statutory code which require the segregation of Negroes and whites in public schools. Va. Const., (Sec.) 140; Va. Code (Sec.) 22-221 (1950). The three-judge District Court, convened under 28 U. S. C. (Secs.) 2281 and 2284, denied the requested relief. The court found the Negro school inferior in physical plant, curricula, and transportation, and ordered the defendants forthwith to provide substantially equal curricula and transportation and to "proceed with all reasonable diligence and dispatch to remove" the inequality in physical plant. But, as in the South Carolina case, the court sustained the validity of the contested provisions and denied the plaintiffs admission to the white schools during the equalizaton program. 103 F. Supp. 337. The case is here on direct appeal under 28 U. S. C. (Sec.) 1253.

In the Delaware case, *Gebhart* v. *Belton,* the plaintiffs are Negro children of both elementary and high school age residing in New Castle County. They brought this action in the Delaware Court of Chancery to enjoin enforcement of provisions in the state constitution and statutory code which require the segregation of Negroes and whites in public schools. Del. Const., Art. X, (Sec.) 2; Del. Rev. Code (Sec.) 2631 (1935). The Chancellor gave judgment for the plaintiffs and ordered their immediate admission to schools previously attended only by white children, on the ground that the Negro schools were inferior with respect to teacher training, pupil-teacher ratio, extra-curricular activities, physical plant, and time and distance involved in travel. 87 A. 2d 862. The Chancellor also found that segregation itself results in an inferior education for Negro children (see note 10, *infra*), but did not rest his decision on that ground. *Id.,* at 865. The Chancellor's degree was affirmed by the Supreme Court of Delaware, which intimated, however, that the defendants might be able to obtain a modification of the decree after equalization of the Negro and white schools had been accomplished. 91 A. 2d 137, 152. The defendants, contending only that the Delaware courts had erred in ordering the immediate admission of the Negro plaintiffs to the white schools, applied to this Court for certiorari. The writ was granted, 344 U. S. 891. The plaintiffs, who were successful below, did not submit a cross-petition.

2 344 U. S. 1, 141, 891.

3 345 U. S. 972. The Attorney General of the United States participated both Terms as *amicus curiae.*

4 For a general study of the development of public education prior to the Amendment, see Butts and Cremin, A History of Education in American Culture (1953), Pts. I, II; Cubberley, Public Education in the United

States (1934 ed.), cc. II-XII. School practices current at the time of the adoption of the Fourteenth Amendment are described in Butts and Cremin, *supra,* at 269-275; Cubberley, *supra,* at 288-339, 408-431; Knight, Public Education in the South (1922), cc. VIII, IX. See also H. Ex. Doc. No. 315, 41st Cong., 2d Sess. (1871). Although the demand for free public schools followed substantially the same pattern in both the North and the South, the development in the South did not begin to gain momentum until about 1850, some twenty years after that in the North. The reasons for the somewhat slower development in the South (*e.g.,* the rural character of the South and the different regional attitudes toward state assistance) are well explained in Cubberley, *supra,* at 408, 423. In the country as a whole, but particularly in the South, the War virtually stopped all progress in public education. *Id.,* at 427-428. The low status of Negro education in all sections of the country, both before and immediately after the War, is described in Beale, A History of Freedom of Teaching in American schools (1941), 112-132, 175-195. Compulsory school attendance laws were not generally adopted until after the ratification of the Fourteenth Amendment, and it was not until 1918 that such laws were in force in all the states. Cubberley, *supra,* at 563-565.

⁵ *Slaughter-House Cases,* 16 Wall. 36, 67-72 (1873); *Strauder* v. *West Virginia,* 100 U. S. 303, 307-308 (1879): "It ordains that no State shall deprive any person of life, liberty, or property, without due process of law, or deny to any person within its jurisdiction the equal protection of the laws. What is this but declaring that the law in the States shall be the same for the black as for the white; that all persons, whether colored or white, shall stand equal before the laws of the States, and in regard to the colored race, for whose protection the amendment was primarily designed, that no discrimination shall be made against them by law because of their color? The words of the amendment, it is true, are prohibitory, but they contain a necessary implication of a positive immunity, or right, most valuable to the colored race, — the right to exemption from unfriendly legislation against them distinctively as colored, — exemption from legal discriminations, implying inferiority in civil society, lessening the security of their enjoyment of the rights which others enjoy, and discriminations which are steps towards reducing them to the condition of a subject race."

See also *Virginia* v. *Rives,* 100 U. S. 313, 318 (1879); *Ex parte Virginia,* (100) U. S. 339, 344-345 (1879).

⁶ The doctrine apparently originated in *Roberts* v. *City of Boston,* 59 Mass. 198, 206 (1849), upholding school segregation against attack as being violative of a state constitutional guarantee of equality. Segregation in Boston public schools was eliminated in 1855. Mass. Acts 1855, c. 256. But elsewhere in the North segregation in public education has persisted until recent years. It is apparent that such segregation has long been a nationwide problem, not merely one of sectional concern.

⁷ See also *Berea College* v. *Ketucky,* 211 U. S. 45 (1908).

⁸ In the *Cumming* case, Negro taxpayers sought an injunction requiring the defendant school board to discontinue the operation of a high school for white children until the board resumed operation of a high school for Negro children. Similarly, in the *Gong Lum* case, the plaintiff, a child of Chinese descent, contended only that state authorities had misapplied the doctrine

by classifying him with Negro children and requiring him to attend a Negro school.

9 In the Kansas case, the court below found substantial equality as to all such factors. 98 F. Supp. 797, 798. In the South Carolina case, the court below found that the defendants were proceeding "promptly and in good faith to comply with the court's decree." 103 F. Supp. 920, 921. In the Virginia case, the court below noted that the equalization program was already "afoot and progressing" (103 F. Supp. 377, 341); since then, we have been advised, in the Virginia Attorney General's brief on reargument, that the program has now been completed. In the Delaware case, the court below similarly noted that the state's equalization program was well under way. 91 A. 2d 137, 149.

10 A similar finding was made in the Delaware case: "I conclude from the testimony that in our Delaware society, State-imposed segregation in education itself results in the Negro children, as a class, receiving educational opportunities which are substantially inferior to those available to white children otherwise similarly situated." 87 A. 2d 862, 865.

11 K. B. Clark, Effect of Prejudice and Discrimination on Personality Development (Midcentury White House Conference on Children and Youth, 1950); Witmer and Kotinsky, Personality in the Making (1952), c. VI; Deutscher and Chein, The Psychological Effects of Enforced Segregation: A Survey of Social Science Opinion, 26 J. Psychol. 259 (1948); Chein, What Are the Psychological Effects of Segregation Under Conditions of Equal Facilities?, 3 Int. J. Opinion and Attitude Res. 229 (1949); Brameld, Educational Costs, in Discrimination and National Welfare (McIver ed., 1949), 44-48; Frazier, The Negro in the United States (1949), 674-681. And see generally Myrdal, An American Dilemma (1944).

12 See *Bolling* v. *Sharpe, infra,* concerning the Due Process Clause of the Fifth Amendment.

13 "4. Assuming it is decided that segregation in public schools violates the Fourteenth Amendment

"(a) would a decree necessarily follow providing that, within the limits set by normal geographic school districting, Negro children should forthwith be admitted to schools of their choice, or

"(b) may this Court, in the exercise of its equity powers, permit an effective gradual adjustment to be brought about from existing segregated systems to a system not based on color distinctions?

"5. On the assumption on which questions 4 (a) and (b) are based, and assuming further that this Court will exercise its equity powers to the end described in question 4 (b).

"(a) should this Court formulate detailed decrees in these cases;

"(b) if so, what specific issues should the decrees reach;

"(c) should this Court appoint a special master to hear evidence with a view to recommending specific terms for such decrees;

"(d) should this Court remand to the courts of first instance with directions to frame decrees in these cases, and if so, what general directions should the decrees of this Court include and what procedures should the courts of first instance follow in arriving at the specific terms of more detailed decrees?"

14 See Rule 42, Revised Rules of this Court (effective July 1, 1954).

[15] *Brown* v. *Board of Education,* — U. S. —.

[16] *Detroit Bank* v. *United States,* 317 U. S. 329; *Currin* v. *Wallace,* 306 U. S. 1, 13-14, *Steward Machine Co.* v. *Davis,* 301 U. S. 548, 585.

[17] *Korematsu* v. *United States,* 323 U. S. 214, 216; *Hirabayashi* v. *United States,* 320 U. S. 81, 100.

[18] *Gibson* v. *Mississippi,* 162 U. S. 565, 591. Cf. *Steele* v. *Louisville & Nashville R. Co.,* 323 U. S. 192, 198-199.

[19] Cf. *Hurd* v. *Dodge,* 334 U. S. 24.

3. Appendix to Appellant's Briefs

THE EFFECTS OF SEGREGATION AND THE CONSEQUENCES OF
DESEGREGATION: A SOCIAL SCIENCE STATEMENT

I

The problem of the segregation of racial and ethnic groups
constitutes one of the major problems facing the American people
today. It seems desirable, therefore, to summarize the contributions which contemporary social science can make toward its
resolution. There are, of course, moral and legal issues involved
with respect to which the signers of the present statement cannot
speak with any special authority and which must be taken into
account in the solution of the problem. There are, however, also
factual issues involved with respect to which certain conclusions
seem to be justified on the basis of the available scientific evidence. It is with these issues only that this paper is concerned.
Some of the issues have to do with the consequences of segregation, some with the problems of changing from segregated to
unsegregated practices. These two groups of issues will be dealt

---

* No. 8. Oliver Brown, Mrs. Richard Lawton, Mrs. Sadie Emmanuel, *et
al.*, *Appellants*, vs. *Board of Education of Topeka, Shawnee County, Kansas,
et al.*

No. 101. *Appellants*, vs. R. W. Elliot, Chairman, J. D. Carson, *et al.*,
Members of the Board of Trustees of School District No. 22, Clarendon
County, S. C., *et al.*

No. 191. Dorothy E. Davis, Bertha M. Davis and Inez D. Davis, etc.,
et al., *Appellants*, vs. County School Board of Prince Edward County, Virginia, *et al.*

with in separate sections below. It is necessary, first, however, to define and delimit the problem to be discussed.

DEFINITIONS

For purposes of the present statement, *segregation* refers to that restriction of opportunities for different types of associations between the members of one racial, religious, national or geographic origin, or linguistic group and those of other groups, which results from or is supported by the action of any official body or agency representing some branch of government. We are not here concerned with such segregation as arises from the free movements of individuals which are neither enforced nor supported by official bodies, nor with the segregation of criminals or of individuals with communicable diseases which aims at protecting society from those who might harm it.

Where the action takes place in a social milieu in which the groups involved do not enjoy equal social status, the group that is of lesser social status will be referred to as the *segregated* group.

In dealing with the question of the effects of segregation, it must be recognized that these effects do not take place in a vacuum, but in a social context. The segregation of Negroes and of other groups in the United States takes place in a social milieu in which "race" prejudice and discrimination exist. It is questionable in the view of some students of the problem whether it is possible to have segregation without substantial discrimination. Myrdal[1] states: "Segregation * * * is financially possible and, indeed, a device of economy only as it is combined with substantial discrimination" (p. 629). The imbededness of segregation in such a context makes it difficult to disentangle the effects of segregation *per se* from the effects of the context. Similarly, it is difficult to disentangle the effects of segregation from the effects of a pattern of social disorganization commonly associated with it and reflected in high disease and mortality rates, crime and delinquency, poor housing, disrupted family life and general sub-standard living conditions. We shall, however, return to this problem after consideration of the observable effects of the total complex in which segregation is a major component.

II

At the recent Mid-century White House Conference on Children and Youth, a fact-finding report on the effects of prejudice, discrimination and segregation on the personality development of children was prepared as a basis for some of the deliberations.[2] This report brought together the available social science and psychological studies which were related to the problem of how racial and religious prejudices influenced the development of a healthy personality. It highlighted the fact that segregation, prejudices and discriminations, and their social concomitants potentially damage the personality of all children — the children of the majority group in a somewhat different way than the more obviously damaged children of the minority group.

The report indicates that as minority group children learn the inferior status to which they are assigned — as they observe the fact that they are almost always segregated and kept apart from others who are treated with more respect by the society as a whole — they often react with feelings of inferiority and a sense of personal humiliation. Many of them become confused about their own personal worth. On the one hand, like all other human beings they require a sense of personal dignity; on the other hand, almost nowhere in the larger society do they find their own dignity as human beings respected by others. Under these conditions, the minority group child is thrown into a conflict with regard to his feelings about himself and his group. He wonders whether his group and he himself are worthy of no more respect than they receive. This conflict and confusion leads to self-hatred and rejection of his own group.

The report goes on to point out that these children must find ways with which to cope with this conflict. Not every child, of course, reacts with the same patterns of behavior. The particular pattern depends upon many interrelated factors, among which are: the stability and quality of his family relations; the social and economic class to which he belongs; the cultural and educational background of his parents; the particular minority group to which he belongs; his personal characteristics, intelligence, special talents, and personality pattern.

Some children, usually of the lower socio-economic classes, may react by overt aggressions and hostility directed toward their own group or members of the dominant group.[3] Anti-social and delinquent behavior may often be interpreted as reactions to these racial frustrations. These reactions are self-destructive in that the larger society not only punishes those who commit them, but often interprets such aggressive and anti-social behavior as justification for continuing prejudice and segregation.

Middle class and upper class minority group children are likely to react to their racial frustrations and conflicts by withdrawal and submissive behavior. Or, they may react with compensatory and rigid conformity to the prevailing middle class values and standards and an aggressive determination to succeed in these terms in spite of the handicap of their minority status.

The report indicates that minority group children of all social and economic classes often react with a generally defeatist attitude and a lowering of personal ambitions. This, for example, is reflected in a lowering of pupil morale and a depression of the educational aspiration level among minority group children in segregated schools. In producing such effects, segregated schools impair the ability of the child to profit from the educational opportunities provided him.

Many minority group children of all classes also tend to be hypersensitive and anxious about their relations with the larger society. They tend to see hostility and rejection even in those areas where these might not actually exist.

The report concludes that while the range of individual differences among members of a rejected minority group is as wide as among other peoples, the evidence suggests that all of these children are unnecessarily encumbered in some ways by segregation and its concomitants.

With reference to the impact of segregation and its concomitants on children of the majority group, the report indicates that the effects are somewhat more obscure. Those children who learn the prejudices of our society are also being taught to gain personal status in an unrealistic and non-adaptive way. When comparing themselves to members of the minority group, they are not required to evaluate themselves in terms of the more basic standards of actual personal ability and achievement. The culture permits and at times, encourages them to direct their feelings of hostility and aggression against whole groups of people the members of which are perceived as weaker than themselves. They often develop patterns of guilt feelings, rationalizations and other mechanisms which they must use in an attempt to protect themselves from recognizing the essential injustice of their unrealistic fears and hatreds of minority groups.[4]

The report indicates further that confusion, conflict, moral cynicism, and disrespect for authority may arise in majority group children as a consequence of being taught the moral, religious and democratic principles of the brotherhood of man and the importance of justice and fair play by the same persons and institutions who, in their support of racial segregation and related practices, seem to be acting in a prejudiced and discriminatory manner. Some individuals may attempt to resolve this conflict by intensifying their hostility toward the minority group. Others may react by guilt feelings which are not necessarily reflected in more humane attitudes toward the minority group. Still others react by developing an unwholesome, rigid, and uncritical idealization of all authority figures — their parents, strong political and economic leaders. As described in *The Authoritarian Personality*,[5] they despise the weak, while they obsequiously and unquestioningly conform to the demands of the strong whom they also, paradoxically, subconsciously hate.

With respect to the setting in which these difficulties develop, the report emphasized the role of the home, the school, and other social institutions. Studies[6] have shown that from the earliest school years children are not only aware of the status differences among different groups in the society but begin to react with the patterns described above.

Conclusions similar to those reached by the Mid-century White House Conference Report have been stated by other social scientists who have concerned themselves with this problem. The following are some examples of these conclusions:

Segregation imposes upon individuals a distorted sense of social reality.[7]

Segregation leads to a blockage in the communications and interaction between the two groups. Such blockages tend to increase mutual suspicion, distrust and hostility.[8]

Segregation not only perpetuates rigid stereotypes and reinforces negative attitudes toward members of the other group, but also leads to the development of a social climate within which violent outbreaks of racial tensions are likely to occur.[9]

We return now to the question, deferred earlier, of what it is about the total society complex of which segregation is one feature that produces the effects described above — or, more precisely, to the question of whether we can justifiably conclude that, as only one feature of a complex social setting, segregation is in fact a significantly contributing factor to these effects.

To answer this question, it is necessary to bring to bear the general fund of psychological and sociological knowledge concerning the role of various environmental influences in producing feelings of inferiority, confusions in personal roles, various types of basic personality structures and the various forms of personal and social disorganization.

On the basis of this general fund of knowledge, it seems likely that feelings of inferiority and doubts about personal worth are attributable to living in an underprivileged environment only insofar as the latter is itself perceived as an indicator of low social status and as a symbol of inferiority. In other words, one of the important determinants in producing such feelings is the awareness of social status difference. While there are many other factor that serve as reminders of the differences in social status, there can be little doubt that the fact of enforced segregation is a major factor.[10]

This seems to be true for the following reasons among others: (1) because enforced segregation results from the decision of the majority group without the consent of the segregated and is commonly so perceived; and (2) because historically segregation patterns in the United States were developed on the assumption of the inferiority of the segregated.

In addition, enforced segregation gives official recognition and sanction to these other factors of the social complex, and thereby enhances the affects of the latter in creating the awareness of social status differences and feelings of inferiority.[11] The child who, for example, is compelled to attend a segregated school may be able to cope with ordinary expressions of prejudice by regarding the prejudiced person as evil or misguided; but he cannot readily cope with symbols of authority, the full force of the authority of the State — the school or the school board, in this instance — in the same manner. Given both the ordinary expression of prejudice and the school's policy of segregation, the former takes on greater force and seemingly becomes an official expression of the latter.

Not all of the psychological traits which are commonly observed in the social complex under discussion can be related so directly to the awareness of status differences — which in turn is, as we have already noted, materially contributed to by the practices of segregation. Thus, the low level of aspiration and defeatism so commonly observed in segregated groups is undoubtedly related to the level of self-evaluation; but it is also, in some measure, related among other things to one's expectations with regard to opportunities for achievement and, having achieved, to the opportunities for making use of these achievements. Similarly, the hypersensitivity and anxiety displayed by many minority group children about their relations with the larger society probably reflects their awareness of status differences; but it may also be influenced by the relative absence of opportunities for equal status contact which would provide correctives for prevailing unrealistic stereotypes.

The preceding view is consistent with the opinion stated by a large majority (90%) of social scientists who replied to a questionnaire concerning the probable effects of enforced segregation under conditions of equal facilities. This opinion was that, regardless of the facilities which are provided, enforced segregation is psychologically detrimental to the members of the segregated group.[12]

Similar considerations apply to the question of what features of the social complex of which segregation is a part contribute to the development of the traits which have been observed in majority group members. Some of these are probably quite closely related to the awareness of status differences, to which, as has already been pointed out, segregation makes a material contribution. Others have a more complicated relationship to the total social setting. Thus, the acquisition of an unrealistic basis for self-evaluation as a consequence of majority group membership probably reflects fairly closely the awareness of status differences. On the other hand, unrealistic fears and hatreds of minority groups, as in the case of the converse phenomenon among minority group members, are probably significantly influenced as well by the lack of opportunities for equal status contact.

With reference to the probable effects of segregation under conditions of equal facilities on majority group members, many of the social scientists who responded to the poll in the survey cited above felt that the evidence is less convincing than with regard to the probable effects of such segregation on minority group members, and the effects are possibly less widespread. Nonetheless, more than 80% stated it as their opinion that the effects of such segregation are psychologically detrimental to the majority group members.[13]

It may be noted that many of these social scientists supported their opinions on the effects of segregation on both majority and minority groups by reference to one or another or to several of the following four lines of published and unpublished evidence.[14] First, studies of children throw light on the relative priority of the awareness of status differentials and related factors as compared to the awareness of differences in facilities. On this basis, it is possible to infer some of the consequences of segregation as distinct from the influence of inequalities of facilities. Second, clinical studies and depth interviews throw light on the genetic sources and causal sequences of various patterns of psychological reaction; and, again, certain inferences are possible with respect to the effects of segregation *per se*. Third, there actually are some relevant but relatively rare instances of segregation with equal or even superior facilities, as in the cases of certain Indian reservations. Fourth, since there are inequalities of facilities in racially and ethnically homogeneous groups, it is possible to infer the kinds of effects attributable to such inequalities in the absence of effects of segregation and by a kind of subtraction to estimate the effects of segregation *per se* in situations where one finds both segregation and unequal facilities.

III

Segregation is at present a social reality. Questions may be raised, therefore, as to what are the likely consequences of desegregation.

One such question asks whether the inclusion of an intellectually inferior group may jeopardize the education of the more intelligent group by lowering educational standards or damage the less intelligent group by placing it in a situation where it is at a marked competitive disadvantage. Behind this question is the assumption, which is examined below, that the presently segregated groups actually are inferior intellectually.

The available scientific evidence indicates that much, perhaps all, of the observable differences among various racial and national groups may be adequately explained in terms of environmental differences.[15] It has been found, for instance, that the differences between the average intelligence test scores of Negro and white children decrease, and the overlap of the distributions increases, proportionately to the number of years that the Negro children have lived in the North.[16] Related studies have shown that this change cannot be explained by the hypothesis of selective migration.[17] It seems clear, therefore, that fears based on the assumption of innate racial differences in intelligence are not well founded.

It may also be noted in passing that the argument regarding the intellectual inferiority of one group as compared to another is, as applied to schools, essentially an argument for homogeneous groupings of children by intelligence rather than by race. Since even those who believe that there are innate differences between Negroes and whites in America in average intelligence grant that considerable overlap between the two groups exists, it would follow that it may be expedient to group together the superior whites and Negroes, the average whites and Negroes, and so on. Actually, many educators have come to doubt the wisdom of class groupings made homogeneous solely on the basis of intelligence.[18] Those who are opposed to such homogeneous grouping believe that this type of segregation, too, appears to create generalized feelings of inferiority in the child who attends a below average class, leads to undesirable emotional consequences in the education of the gifted child, and reduces learning opportunities which result from the interaction of individuals with varied gifts.

A second problem that comes up in an evaluation of the possible consequences of desegregation involves the question of whether segregation prevents or stimulates inter-racial tension and conflict and the corollary question of whether desegregation has one or the other effect.

The most direct evidence available on this problem comes from observations and systematic study of instances in which desegregation has occurred. Comprehensive reviews of such instances[19] clearly establish the fact that desegregation has been carried out successfully in a variety of situations although outbreaks of violence had been commonly predicted. Extensive desegregation has taken place without major incidents in the armed services in both Northern and Southern installations and involving officers and enlisted men from all parts of the country, including the South.[20] Similar changes have been noted in housing[21] and industry.[22] During the last war, many factories both in the North and South hired Negroes on a non-segregated, non-discriminatory basis. While a few strikes occurred, refusal by management and unions to yield quelled all strikes within a few days.[23]

Relevant to this general problem is a comprehensive study of urban race riots which found that race riots occurred in segregated neighborhoods, whereas there was no violence in sections of the city where the two races lived, worked and attended school together.[24]

Under certain circumstances desegregation not only proceeds without major difficulties, but has been observed to lead to the emergence of more favorable attitudes and friendlier relations between races. Relevant studies may be cited with respect to housing,[25] employment,[26] the armed services[27] and merchant marine,[28] recreation agency,[29] and general community life.[30]

Much depends, however, on the circumstances under which members of previously segregated groups first come in contact with others in unsegregated situations. Available evidence suggests, first, that there is less likelihood of unfriendly relations when the change is simultaneously introduced into all units of a social institution to which it is applicable — *e.g.*, all of the schools in a school system or all of the shops in a given factory.[31] When factories introduced Negroes in only some shops but not in others the prejudiced workers tended to classify the desegregated shops as inferior, "Negro work." Such objections were not raised when complete integration was introduced.

The available evidence also suggests the importance of consistent and firm enforcement of the new policy by those in authority.[32] It indicates also the importance of such factors as: the absence of competition for a limited number of facilities or benefits;[33] the possibility of contacts which permit individuals to learn about one another as individuals;[34] and the possibility of equivalence of positions and functions among all of the participants within the unsegregated situation.[35] These conditions can generally be satisfied in a number of situations, as in the armed services, public housing developments, and public schools.

IV

The problem with which we have here attempted to deal is admittedly on the frontiers of scientific knowledge. Inevitably, there must be some differences of opinion among us concerning the conclusiveness of certain items of evidence, and concerning the particular choice of words and placement of emphasis in the preceding statement. We are nonetheless in agreement that this statement is substantially correct and justified by the evidence, and the differences among us, if any, are of a relatively minor order and would not materially influence the preceding conclusions.

FLOYD H. ALLPORT, Syracuse, New York
GORDON W. ALLPORT, Cambridge, Mass.
CHARLOTTE BABCOCK, M.D., Chicago, Ill.
VIOLA W. BERNARD, M.D., N. Y., N. Y.
JEROME S. BRUNER, Cambridge, Mass.
HADLEY CANTRIL, Princeton, New Jersey
ISIDOR CHEIN, New York, New York
KENNETH B. CLARK, New York, N. Y.
MAMIE P. CLARK, New York, New York
STUART W. COOK, New York, New York
BINGHAM DAI, Durham, North Carolina
ALLISON DAVIS, Chicago, Illinois
ELSE FRENKEL-BRUNSWIK, Berkeley, Calif.
NOEL P. GIST, Columbia, Missouri
CHARLES S. JOHNSON, Nashville, Tennessee

DANIEL KATZ, Ann Arbor, Michigan

OTTO KLINEBERG, New York, New York

DAVID KRECH, Berkeley, California

ALFRED MCCLUNG LEE, Brooklyn, N. Y.

R. N. MACIVER, New York, New York

PAUL F. LAZARSFELD, New York, N. Y.

ROBERT K. MERTON, New York, N. Y.

GARDNER MURPHY, Topeka, Kans.

THEODORE M. NEWCOMB, Ann Arbor, Mich.

ROBERT REDFIELD, Chicago, Illinois

IRA DEA. REID, Haverford, Pennsylvania

ARNOLD M. ROSE, Minneapolis, Minn.

GERHART SAENGER, New York, New York

R. NEVITT SANFORD, Poughkeepsie, N. Y.

S. STANFIELD SARGENT, New York, N. Y.

M. BREWSTER SMITH, New York, N. Y.

SAMUEL A. STOUFFER, Cambridge, Mass.

WELLMAN WARNER, New York, N. Y.

GOODWIN WATSON, New York, New York

ROBIN M. WILLIAMS, Ithaca, New York

Dated: September 22, 1952.

FOOTNOTES

[1] Myrdal, G., *An American Dilemma*, 1944.

[2] Clark, K. B., *Effect of Prejudice and Discrimination on Personality Development*, Fact Finding Report Mid-century White House Conference on Children and Youth, Children's Bureau, Federal Security Agency, 1950 (mimeographed).

[3] Brenman, M., The Relationship Between Minority Group Identification in A Group of Urban Middle Class Negro Girls, *J. Soc. Psychol.*, 1940, 11, 171-197; Brenman, M. Minority Group Membership and Religious, Psychosexual and Social Patterns in A Group of Middle-Class Negro Girls. *J. Soc. Psychol.*, 1940, 12, 179-196; Brenman, M., Urban Lower-Class Negro Girls, *Psychiatry*, 1953, 6, 307-324; Davis, A., The Socialization of the American Negro Child and Adolescent, *J. Negro Educ.*, 1939, 8, 264-275.

[4] Adorno, T. W.; Frenkel-Brunswik, E.; Levinson, D. J.; Sanford, R. N., *The Authoritarian Personality*, 1951.

[5] Adorno, T. W.; Frenkel-Brunswik, E.; Levinson, D. J.; Sanford, R. N., *The Authoritarian Personality*, 1951.

[6] Clark, K. B. & Clark, M. P., Emotional Factors in Racial Identification and Preference in Negro Children, *J. Negro Educ.*, 1950, 19, 341-350; Clark, K. B. & Clark, M. P., Racial Identification and Preference in Negro Children, *Readings in Social psychology*, Ed. by Newcomb & Hartley, 1947; Radke, M.; Trager, H.; Davis, H., Social Perceptions and Attitudes of Children, *Genetic Psychol. Monog.*, 1949, 40, 327-447; Radke, M.; Trager, H.; Children's Perceptions of the Social Role of Negroes and Whites, *J. Psychol.*, 1950, 29, 3-33.

[7] Reid, Ira, What Segregated Areas Mean; Brameld, T., Educational Cost, *Discrimination and National Welfare*, Ed. by MacIver, R. M., 1949.

[8] Frazier, E., *The Negro in the United States*, 1949; Krech, D. & Crutchfield, R. S., *Theory and Problems of Social Psychology*, 1948; Newcomb, T., *Social Psychology*, 1950.

[9] Lee, A. McClung and Humphrey, N. D., *Race Riot*, 1943.

[10] Frazier, E., *The Negro in the United States*, 1949; Myrdal, G., *An American Dilemma*, 1944.

[11] Reid, Ira, What Segregated Areas Mean. *Discrimination and National Welfare*, Ed. by MacIver, R. M., 1949.

[12] Deutscher, M. and Chein, I., The Psychological Effects of Enforced Segregation: A Survey of Social Science Opinion, *J. Psychol.*, 1948, 26, 259-287.

[13] Deutscher, M. and Chein, I. The Psychological Effects of Enforced Segregation: A Survey of Social Science Opinion, *J. Psychol.*, 1948, 26, 259-287.

[14] Chein, I., What Are the Psychological Effects of Segregation Under Conditions of Equal Facilities?, *International J. Opinion and Attitude Res.*, 1949, 2, 229-234.

[15] Klineberg, O., *Characteristics of American Negro*, 1945; Klineberg, O., *Race Differences*, 1936.

[16] Klineberg, O., *Negro Intelligence and Selective Migration*, 1935.

[17] Klineberg, O., *Negro Intelligence and Selective Migration*, 1935.

[18] Brooks, J. J., Interage Grouping on Trial—Continuous Learning, *Bulletin No. 87, Association for Childhood Education*, 1951; Lane, R. H., Teacher in Modern Elementary School, 1941; Educational Policies Commission of the National Education Association and the American Association of School Administration Report in *Education For All Americans*, published by the N. E. A. 1948.

[19] Delano, W., Grade School Segregation: The Latest Attack on Racial Discrimination, *Yale Law Journal*, 1952, 61, 5, 730-744; Rose, A., The Influence of Legislation on Prejudice; Chapter 53 in *Race Prejudice and Discrimination*, Ed. by Rose, A., 1951; Rose, A., *Studies in Reduction of Prejudice*, Amer. Council on Race Relations, 1948.

[20] Kenworthy, E. W., The Case Against Army Segregation, *Annals of the American Academy of Political and Social Science*, 1951, 275, 27-33; Nelson, Lt. D. D., *The Integration of the Negro in the U. S. Navy*, 1951; Opinions About Negro Infantry Platoons in White Companies in Several Divisions, *Information and Education Division, U. S. War Department, Report No. B.157*, 1945.

[21] Conover, R. D., *Race Relations at Codornices Village, Berkeley-Albany, California; A Report of the Attempt to Break Down the Segregated Pattern*

on *A Directly Managed Housing Project,* Housing and Home Finance Agency, Public Housing Administration, Region I, December 1947 (mimeographed); Deutsch, M. and Collins, M. E., *Interracial Housing, A Psychological Study of A Social Experiment,* 1951; Rutledge, E., *Integration of Racial Minorities in Public Housing Project: A Guide for Local Housing Authorities on How to Do It,* Public Housing Administration, New York Field Office (mimeographed).

22 Minard, R. D., The Pattern of Race Relationships in the Pocahontas Coal Field, *J. Social Issues,* 1952, 8, 29-44; Southall, S. E., *Industry's Unfinished Business,* 1951; Weaver, G. L-P, *Negro Labor, A National Problem,* 1941.

23 Southall, S. E., *Industry's Unfinished Business,* 1951; Weaver, G. L-P, *Negro Labor, A National Problem,* 1941.

24 Lee, A. McClung and Humphrey, N. D., *Race Riot,* 1943; Lee, A. McClung, Race Riots Aren't Necessary, *Public Affairs Pamphlet,* 1945.

25 Deutsch, M. and Collins, M. E., *Interracial Housing, A Psychological Study of A Social Experiment,* 1951; Merton, R. K.; West, P. S.; Jahoda, M., *Social Fictions and Social Facts: The Dynamics of Race Relations in Hilltown,* Bureau of Applied Social Research, Columbia Univ., 1949 (mimeographed); Rutledge, E., *Integration of Racial Minorities in Public Housing Projects; A Guide for Local Housing Authorities on How To Do It,* Public Housing Administration, New York Field Office (mimeographed); Wilner, D. M.; Walkley, R. P., and Cook, S. W., Intergroup Contact and Ethnic Attitudes in Public Housing Projects, *J. Social Issues,* 1952, 8, 45-69.

26 Harding, J., and Hogrefe, R., Attitudes of White Department Store Employees Toward Negro Co-workers, *J. Social Issues,* 1952, 8, 19-28; Southall, S. E., *Industry's Unfinished Business,* 1951; Weaver, G. L-P., *Negro Labor, A National Problem,* 1941.

27 Kenworthy, E. W., The Case Against Army Segregation, *Annals of the American Academy of Political and Social Science,* 1951, 275, 27-33; Nelson, Lt. D. D., *The Integration of the Negro in the U. S. Navy,* 1951; Stouffer, S., et al., *The American Soldier,* Vol. I, Chap. 19, A Note on Negro Troops in Combat, 1949; Watson, G., *Action for Unity,* 1947; Opinions About Negro Infantry Platoons in White Companies in Several Divisions, *Information and Education Division, U. S. War Department, Report No. B-157,* 1945.

28 Brophy, I. N., The Luxury of Anti-Negro Prejudice, *Public Opinion Quarterly,* 1946, 9, 456-466 (Integration in Merchant Marine), Watson, G., *Action for Unity,* 1947.

29 Williams, D. H., *The Effects of an Interracial Project Upon the Attitudes of Negro and White Girls Within the Young Women's Christian Association,* Unpublished M.A. thesis, Columbia University, 1934.

30 Dean, J. P., *Situational Factors in Intergroup Relation: A Research Progress Report.* Paper Presented to American Sociological Society, 12/28/49 (mimeographed); Irish, D. P., Reactions of Residents of Boulder, Colorado, to the Introduction of Japanese Into the Community, *J. Social Issues,* 1952, 8, 10-17.

31 Minard, R. D., The Pattern of Race Relationships in the Pocahontas Coal Field, *J. Social Issues,* 1952, 8, 29-44; Rutledge, E., *Integration of Racial Minorities in Public Housing Projects; A Guide for Local Housing*

Authorities on How to Do It, Public Housing Administration, New York Field Office (mimeographed).

[32] Deutsch, M. and Collins, M. E., *Interracial Housing, A Psychological Study of A Social Experiment*, 1951, Feldman, H., The Technique of Introducing Negroes Into the Plant, *Personnel*, 1942, 19, 461-466; Rutledge, E., *Integration of Racial Minorities in Public Housing Projects; A Guide for Local Housing Authorities on How to Do It*, Public Housing Administration, New York Field Office (mimeographed); Southall, S. E., *Industry's Unfinished Business*, 1951; Watson, G., *Action for Unity*, 1947.

[33] Lee, A. McClung and Humphrey, N. D., *Race Riot*, 1943; Williams, R., Jr., *The Reduction of Intergroup Tensions*, Social Science Research Council, New York, 1947; Windner, A. E., *White Attitudes Towards Negro-White Interaction In An Area of Changing Racial Composition.* Paper Delivered at the Sixtieth Annual Meeting of the American Psychological Association, Washington, September 1952.

[34] Wilner, D. M.; Walkley, R. P.; and Cook, S. W., Intergroup Contact and Ethnic Attitudes in Public Housing Projects, *J. Social Issues*, 1952, 8, 45-69.

[35] Allport, G. W., and Kramer, B., Some Roots of Prejudice, *J. Psychol.*, 1946, 22, 9-39; Watson, J., Some Social and Psychological Situations Related to Change in Attitude, *Human Relations*, 1950, 3, 1.

REFERENCES

Adorno, T. W.; Frenkel-Brunswik, E. Levinson, D. J.; Sanford, R. N., *The Authoritarian Personality*, 1951.

Allport, G. W., and Kramer, B., Some Roots of Prejudice, *J. Psychol.*, 1946, 22, 9-39.

Bauer, C., Social Questions in Housing and Community Planning, *J. of Social, Issues.* 1951, VII, 1-34.

Brameld, T., Educational Costs *Discrimination and National Welfare*, Ed. by MacIver, R. M., 1949.

Brenman, M., The Relationship Between Minority Group Identification in A Group of Urban Middle Class Negro Girls, *J. Soc. Psychol.*, 1940, 11, 171-197.

Brenman, M., Minority Group Membership and Religious, Psychosexual and Social Patterns In A Group of Middle-Class Negro Girls, *J. Soc. Psychol.*, 1940, 12, 179-196.

Brenman, M., Urban Lower-Class Negro Girls, *Psychiatry*, 1943, 6, 307-324.

Brooks, J. J., Interage Grouping on Trial, Continuous Learning, *Bulletin No. 87 of the Association for Childhood Education*, 1951.

Brophy, I. N., The Luxury of Anti-Negro Prejudice, *Public Opinion Quarterly*, 1946, 9, 456-466 (Integration in Merchant Marine).

Chein, I., What are the Psychological Effects of Segregation Under Conditions of Equal Facilities?, *International J. Opinion & Attitude Res.*, 1949, 2, 229-234.

Clark, K. B., Effect of Prejudice and Discrimination on Personality Development, *Fact Finding Report Mid-Century White House Conference on Children and Youth*, Children's Bureau-Federal Security Agency, 1950 (mimeographed).

Clark, K. B. and Clark, M. P., Emotional Factors in Racial Identification and Preference in Negro Children, *J. Negro Educ.*, 1950, 19, 341-350.

Clark, K. B. and Clark, M. P., Racial Identification and Preference in Negro Children, *Readings in Social Psychology*, Ed. by Newcomb & Hartley, 1947.

Conover, R. D., *Race Relations at Codornices Village, Berkeley-Albany, California: A Report of the Attempts to Break Down the Segregated Pattern On A Directly Managed Housing Project*, Housing and Home Finance Agency, Public Housing Administration, Region I, 1947 (mimeographed).

Davis, A., The Socialization of the American Negro Child and Adolescent, *J. Negro Educ.*, 1939, 8, 264-275.

Dean, J. P., *Situational Factors in Intergroup Relations: A Research Progress Report*, paper presented to American Sociological Society, Dec. 28, 1949 (mimeographed).

Delano, W., Grade School Segregation: The Latest Attack on Racial Discrimination,*Yale Law Journal*, 1952, 61, 730-744.

Deutscher, M. and Chein, I., The Psychological Effects of Enforced Segregation: A Survey of Social Science Opinion, *J. Psychol.*, 1948, 26, 259-287.

Deutsch, M. and Collins, M. E., *Interracial Housing, A Psychological Study of a Social Experiment*, 1951.

Feldman, H., The Technique of Introducing Negroes Into the Plant, *Personnel*, 1942, 19, 461-466.

Frazier, E., *The Negro In the United States*, 1949.

Harding, J., and Hogrefe, R., Attitudes of White Department Store Employees Toward Negro Co-Workers. *J. Social Issues*, 1952, 8, 19-28.

Irish, D. P., Reactions of Residents of Boulder, Colorado to the Introduction of Japanese Into the Community, *J. Social Issues*, 1952, 8, 10-17.

Kenworthy, E. W., The Case Against Army Segregation, *Annals of the American Academy of Political and Social Science*, 1951, 275, 27-33.

Klineberg, O., *Characteristics of American Negro*, 1945.

Klineberg, O., *Negro Intelligence and Selective Migration,* 1935.
Klineberg, O., *Race Differences,* 1936.
Krech, D. & Crutchfield, R. S., *Theory and Problems of Social Psychology,* 1948.

Lane, R. H., *Teacher in Modern Elementary School,* 1941.
Lee, A. McClung and Humphrey, N. D., *Race Riot,* 1943.
Lee, A. McClung, Race Riots Aren't Necessary, *Public Affairs Pamphlet,* 1945.

Merton, R. K.; West, P. S.; Jahoda, M., *Social Fictions and Social Facts: The Dynamics of Race Relations in Hilltown;* Bureau of Applied Social Research, Columbia University, 1949 (mimeographed).
Minard, R. D., The Pattern of Race Relationships in the Pocahontas Coal Field, *J. Social Issues,* 1952, 8, 29-44.
Myrdal, G., *An American Dilemma,* 1944.

Newcomb, T., *Social Psychology,* 1950.
Nelson, Lt. D. D., *The Integration of the Negro in the U. S. Navy,* 1951.

Rackow, F., Combatting Discrimination in Employment, *Bulletin No. 5, N. Y. State School of Industrial and Labor Relations,* Cornell Univ., 1951.
Radke, M., Trager, H., Davis, H., Social Perceptions and Attitudes of Children, *Genetic Psychol, Monog.,* 1949, 40, 327-447.
Radke, M., Trager, H., Children's Perceptions of the Social Role of Negroes and Whites, *J. Physcol.,* 1950, 29, 3-33.
Reid, Ira., What Segregated Areas Mean, *Discrimination and National Welfare,* Ed. by MacIver, R. M., 1949.
Rose, A., The Influence of Legislation on Prejudice Chapter 53 in *Race Prejudice and Discrimination,* Ed. by Rose, A., 1951.
Rose, A., *Studies in Reduction of Prejudice,* Amer. Council on Race Relations, 1948.
Rutledge, E. *Integration of Racial Minorities in Public Housing Projects; A Guide for Local Housing Authorities on How to Do It.* Public Housing Administration, New York Field Office (mimeographed).

Saenger, G. and Gilbert, E., Customer Reactions to the Integration of Negro Sales Personnel, *International Journal of Attitude and Opinion Research,* 1950, 4, 57-76.
Saenger, G. & Gordon, N. S., The Influence of Discrimination on Minority Group Members in its Relation to Attempts to Combat Discrimination, *J.Soc. Psychol.,* 1950, 31.
Southall, S. E., *Industry's Unfinished Business,* 1951.

Stouffer, S. et al., *The American Soldier,* Vol. I, Chap. 19, A Note on Negro Troops in Combat, 1949.

Watson, G., *Action for Unity,* 1947.

Watson, J., Some Social and Psychological Situations Related to Change in Attitude, *Human Relations,* 1950, 3, 1.

Weaver, G. L-P., *Negro Labor, A National Problem,* 1941.

Williams, D. H., *The Effects of an Interracial Project Upon the Attitudes of Negro and White Girls Within the Young Women's Christian Association,* Unpublished M. A. thesis, Columbia University, 1934.

Williams, R., Jr., *The Reduction of Intergroup Tensions,* Social Science Research Council, 1947.

Wilner, D. M., Walkley, R. P.; and Cook, S. W., Intergroup Contact and Ethnic Attitudes in Public Housing Projects, *J. Social Issues,* 1952, 8, 45-69.

Windner, A. E., *White Attitudes Towards Negro-White Interaction in in an Area of Changing Racial Composition,* Paper delivered at the Sixtieth Annual Meeting of The American Psychological Association, Washingtion, September 1952.

Opinions about Negro Infantry Platoons in White Companies in Several Divisions, *Information and Education Divisions, U. S. War Department, Report No. B-157,* 1945.

Educational Policies Commission of the National Education Association and the American Association of School Administration Report in, *Education for All Americans* published by the N.E.A. 1948.

Appendix 4. The Desegregation Cases: Criticism of the Social Scientist's Role

by Kenneth B. Clark

Basic to the direct and indirect criticisms which have been raised concerning the role of social scientists in the school desegregation cases is the generally unstated question of the propriety of social scientists playing any role in this type of legal controversy. It is clear that the public school desegregation cases are crucially related to the delicate and specific problems of the relative status of the Negro and white groups in American culture and the equally delicate and general problem of social change. Before one attempts to discuss the specific criticisms or the fundamental questions which they appear to reflect, it might be valuable to attempt an analysis of the social dynamics, the context within which such discussions seem either necessary or desirable. Serious discussion of whether social scientists should play a role in the legal processes related to the desegregation of the public schools would seem no more or less justified than discussions of the following questions:

Should social scientists play a role in helping industry function more efficiently—make larger profits—develop better labor management relations—increase the sense of satisfaction among the workers?

Should social scientists play a role in helping governmental agencies and key policy makers make more effective and valid decisions?

Should social scientists play a role in attempting to solve the many human and psychological problems faced by the military arm of our government?

The psychological significance of the fundamental problem posed by questioning the relationship between social scientists and the desegregation cases may be even more clearly illustrated by asking the analogous question:

Should biological scientists play a role in guiding medical research and practices?

The answers to the above questions would seem so obviously positive that one is forced to question the validity of the question which is implicit in the criticisms which have been raised concerning the role of the social scientists in the desegregation cases. In searching for an answer, one must look in the direction of understanding the complexity of the power structure of our society and particularly the types of threats to the existing social structure which are inherent in the recent decisions of the United States Supreme Court which ruled that racial segregation in public schools and other forms of state-supported public accommodations violate the equal protection clause of the fourteenth amendment of the United States Constitution. These decisions must be seen as demanding fundamental changes in the power alignments and group status patterns which prevail in our society. The social scientists who collaborated with the lawyers who argued and won these cases were certainly accessories to this demand for a significant form of social change. They themselves might not have been psychologically prepared to accept with equanimity the directness of the involvement or the sweeping demand for social change which the Court's decision precipitated. It is also possible that these changes are not only contrary to the prevailing status hierarchy among the racial groups in our society but also inimical to an important aspect of the continued controlling power pattern of this society. If this is true, the accessory role of social scientists in these decisions subjects them to the criticisms of those who are identified with and seek to perpetuate the racial status quo and the related power controls.

It may be, therefore, that the continued preoccupation of social scientists and their critics with the question of whether they should be involved in this phase of the legal processes reflects their anxiety in the face of these criticisms; and reflects even more concretely the possibility that these criticisms may lead to more punitive controls of those social scientists who continue to identify themselves with "controversial causes" — *i.e.*, causes which threaten the prevailing power alignments in the society.

Social scientists, like other knowledgeable individuals in our society, must be sensitive to the problems of power and the techniques of social control which are operative in the society in which they work. In spite of the demand for objectivity and integrity in the search for truth, the important determinant of serious scientific work, social scientists are influenced indirectly and sometimes directly, subtly and sometimes crudely, by the prevailing social biases and uncritically accepted frames of reference of their society.

Given this perspective, one can then begin to evaluate the specific criticisms which have been raised against the social scientists who have been involved in these desegregation cases. The implications of any of these criticisms are not restricted to the more academic problems of social science theory, methodology, and the nature of social science evidence. Nor are they limited to the more complex problems of the delicate relationship between the social sciences and the law. These are indeed crucial problems which merit continuous discussion and debate in the relatively young and dynamic social sciences. The full import of a given criticism must be understood in terms of whether it clarifies or distorts the larger social issues; specifically, the practical reality of the nature, function, and consequences of racial segregation in American life, the stresses and strains inevitably involved in attempts to change institutionalized patterns of social injustices, and the role of the courts and other governmental agencies in the competition among groups for changes in, or maintenance of, the status quo.

Some of the most intense criticisms have come from political leaders of the deep southern states. Men like Senators Eastland and Talmadge, former Governor Byrnes and Governor Faubus have attacked the Supreme Court's decision not only on the grounds that it violated "states rights" but also, significantly for the purposes of this paper, on the grounds that it attempted to substitute psychological and sociological theories for the law. There is a question whether these types of criticisms should be taken seriously by social scientists since they seem motivated largely by political considerations.

Attacks on the role of social scientists in these cases have not been restricted to politicians who object to the Court's decision and the social changes which they fear may result, but have come also from serious students of jurisprudence and more recently from social scientists. One of the most consistent of the legal critics is the distinguished professor of jurisprudence, Edmond Cahn, of New York University Law School. Earnest van den Haag is an example of a critic from within the field of social sciences. The bulk of this paper will be devoted to an analysis of the criticisms of Professor Cahn and Dr. van den Haag because Professor Cahn has undoubtedly influenced the thinking of other students of jurisprudence[1] and Dr. van den Haag has presented the most specific and intense critical comments that have so far been published by a social scientist.

EDMOND CAHN'S CRITICISMS

The criticisms of Professor Cahn take many forms.[2] Essentially, however, he states that it is incorrect to believe that the *Brown* decision[3] was "caused by the testimony and opinions of the scientists" and that the constitutional rights of Negroes or any other Americans should not "rest on any such flimsy founda-

tion as some of the scientific demonstrations in these records."
He contends that the cruelty inherent in racial segregation "is
obvious and evident."

Among his other charges are: (1) that this writer exaggerated
the contribution of social science experts to these cases; and (2)
that in writing a report of the role of social scientists which was
published before May 17, 1954, the writer could not have known
that Chief Justice Warren's opinion would not mention either
the testimony of the expert witnesses or the statements submitted
by the thirty-two social scientists. Professor Cahn added so-
licitously:

> The Chief Justice cushioned the blow to some extent by citing
> certain professional publications of the psychological experts in a
> footnote, alluding to them graciously as 'modern authority.' In view of
> their devoted efforts to defeat segregation, this was the kind of gesture
> a magnanimous judge would feel impelled to make, and we are bound
> to take satisfaction in the accolade.

In speculating on why the Court did not mention the social
scientists' brief in its opinion, Professor Cahn states his personal,
subjective reaction that the text of this statement conveyed little
or no information beyond what is known as "literary psychology." The fact is, however, that all but one of the references cited
by the Court in footnote 11 of the *Brown* decision were cited as
references in the social science brief which had been submitted
to the Court. The one reference which had not been listed but
cited by the Court was Witmer and Kotinsky's *Personality in the
Making*, the relevant portion of which was a summary of this
writer's White House Conference manuscript on the effects of
prejudice and discrimination on personality development.

Whatever might be one's degree of agreement or disagreement
with Professor Cahn's estimate of the worth of the social scientists' testimony in these cases or the degree of the Court's
regard for the social scientists' material presented in the brief
or in the trial records, one must take seriously his argument that
the constitutional rights of Negroes or other Americans should

not rest on social scientists' testimony alone. If he had concentrated and elaborated on this issue on a high level of academic discourse, he might have made an important contribution to thought in a field in which he is competent. When he leaves the area of the law, constitutional rights, and matters of jurisprudence and invades the area of social sciences, making broad and general comments about the validity of social science methods, premises, approaches, findings and conclusions, and when he explicitly or implicitly attacks or suggests that the social scientists who participated in these cases as witnesses and consultants did not do so with the utmost personal and scientific integrity, he gratuitously leaves his field of competence and communicates his personal opinions, biases and misconceptions as if they were facts. His prèstige in a field in which he has been trained thereby disguises his ignorance in a field in which he has no training. For these reasons, it is necessary to answer these charges and generalizations with clarity.

SOME RELEVANT FACTS

Before one enters a general appraisal of the validity of some of the many assumptions, implications, and charges raised by Professor Cahn, it is necessary to clarify certain points of fact which are relevant to opinions about the role of social scientists in these cases:

(1) The social scientists who participated in these cases were invited to do so by the lawyers of the NAACP. It was these lawyers who had the primary and exclusive responsibility for developing the legal rationale and approach upon which these cases would be tried and appealed. It was they who made the decision to bring the legal attack on the problem of overruling the *Plessy* "separate but equal" doctrine[4] by attempting to demonstrate that state laws which required or permitted segregation in public schools violated the equal protection clause of the fourteenth amendment. It was their decision that the chances of successs would be greater if it could be demonstrated that racial segregation, without regard to equality of facilities, damaged Negro children. Futhermore, it was their decision to determine

whether they could find acceptable evidence from social psychology and other social sciences which would support their belief that psychological damage resulted from racial segregation. Social scientists were not involved and did not participate in any way in these initial and important policy or legal strategy decisions. Only after these decisions were made by the lawyers of the NAACP were the social scientists approached and invited by the lawyers to participate in these cases. The social scientists were asked whether there were any relevant scientific studies on the psychological effects of racial segregation. Finally, it was the judgment of these lawyers that the studies and evidence offered by the social scientists were relevant and crucial enough to form an integral part of their trial and appellate case.

(2) The studies which were relied upon by the social scientists in arriving at the conclusion that racial segregation damaged the human personality were not studies which were conducted specifically for these legal cases. Systematic research on the psychological aspects of racial prejudice, discrimination, and segregation had been going on for more than fifteen years. The White House Conference manuscript, which was cited by the United States Supreme Court in footnote 11 in the *Brown* decision, was a compilation of all of the available knowledge of the effects of prejudice and discrimination on personality development in children and was prepared by this writer months before he was aware of the fact that the NAACP intended to bring cases before the federal courts challenging the validity of segregated schools.

(3) The studies cited in this White House Conference manuscript and the joint primary research of this writer and his wife formed the bulk of his testimony in three of these five cases. The primary research studies were conducted ten years before these cases were heard on the trial court level. Professor Cahn's allegation that the writer served in the role of advocate rather than that of an objective scientists in his participation in these cases seems difficult to sustain in the face of testimony given on the basis of research conducted ten years before these cases were heard. One would have to be gifted with the power of a seer in order to prepare himself for the role of advocate in these specific cases ten years in advance.

(4) The use of the "Dolls Test" (actual dolls, not pictures of dolls, were used in this research) on some of the plaintiffs was to determine whether the general findings from the larger number of Negro children who had been tested years before were true also for the children who were the actual plaintiffs in these cases. The decision to test some of these plaintiffs was a legal one made by the lawyers of the NAACP. It was their assumption as lawyers that general scientific findings would have more weight in a courtroom if it could be demonstrated that they also applied in the specific cases and for the particular plaintiffs before the court. When these plaintiff children were tested and interviewed

by this writer, it was his judgment that some of these children showed evidence of the same type of personality damage related to racial prejudice, segregation, and discrimination which was found in the larger number of subjects who were studied in the original, published research. This opinion was presented to the courts in the form of sworn testimony.

(5) The justices of the federal district courts were at all times free to rule that the testimony of the social scientists was irrelevant and immaterial. The United States Supreme Court could have refused to accept the Social Science statement which was submitted to it in the form of an appendix to the legal brief of the appellants. If either of these had been done, there would now be no question of whether the courts did or did not reply on the findings and opinions of social scientists.

It is still a matter of social reality that social scientific findings and opinions are not incorporated into, nor do they determine, policy decisions, legislative action, or judicial decisions except to the extent that those who have the power to make these practical decisions choose to accept or reject the relevant findings of scientists. Whether this should continue to be so is, of course, debatable.

"FIDELITY," "TRUTH," AND ACADEMIC COURTESY

Professor Cahn implies that the primary motive of the social psychologists who participated in these cases was not "strict fidelity to objective truth." This is a serious, grave, and shocking charge.

Professor Cahn did not present evidence to support his implication that the social scientists who particpated in these cases, and particularly this writer, betrayed their trusts as scientists. He merely makes the assertion that some day judges will be wise and will be able to notice "where objective science ends and advocacy begins." For the present, however, "it is still possible for the social psychologists to 'hoodwink' a judge who is not overwise. . . ."

It is difficult to take this type of comment seriously. Since it has been published over the signature of an individual who commands the respect of his legal colleagues, it cannot be dismissed. It cannot be waived aside as evidence that Professor Cahn believes himself wiser than the entire legal staff of the NAACP, the battery of lawyers employed by the opposition — including the late John W. Davis, who devoted a considerable amount of space in his Supreme Court brief and in his first arguments before the United States Supreme Court to the social science testimony — or the lawyers of the Department of Justice of the United States, and, finally, the Justices of the United States Supreme Court.

This point must be answered by a description of concrete facts in the relationship between the NAACP lawyers and the social scientists who were involved in these cases. The social scientists who testified in these cases or endorsed the Social Science appendix at the invitation of this writer were not the type of human beings who were capable, personally or professionally, of testifying to a fact or stating an opinion which they did not believe to be consistent with the scientific evidence as they knew it. These men are neither infallible nor all-wise; but they are the outstanding experts in this field. What is even more important, they are men of integrity.

When the lawyers of the NAACP, in their understandable zeal to develop the strongest possible case, asked the social scientists whether it was possible to present evidence showing that *public school segregation*, in itself, damaged the personalities of Negro children, it was pointed out to them that the available studies had so far not isolated this single variable from the total social complexity of racial prejudice, discrimination, and segregation. It was therefore not possible to testify on the psychologically damaging effects of segregated schools alone. Such specific evidence, if available at all, would have to come from educators and educational philosophers. Some of the more insistent lawyers felt that only this type of specific testimony would be of value to them in these cases. It was pointed out to these lawyers that if this were so then the social psychologists and other social scientists could not be of any significant, direct help to them. A careful examination of the testimony of the social scientists, found in the record of these cases and the Social Science appendix submitted to the United States Supreme Court, will show that the social scientists presented testimony, opinions, and information consistent with the available empirical studies, conclusions, and observations. They presented this information with caution and restraint befitting their roles as trained and disciplined scientists. As expert witnesses, they made not a single concession to expediency, to the practical and legal demands of these cases, or even to the moral and humane issues involved as they adhered to their concept of "strict fidelity to objective truth." Certainly Professor Cahn cannot be the judge of whether his concept of "strict fidelity to objective truth" in the field of social science is more acceptable or valid than theirs.

It must also now be stated that one of the responsibilities assigned to this writer in his role of social science consultant to the legal staff of the NAACP was to advise the lawyers not only about those studies and individuals who were scientifically acceptable, but also to advise and warn them away from studies and individuals of questionable scientific repute. At least one well-publicized report on the damaging effects of segregation on the personality of Negroes was not used in these cases because it was the judgment of this writer, which was communicated to and accepted by the lawyers, that its methodology was scientifically questionable, its selection of subjects and sampling were clearly biased, and that its conclusions bordered on the sensational. In short, it was believed that in spite of the fact that this study purported to present clear evidence in support of the hypothesis that racial oppression damaged the personality of Negroes, its flaws and scientific inadequacy were so clear it could not be defended in court.

It is difficult to determine precisely what Professor Cahn means by "objective truth." According to his article "most of mankind already acknowledged . . ." that segregation is cruel to Negro children, involves stigma and loss of status, and may ultimately shatter their "spines" and deprive them of self-respect. The "shattering of spines" is Professor Cahn's contribution to the knowledge of the detrimental effects of racial segregation. No social scientist testified to this "fact." Professor Cahn contends, however, that when scientists attempt to demonstrate these same "well-known facts" through their use of the methods and approaches of science, they "provide a rather bizarre spectacle." What is more, he maintains they exaggerate their role, their methods are questionable, their logic and interpretation weak and fallacious, and they distort their findings as they become advocates who seek to "hoodwink" the judges. A serious question would be: How could the social scientists be so unreliable yet nonetheless come out with a picture of social reality which Professor Cahn and everyone else "already knew"?[5]

Professor Cahn presents a novel concept of the relationship between common knowledge and scientific knowledge. The logic of his position rests upon the premise that science concerns itself with one order of reality which is distinct from other forms of reality or truth — that a scientific "fact" has different attributes or characteristics than a "fact" of common knowledge. Another related theme which runs through his comments is that a "legal fact" is distinct from both a "scientific fact" and a "fact of common knowledge."

Cahn's pluralistic approach to the nature of "facts," while not a novel philosophical position, seems to involve a mystical semantic confusion which is inconsistent with the assumptions imperative for a scientific approach to the understanding of the nature of man, his society, and his environment.

Science is merely the last of many approaches that man has used in his attempt to determine the "facts" and truth of nature. As the late Professor Einstein has observed: "Scientific thought is a development of pre-scientific thought." Before and coincident with science, man tried mysticism, religion, and philosophy in his attempts to determine the facts of nature. In his quest to control his environment and his relations with his fellow human beings, he attempted to implement his various types of "knowledge" by seemingly compatible techniques of control, *e.g.*, magic, prayers, reason, law, and technology. These various approaches in the quest of truth and the control of the environment were not seeking different types of truth. Indeed, it must be assumed that science and technology developed precisely because earlier approaches to the nature of "truth" and "fact" left much to be desired by way of successful demonstration of the practical utility or the human consequences of these "truths" and "facts."

The development of science as an approach to the determination of truth involved the development of methods for the control of errors in human observation, judgment, biases, and vested interests. These were the factors which seemed to have distorted man's concept of, or blocked his contact with, the "truth" or "facts" of experience. When they are operative, man's "common knowledge" becomes inconsistent with "scientific knowledge." When they are controlled or for some other reason non-operative, "common knowledge" and "scientific knowledge" are coincident — both reflecting the nature of reality, truth, or facts, as these are knowable to the human senses and intelligence.

Science is essentially a method of controlled observation and verification for the purpose of reducing human errors of observation, judgment, or logic. Science begins with observation and ends by testing its assumptions against experience. It is not a creation of another order of reality. In a very basic sense there cannot be a "legal fact" or a "fact of common knowledge" which is not at the same time a "scientific fact." Whenever this appears to be true, one or the other type of "fact" is not a fact.

THE BASIC ISSUE

After one has cut through the emotional irrelevancies of Professor Cahn's article, one is confronted with the basic circuitous plea that the law and the courts of the land should be isolated in Olympian grandeur from the other intellectual and scientific activities of man. Specifically, Cahn seems primarily — even if unconsciously — disturbed by the fact that the upstarts of the new social sciences should have been involved at all in these important cases which belonged exclusively to lawyers and students of jurisprudence. It is to be hoped that a decreasing number of lawyers believe that laws and courts are sacred and should be kept antiseptically isolated from the main stream of human progress. Such isolation cannot be and never has been true except in the classrooms of some puristic law school professors.

The law is concerned with society and the regulation of human affairs. Social science, government, philosophy, and religion are also concerned with society, its understanding and regulation. Man's relations with his fellow man involve matters far too grave and crucial to be left to lawyers and judges alone. Respect for the law, intelligently and ethically conceived and executed, is essential for stable government. Intelligence and ethics cannot stem from the law alone but must be fed to it through the ceaseless struggles of scholars, scientists, and others toward truth and understanding. This may be difficult for Professor Cahn to accept. It nonetheless remains a fact.

As Brandeis once said: "A judge is presumed to know the elements of law, but there is no presumption that he knows the facts."[6] With the vast range and types of cases which come before the courts, it is unlikely that even the wisest judges and lawyers could be competent in all fields of human knowledge. One may presume that it was a recognition of these facts among others that influenced the decision of the lawyers of the NAACP to seek the help of social scientists in their attempt to overrule the *Plessy v. Ferguson* "separate but equal" doctrine which had dominated civil rights litigation since 1896.

Another important fact which was ignored by Professor Cahn in his castigation of the social scientists' role in these segregated school cases was the fact that this was not the first time that the lawyers of the NAACP had sought to convince the United States Supreme Court that segregation in and of itself was unconstitutional. In the *Sweatt*[7] and *McLaurin*[8] cases they sought a decision on the issue of segregation *per se* by relying on the traditional legal approach. Substantially the same United States Supreme Court which handed down the *Brown* and *Bolling*[9] decisions, however, decided the *Sweatt* and *McLaurin* cases within the framework of the *Plessy* "separate but equal" doctrine. It may merely be coincidental that the lawyers of the NAACP succeeded in overruling the *Plessy* doctrine only after they enlisted an impressive array of social science testimony and talent and attacked this problem with this approach.

ANOTHER POINT OF VIEW

Some astute students of jurisprudence hold opinions on this issue which differ from those presented by Professor Cahn. The late Alexander Pekelis, in making his case for a jurisprudence of welfare, stated:

A great many contemporary judicial decisions show this three fold leitmotif—awareness of freedom, confession of fallibility, and quest for extra-legal guidance. . . .

A participation of the social sciences in the development of a welfare jurisprudence may bring the normative elements in social science into the light of consciousness, and thus contribute to a healthy development of social theory. . . .

The economic and social facts of life, which legal realism has taught us, have banished the belief that judicial decisions are brought ready-made by constitutional storks. . . . Similarly, society cannot be built upon judicial whim or expediency alone.

We cannot turn back the clock. Social scientists (economists, sociologists and psychologists) are with us for good, and are going to remain in the very midst of government. . . . Judges may and should become acquainted with the various non-legal disciplines. . . . A judge should know more about social studies precisely in order to acquire the conviction that they can furnish no more certainty than constitutions, statutes or precedents.[10]

It would be fatuous to argue that because there is difference of opinion among eminent students of jurisprudence that, therefore, judicial opinions should not be taken seriously. Of course there are dangers involved in the use of science in any area of human activity. There are undoubtedly some social scientists who might be willing to sell their intelligence, training, and themselves to the highest bidder. There are those who will be easily intimidated by the practical demands of vested interests and men of power. There are those who will rationalize their subservience by demonstrating their affluence and tough-minded practicality — or even their scientific purity. But this is not new. Science has nonetheless continued its advance and contributions to the ethical and material progress of mankind.

ERNEST VAN DEN HAAG'S CRITICISM

The most serious and significant forms of criticisms are those which are now beginning to come from social scientists. Dr. Bruno Bettelheim of the University of Chicago has publicly stated that there is no scientific evidence that racial segregation damages the human personality. More recently, Ralph Ross and Ernest van den Haag published a book entitled THE FABRIC OF SOCIETY. The criticisms by Dr. van den Haag must be seen as distinct from the criticisms of politicians and students of jurisprudence. These are the criticisms of a social scientist who bears the responsibility and must be held to the rules of social science.

In an appendix to chapter 14 of THE FABRIC OF SOCIETY entitled "Prejudice About Prejudice," Dr. van den Haag, who is responsible for this section of the book, makes the following statements among others:

Whether humiliation leaves deep and lasting traces and whether it increases the incidence of personality disorders among Negroes, we do not know (nor do we know whether congregation would obviate them).

It (the United States Supreme Court) did not depend on the attempt of the social scientists to detect and prove the psychological injuries by 'scientific' tests—which is fortunate for the evidence presented *is so flimsy* as to discredit the conclusion. . . .

Dr. van den Haag then proceeds to repeat, with some elaborations, Edmond Cahn's criticisms of the role of social scientists in the desegregation cases. According to van den Haag, although the Court "did not depend" upon social scientists, "much weight was given certain 'generally accepted tests' which Professor Kenneth B. Clark undertook with certain Negro children in a segregated school."

Professor Clark tested sixteen children between the ages of six to nine in Clarendon County, South Carolina, and elsewhere about three hundred children. This number would be too small to test the reaction to a new soap. Professor Clark seems not to have made sure that his sample is unbiased. . . . It appears finally, that no attempt was made to compare the reactions of Negro children in segregated schools with those of Negro children in non-segregated schools. . . . He found then that the behavior he had attributed to segregation in his testimony—rejection of colored dolls by Negro children—occurs more often when children are in *non-segregated* schools.

Professor Clark presented *drawings* (K.B.C.) of dolls to the children, . . . Professor Clark concluded that prejudice had led them (the Negro children) to identify white and nice; and even to identify with the white dolls despite their own dark color.

His general interpretation—that the identification of 'white' with 'nice' is a result of anti-Negro prejudice—is truly astounding. . . .

The 'scientific' evidence for the injury is no more 'scientific' than the evidence presented in favor of racial prejudice. . . . We need not try 'scientifically' to prove that prejudice is clinically injurious. This is fortunate for we cannot.

In attempting to answer Dr. van den Haag's criticism of the wisdom of the May 17, 1954, decision of the United States Supreme Court and his criticism of the social science testimony which was presented to the federal courts at the trial level of these cases, one is confronted with a difficult task. To those students who are familiar with the facts of the Supreme Court's decision and the limited role of social scientists in the cases which led to this decision, it will be apparent that Dr. van den Haag's criticisms of this decision and the role of the social scientists are not based upon his direct knowledge of the facts. Either Dr. van den Haag did not read or did not understand the basic documents which are relevant to a scholarly discussion or criticism of these problems.

For example, he states that in its 1954 decision, the United States Supreme Court not only prohibited compulsory segregation but required "compulsory congregation." A careful reading of this decision reveals that nowhere does the Court demand what Dr. van den Haag calls "compulsory congregation." And certainly the Court does not attempt "to compel equal esteem of groups for each other." The Court, after reviewing the legal background and precedence and after alluding to the effects of state enforced segregation on the Negro plaintiffs, concluded ". . . that in the field of public education 'separate but equal' has no place. Separate educational facilities are inherently unequal. Therefore, we hold that the plaintiffs and others similarly situated . . . are, by reason of the segregation complained of, deprived of the equal protection of the laws guaranteed by the Fourteenth Amendment."

In reference to his attack on the role of the social scientist and particularly the role of the writer in these cases, it is equally clear that Dr. van den Haag relied upon secondary sources for his "facts" and published his critical analysis without reading the original reports of these research studies and without reading the Appendix to the Appellant's Briefs written by three social scientists and endorsed by thirty-two outstanding research workers in the field of race relations in America. Dr. van den Haag betrays himself by repeating a crucial error which was first found in Professor Cahn's criticism of the role of social scientists in these cases. He repeats Cahn's error that "Professor Clark presented *drawings* of dolls to the children." A reading of the original reports of this research would have revealed that one of the three methods used in this study was the presentation of *actual dolls* rather than the *drawings* of dolls.

Dr. van den Haag contends that "Professor Clark tested sixteen children between the ages of six and nine in Clarendon County, South Carolina" and "elsewhere about three hundred children."

He maintains "that this number would be too small to test the reaction to a new soap." The record of the testimony in the *Briggs* case,[11] reveals that the results of the tests of those sixteen children were not presented as an "unbiased" sample. It was clearly stated that these were the results of the testing of the plaintiffs in these cases.

The writer's testimony in these cases was not based exclusively on his own research findings but on his evaluation of the weight of evidence from other investigations of this problem. The record states:

> I have reached the conclusion from the examination of my own results and from an examination of the literature in the entire field that discrimination, prejudice, and segregation have definitely detrimental effects on the personality development of the Negro child.

Dr. van den Haag's criticism of the "flimsy" nature of the scientific evidence would have to be taken more seriously if he had examined carefully the nearly sixty references which were used as the basis of the social science brief which was submitted to the United States Supreme Court. If this were too arduous a task, then he could have examined the seven references cited by the United States Supreme Court in footnote 11 of the *Brown* decision.

Further evidence that Dr. van den Haag did not read the original reports of these research studies is found in his distortion of the findings and interpretation of the results of the dolls test and other methods which were used to explore the dynamics of racial identification and preference in Negro children. He states categorically that "Professor Clark concluded that prejudice had led them to identify white and nice." At no point in the report of this original research was this conclusion stated. In fact, the term "prejudice" was not used in the article referred to by van den Haag as the source of his statement. The preferences and identification of these Negro children were interpreted in terms of conflicts in self-esteem and the types of ego pressures which result when the attitudes of a larger society negate the normal self-esteem needs of human beings. If Dr. van den Haag had examined the original sources, he would have learned that these studies were conducted more than ten years before the authors had any knowledge that these findings could have any specific practical use. Originally, these were studies in the relatively technical and complex field of the determinants and dynamics of the development of the concept of the self. He would have learned, also, that nowhere in the reports of these early studies or in the social science brief presented to the United States Supreme Court was it ever contended that racial segregation, in itself, accounted for the observed damage in the ego structure of these children. The social science brief submitted to the United States Supreme Court was explicit on this fact:

> In dealing with the question of the effects of segregation, it must be recognized that these effects do not take place in a vacuum, but in a social context. The segregation of Negroes in the United States takes place in a social milieu in which 'race' prejudice and discrimination exist. It is questionable in the view of some students of the problem, whether it is possible to have segregation without substantial discrimination. . . . The imbedness of segregation in such a context makes it difficult to disentangle the effects of segregation per se from the effects of the context.

In his insistence that "we need not try scientifically to prove that prejudice is clinically injurious" and that this is fortunate "for we cannot," Dr. van den Haag betrays a peculiar concept of science. The assertion that we cannot prove, through the methods of science, the personality damage associated with social humiliation, stigma, and other forms of prolonged adverse social situations is a curious position for a contemporary social scientist to hold.

Probably the most disturbing and revealing aspect of Dr. van den Haag's criticism is the fact that an examination of other portions of his book demonstrates that he maintains a double standard of what he considers scientific objectivity and acceptable evidence. On the one hand, he contends that the writer's work and findings were unscientific and based on a number of cases that "would be too small to test the reaction to a new soap" and on the other hand, he accepts and presents the sweeping conclusions of Rene Spitz based on an unstated total number of children. Whatever the merits or defects of Spitz's work, the question still remains whether the following conclusions drawn by van den Haag are justified:

> The infant reaching the outside world after dreadful travail, must be made to feel at home if he is to stay. Even the greatest maternal comfort cannot replace what he has left behind.
> . . . It seems entirely possible that lack of maternal affection in the first few years of life deals a blow which cannot be mended later.

Dr. van den Haag seems to have one set of standards for the scientific acceptability of findings concerning the effects of hospitalism and maternal deprivation on infants and another set of standards for findings concerning the effects of the total pattern of racial prejudice, discrimination, and segregation on the personality development of children. Nowhere does he reveal the basis for his judgment that the evidence in the latter case is flimsy whlie the evidence in support of the former can be accepted uncritically as he presents it.

CONCLUSIONS

Those who attempt to use the methods of social science in dealing with problems which threaten the status quo must realistically expect retaliatory attacks, direct or oblique, and must be prepared to accept the risks which this role inevitably involves. Attacks motivated by understandable political opposition or the criticisms which reflect the vested interest or limitations of other disciplines must be expected.

Differences of opinion and interpretation concerning the relative weight to be given to the available evidence must, of course, be expected among conscientious social scientists. In this latter instance, however, certain fundamental rules of social scholarship, consistency and logic must prevail if the controversy is to be intellectually constructive and socially beneficial.

It is a fact that the collaboration between psychologists and other social scientists which culminated in the *Brown* decision will continue[12] in spite of criticisms. Those who question the propriety of this collaboration will probably increase the intensity of their criticism — particularly as social controversy and conflict increase. Nevertheless, some social scientists will continue to play a role in this aspect of the legal and judicial process because as scientists they cannot do otherwise. They are obligated by temperament, moral commitment and their concept of the role and demands of science. They will continue to do so in spite of criticisms or threats. They will do so because they see the valid goals of the law, government, social institutions, religion and science as identical; namely to secure for man personal fulfillment in a just, stable, and viable society.

FOOTNOTES

[1] See Blaustein and Ferguson, *Desegregation and the Law*, 135-37 (1957).

[2] Cahn, Chapter on Jurisprudence, *Annual Survey of American Law*, 30 N.Y.U. L. Rev. 150-69 (1955).

[3] *Brown v. Board of Educ.*, 347 U.S. 483 (1954).

[4] *Plessy v. Ferguson*, 163 U.S. 537 (1896).

[5] It may be noted parenthetically that it is questionable whether all judges share this "common knowledge," as is evidenced by the prior decision that upheld the "separate but equal" doctrine. At any rate, Professor Cahn does not explain why these judges did not act upon their knowledge. In fact, he does not explain how a person not gifted with superior insights can determine what is and what is not "common knowledge" as distinct from the personal biases of judges. Nor does Professor Cahn suggest any means, other than through the medium of expert witnesses, for getting "common knowledge," critically examined, into the court record so that it may be considered by judges who have the responsibility for the final decision.

[6] Mason, Brandeis, *A Free Man's Life* (1946).

[7] *Sweatt v. Painter*, 339 U.S. 629 (1950).

[8] *McLaurin v. Oklahoma State Regents*, 339 U.S. 637 (1950).

[9] *Bolling v. Sharpe*, 347 U.S. 497 (1954) (decided the same day, as the *Brown* decision). The Court held segregated schools in the District of Columbia to be unconstitutional.

10 Pekelis, *The Case For a Jurisprudence of Welfare*, 2 *Social Research* No. 3, reprinted in 6 *Lawyer's Guild Review* No. 5 (1946).

11 *Briggs* v. *Elliot*, 347 U.S. 483 (1954) (companion to the *Brown* case).

12 A group of psychologists are now working with the lawyers of the NAACP in an attempt to determine the most effective legal attack on the various types of plans developed by some southern states in an attempt to evade the letter and spirit of the *Brown* decision.

Appendix 5. The Role of the Social Sciences in Desegregation*

by Kenneth B. Clark

There is probably no more ominous and pervasive issue facing America and the world today than the problems involved in the rapidly changing status of nonwhite groups in their relationship to the previously dominant white Europeans. The delicacy of the relationship between China and the Soviet Union, the seething surge toward an independent nationalism on the part of the peoples of Asia and Africa, and the reorganization of the British Empire into a multi-racial Commonwealth of equal status partners are some of the contemporary manifestations of the profound social and psychological revolution precipitated by the infectiousness of the democratic idea. Racial desegregation in the United States must be seen as a crucial aspect of this world wide pattern of democratic social change.

The magnitude and implications of the desegregation problem make it imperative that American social scientists assume the responsibility inherent in their role as objective students of our society and attempt to understand the dynamics and complexities of this aspect of social change. This obligation must be fulfilled in spite of the fact that the desegregation problem in America

---

* An expanded version of the presidential address to the Society for the Psychological Study of Social Issues, delivered in Chicago on 5 September, 1960.

and the contextual problem of the changing status of racial groups throughout the world are issues fraught with subtle and flagrant biases, intensified by emotional entanglements, and confused by historical, economic, political, and international factors and practical power considerations. It is precisely because of these complicating variables that the responsibility of the social scientists to contribute their knowledge, insights, and approach toward an effective and democratic resolution of these problems becomes more challenging and imperative.

THE DILEMMA

The dilemma of the social scientists in employing the techniques and objectivity of science here is highlighted by the fact that complex social problems have historically been resolved not so much through the application of facts or principles of right or justice, but through the effective use of economic, social, political, or military power. In our past and present social and political system, social scientists lack this kind of primary effective power. Whatever power they may have is secondary and ancillary, derived through the sufferance or request of those who control primary power in our society. Social scientists do not establish policy or make definitive decisions on crucial social issues. At best, they sometimes advise the decision makers, and their advice may be accepted in whole, or in part, or not at all.

The following hypothesis seems relevant: The knowledge and advice of social scientists is sought and accepted in inverse relationship to the degree of controversy, intensity of feelings and emotions, and complexity of political, economic, and other power considerations and vested interest competitions which are involved in the particular social problem. A related and subsidiary hypothesis is that when social scientists are involved in controversial and power-weighted problems, the acceptance or rejection of their facts, knowledge, and advice is determined by the degree to which these are compatible with the prevailing power-determined point of view.

If these hypotheses are valid, then it follows that the advice of social scientists, based upon the best available empirical knowledge, on effective techniques for the desegregation of the public schools and other social institutions will be accepted and used only when it is regarded as to the advantage of the dominant or controlling power group. In the solution of a complex social problem, objective knowledge generally is not used until passions, politics, and other power considerations prove ineffective.

A most troublesome dilemma is faced then by those social scientists who persist in an attempt at objective study of crucial and controversial social problems. Their findings may be used as effectively by those who seek to maintain the *status quo* and to block progress as well as by those who seek to facilitate democratic social change. As is the case in the physical sciences, the discoveries of the social sciences may be used either for the benefit or the detriment of mankind. So far, there are no sure safeguards against the use of social science by a Faubus to create confusion and retard the desegregation process, just as there are no safeguards to insure that the physics of the atom will not be used to precipitate the ultimate catastrophy. The dilemma is further heightened by the yawning gap between the immediate determinants of power decisions and the values, intent, and general perspectives of the scientists who seek to obtain the factual answers to human problems. Within the past two or three decades, it has become stridently clear that "factual," "scientific" answers do not bring with them human and moral solutions.

But responsibility of the scientist to test and retest his hypotheses, to seek his facts, and to check on the accuracy of his predictions remain in spite of — and because of — the many obstacles which he is required to face and surmount. Only through maintaining his role as an objective searcher after truth can he hope to make any contribution toward a positive resolution of the survival problems of man.

An analysis of the past and present role of social scientists in the public school desegregation issue, a re-examination of the findings, and an evaluation of the accuracy of their predictions after five or six years may provide a basis for a more systematic understanding of the role, value, and possible contributions of social science in dealing with other complex social problems.

SOCIAL SCIENCE AND THE LAW

In February, 1951, Robert L. Carter, one of the lawyers for the National Association for the Advancement of Colored People, visited me to inquire whether psychologists had any findings which were relevant to the effects of racial segregation on the personality development of Negro children. He stated that the legal staff of the NAACP had decided to challenge the constitutionality of state laws which required or permitted racial segregation in public schools. These proposed cases would be tried in an attempt to overrule the *Plessy vs. Ferguson* "separate but equal" doctrine and to demonstrate that segregated facilities are inherently unequal. Carter and his legal colleagues believed that in order to increase the chances of successfully demonstrating before the Federal Courts that segregation violated the equal protection clause of the Fourteenth Amendment of the Constitution, the help of psychologists was necessary to evaluate the thesis that racial segregation inflicts psychological damage on its victims. He invited me to collaborate with the lawyers in planning for the most effective use of social psychologists and other social scientists in the courts of first instance and appeal when these cases were heard.

On the trial level, social scientists participated as expert witnesses, giving testimony on the nature of racial segregation, its psychological and personality consequences, and the probable consequences of desegregation (4). The first of these cases was heard before a Federal Court in Charleston, South Carolina, on May 28 and 29, 1951. The last of the four cases which challenged the constitutionality of state laws requiring or permitting segregated public schools was held in the Federal Court at Richmond, Virginia, starting on February 25, 1952.

On the appeal of these cases to the United States Supreme Court, the role of the social scientists was restricted to the preparation of materials related to the psychological effects of segregation, the consequences of desegregation, and finally an empirical analysis of techniques for desegregation. The data were collected and analyzed by social scientists and presented to the NAACP attorneys to be used in whatever ways they believed most effective in the presentation of their case. For the first argument in the October, 1952, term of the Supreme Court, the lawyers decided that the social psychological data should be presented in the form of a special social science brief as an appendix to the regular legal appellant's briefs. This precedent setting document (*10*), entitled "The Effects of Segregation and the Consequences of Desegregation: A Social Science Statement," was prepared by Stuart Cook, Isidor Chein, and me. Thirty-two outstanding American social scientists reviewed and endorsed it for presentation to the highest court of our land.

The Supreme Court, instead of handing down its decision during this year of the first argument, asked for a re-argument of these cases in terms of five questions posed by the Court itself. Appropriate preparation required a continued and broadened collaboration between social scientists and the legal staff of the NAACP because some of the Court's questions levied more heavily on social science than the law. Two of the queries concerned the history of the adoption of the Fourteenth Amendment; one was concerned with the power of the Court, and the last two were concerned with the method of transition from segregated to nonsegregated schools.

For example, the Court's fourth question asked the following:

Assuming it is decided that segregation in public schools violates the Fourteenth Amendment, (a) would a decree necessarily follow providing that, within the limits set by normal geographic school districting, Negro children should forthwith be admitted to schools of their choice, or (b) may this court, in the exercise of its equity powers, permit an effective gradual adjustment to be brought about from existing segregated systems to a system not based on color distinctions?

It was decided that this question should not be answered by speculation but through an objective empirical study of actual instances of desegregation. It was also decided that such a study and analysis should be the responsibility of social psychologists. I was assigned the responsibility of developing a research plan to obtain empirical evidence on this question. Again, this responsibility could be successfully discharged only through the contributions and involvement of many social scientists like Otto Klineberg, Robert K. Merton, Gordon Allport, Viola Bernard, Alfred McClung Lee, Gardner Murphy, Robin M. Williams, John Dean, Robert Johnson, and of course Stuart Cook, Isidor Chein, and Brewster Smith. This phase of the collaboration resulted in the publication of the monograph, "Desegregation: An Appraisal of the Evidence" (4), published under the auspices of the Society for the Psychological Study of Social Issues.

On May 17, 1954, the United States Supreme Court handed down its historic decision, ruling that all state laws which required or permitted racial segregation in public schools violated the equal protection clause of the Constitution. It is difficult to overestimate the significance of this decision. Its significance for constitutional law and civil rights litigation lies in its displacing the *Plessy vs. Ferguson* "separate but equal" doctrine, which has determined the framework of the legal struggle for unqualified equality of America's Negro citizens from 1896. This primary goal had been unequivocably won. Perhaps it is too early to evaluate the decision's vast educational, political, social, and international implications, but it is clear that they are of enormous weight.

Of special interest is the fact that the Court, in spite of criticisms (2), based its rejection of the old *Plessy vs. Ferguson* doctrine on contemporary psychological knowledge. The text of its decision ran as follows:

To separate Negro students from others of similar age and qualifications solely because of their race generates a feeling of inferiority as to their status in the community that may effect their hearts and minds in a way unlikely ever to be undone.

The Court then quotes from the decision of the trial judges in the Kansas case.

Segregation of white and colored children in public schools has a detrimental effect upon the colored children. The impact is greater when it has the sanction of the law; for the policy of separating the races is usually interpreted as denoting the inferiority of the Negro group. A sense of inferiority affects the motivation of a child to learn. Segregation with the sanction of law, therefore, has a tendency to retard the educational and mental development of Negro children and to deprive them of some of the benefits they would receive in a racially integrated school system.

The passage then concludes with these words:

Whatever may have been the extent of psychological knowledge at the time of *Plessy vs. Ferguson,* this finding is amply supported by modern authority. Any language in *Plessy vs. Ferguson* contrary to this finding is rejected. We conclude that in the field of public education the doctrine of "separate but equal" has no place. Separate educational facilities are inherently unequal . . .

In support of its reference to "modern authority," the Court cited seven social science documents in its famous eleventh footnote. Six of these seven came from the documents presented in the Social Science Appendix to the Appellant's Brief submitted at the October, 1952, term of the Court by the 32 social scientists. This fact, together with the emphasis placed on the psychological damage inherent in racial segregation in the May 17, 1954, decision, supports the belief that the U. S. Supreme Court gave careful consideration to the findings of social science in these crucial desegregation cases.

After establishing the primary legal fact of the unconstitutionality of racial segregation in public education by the *Brown* decision of May, 1954, the Court postponed the formulation of specific implementation decrees and consideration of appropriate relief for the plaintiffs. Because such decrees involved "problems of considerable complexity," among other reasons, it was necessary for the litigants, the Attorney General of the United States, and the Attorneys General of the states requiring or permitting segregation in public education, to submit briefs and "to present further arguments on Questions IV and V previously propounded by the Court for re-argument this term." The emphasis in this final argument was specifically and exclusively in terms of implementation of the previous decision and a determination of the most effective ways of bringing about the transition from "existing segregated systems to a system not based on color distinctions."

The task of the social scientist here was to provide the lawyers with the kind of information which, within the framework of the law, would differentiate fact from opinion, knowledge from prejudice, and predictions based upon past biases from those based upon careful and detailed analyses of past events. The aim was twofold: (1) to answer Question IV through the collection and analysis of all available instances of desegregation with particular emphasis on those instances in southern or southwestern states, and (2) to present this evidence in as specific and as concrete form as possible to clarify the conditions under which a change from segregation to desegregation could be smoothly and effectively accomplished.

This process primarily involved a re-examination of the results of the previous empirical study of problems of desegregation. The materials collected, analyzed, and presented in "Desegregation: An Appraisal of the Evidence" and by Harry Ashmore (1) had to be re-evaluated in the light of additional data, and their generalizations and conclusions had to be subjected to the rigorous scrutiny of outstanding scholars and students of the problem. Time made it necessary to call an emergency conference of these persons on July 23, 1954, to identify the most effective techniques of desegregation on the basis of available evidence. Those who attended that conference were Viola Bernard, Isidor Chein, Kenneth Clark, Mamie Clark, Stuart Cook, John Dean, Alfred McClung Lee, Theodore Newcomb, Elsa Robinson, Arnold Rose, Samuel Stouffer, and Goodwin Watson.[1] In addition to the contributions made by those present at the conference, I corresponded with Gordon Allport, Jerome Bruner, Bingham Dai, Gardner Murphy, and Ira Reid in order to obtain their judgment on the problems presented to us. Extensive and repeated personal conversations were held with Otto Klineberg and Robert Merton.

On the basis of the conference, correspondence, and personal discussions, I prepared and presented to the lawyers a preliminary memo on the techniques and methods for effective desegregation. It was their responsibility to decide how this memorandum should be used. After careful analysis and extensive discussion, they decided to integrate the social science data into a single legal brief which dealt specifically with the problem of effective implementation of the May 17, 1954, decision.[2]

On May 31, 1955, the Court handed down its decree, ignoring the main lines of evidence furnished by the social scientists, establishing the framework for the desegregation of the public schools. The subsequent pace and problems of public school desegregation may have been influenced, among other things, by the varying and contradictory interpretations of the meaning and forcefulness of this implementation decree. Its essential ambiguity is indicated by the belief, at the very time of its promulgation, by some proponents of segregation that it was a decided victory for the South and that the "Court has not had the courage of its previously avowed convictions."

Some pro-segregationists were not so sure, however, that the May 31st decree was a clear victory. A member of the state legislature of South Carolina exclaimed, "Insofar as the decision seems to indicate integration of the two races in the school system, I think no such plan can be put into operation in Clarendon

County or in South Carolina either, now or in the foreseeable future." The then Governor of Georgia, Marvin Griffin, stated the negative pro-segregationist position most forcefully: "No matter how much the Supreme Court seeks to sugar coat its bitter pill of tyranny, the people of Georgia and the South will not swallow it."

Negro leaders were also divided in their reaction. The chief officers of the NAACP publicly stated their gratification with the positive and specific quality of the Court's implementation decree. On the other hand, the president of the Mississippi State Conference of the NAACP commented prophetically and with undisguised bitterness: "It looks like the Supreme Court doesn't believe in our Constitution. The ruling will do some good, but it will require a lot of litigation on our part that could have been avoided had they rendered a forthright decision."

Events since 1955 have disturbingly and persistently reflected this confusion. The decisions handed down by the Federal District Courts in the Clarendon County, South Carolina, and the Prince Edward County, Virginia, cases after the May 31st decree were most liberal interpretations of the Court's implementation plan. In these decisions, local school officials were permitted an apparently indefinite time to present a scheme for the desegregation of their schools. Nor did these Courts require specific assurances that the problem would be systematically studied, that desegregation would proceed in "good faith," or that a deadline for its completion be stated and enforced. As a matter of fact, these decisions have allowed the continuation of segregated schools in Clarendon County, South Carolina, and Prince Edward County, Virginia, right up to the present. Even more disturbing, attorneys have not yet found a formula for obtaining compliance with the Supreme Court's decision in these and other communities, and there has not yet been established a legal basis for obtaining a clarification from the Supreme Court of its implementation decree. As of now, that decision is characterized by the ambiguities of "deliberate speed," "variety of local problems," "practical flexibility," the need to reconcile "public and private needs," "a prompt and reasonable start toward full compliance," "the courts may find that additional time is necessary to carry out the ruling in an effective manner," and "consistent with good faith and compliance at the earliest practicable date."

With the passage of time, the practical significance of these ambiguities have become unmistakably clear to students of the desegregation process. Probably the most pivotal inadequacy — lack of clarity and specificity — is a function of the Court's failure to set a specific deadline for the *termination* of desegregation. This omission gives substance to the argument that the implementation decree approached the problem of an effective transition on the basis of a doctrine of "gradualism."

In evaluating the wisdom of the Court's adoption of a gradualist approach, even under the stated conditions of a "prompt and reasonable start" and evidence of "good faith and compliance," one must keep in mind that this position was contrary to the recommendations presented by the social scientists on the strength of their findings. These findings clearly indicated that an unwarranted and prolonged period of time for desegregation arouses doubt, conflict, and anxiety among the individuals involved and makes more difficult positive and effective social change. A 1955 analysis (3) of this decision warned:

> There is a possible danger that the Supreme Court's concept of "additional time" may be interpreted in some communities as meaning indefinite postponement. It would then be the responsibility of the District Courts or eventually the Supreme Court itself to define positively and with precision the meaning of additional time so that it would be socially beneficial rather than detrimental. With this type of definite interpretation of this term by our Federal Courts, there will be less danger that the general public will interpret the decision as evidence of vacillation and indecision on the part of our judicial authorities.

This analysis concluded that the implementation decree was written by reasonable men in an attempt to communicate with other reasonable men concerning the most effective method of resolving a complex social problem. The problem which remains to be decided by the future is whether some of the individuals to whom the Court addressed its reasonable appeal are really reasonable men. Events within the past five years have indicated that many of the individuals who control the political, social, and economic power necessary to effect significant and positive social change in race relations are not willing to do so but are willing to take the unreasonable risks of exploiting racial issues for the perpetuation of personal political power, or are blinded by passion and prejudice, or are immobilized by conflict and apathy. For these men, a more precise, definite, and specific implementation decree, based upon the empirical findings of social science, could not have been any more threatening and might have contributed to a more effective and accelerated pattern of public school desegregation.

The findings and predictions of social scientists and social psychologists concerning the factors related to effective and ineffective approaches to public school desegregation are to be found in many published documents and some unpublished manuscripts (*1, 4, 6, 10*).[3]

The evidence from various sources indicates, of course, that the problem of an effective transition from segregated to nonsegregated patterns of living in various areas and social institutions involves many considerations. Some factors when present assure smoothness. Others are associated with delay, confusion, social disruption, and, at times, overt violence. The following factors seem to be of critical importance, and at least some of them are found in all known instances of effective desegregation:

(1) A clear and unequivocal statement of the policy of desegregation by leaders, prestige figures, and other authorities.

(2) Firm enforcement of the desegregation policy by enforcement officers and other authorities, and persistence in the execution of this policy in the face of initial resistance.

(3) A willingness on the part of the responsible authorities to deal with violations, attempted violations, and incitements to violations of desegregation by a resort to the law and dramatic enforcement action.

(4) Refusal by the authorities to resort to, engage in, or tolerate subterfuges, gerrymandering, or other devices for evading the policy and fact of desegregation.

(5) An appeal to the public in terms of the religious principles of brotherhood and the acceptance of the American democratic traditions of fair play and equal justice.

The examples of effective desegregation of the public schools in Washington, D. C., Baltimore, St. Louis, Louisville, and other communities tend to validate these principles.

Factors which are associated with an increase in resistance and opposition to desegregation and contribute to ineffectiveness in its accomplishment include the following:

(1) An equivocal, ambiguous, or vacillating position among authorities.

(2) Competition between government agencies and the exploitation of the issue of desegregation for political purposes.

(3) A weak or inconsistent position among law enforcement officers or their alliance with opponets of desegregation.

(4) Attempts on the part of the authorities or law enforcement officers to resist or evade the policy of desegregation.

(5) The setting of an unnecessarily remote date for the completion of desegregation with or without specifying the way in which that interval of time should be used—permitting a long time for public debate, public opinion polls, or prolonged arguments concerning the advisability of desegregation or the proper processes for desegregation.

(6) Resorting to various types of segmentalized or piecemeal processes of desegregation.

(7) Leaving the problem of desegregation as a matter of choice for whites or Negroes.

The unhappy events surrounding the desegregation of the public schools in Little Rock — particularly the role of Governor Faubus of Arkansas — reinforce these observations. There is now no question that Governor Faubus successfully exploited the desegregation issue for political purposes and was clearly allied with the opponents of desegregation. There also seems to be little doubt that the role of President Eisenhower in the Little Rock crisis was inconsistent — on one occasion strong and forceful, but generally vacillating, ambiguous, and equivocal.

Ironically, an analysis of the Little Rock and similar incidents of prolonged resistance to public school desegregation suggests that the opponents to this form of social change were quite familiar with the findings of the social scientists. They could not have been more effective in blocking desegregation if they had articulately applied these findings in order to obtain their destructive ends.

It seems clear that violence can be perpetrated by a small minority of frustrated and disgruntled individuals whose basic motivations are not necessarily directly related to race. Though rare, violence has been found under conditions of ambiguous, inconsistent, or dilatory desegregation policy on the part of authorities, ineffective, weak, and at times conspiratorial police action, and as a reflection of the type of inconsistency which is associated with conflicting and competing governmental agencies and authorities. Some or all of these observations were confirmed in every instance of violence associated with public school desegregation. What was not foreseen was that violence would or could be openly incited by governmentally constituted authority figures.

Similarly, there are many techniques which can be used intentionally or unintentionally to delay or evade desegregation. Almost any procedure, other than the assignment of students to schools without regard to race within a specified interval of time required for administrative changes, can be manipulated in such a way as to become a technique of evasion. Some of the more or less obvious devices which are used to give the impression of compliance with the desegregation decree, but which nonetheless maintain the fact of segregation, include the following:

(1) The maintenance of segregated facilities along with a policy of "voluntary desegregation" or "choice."

(2) Gerrymandering or other manipulation of school district lines in order to insure that schools will remain in effect racially segregated.

(3) The introduction of a series of delays, including prolonged periods of "public education," debates, discussions, seminars, and other forms of "preparation" for desegregation.

(4) Specific devices and procedures which may be proposed as sound educational methods, but which can in effect maintain segregated schools or segregated classes within schools: homogeneous groupings according to intelligence determined by group rather than individual tests, homogeneous classes in terms of level of achievement, rapid and slow classes, specialized classes, and specialized schools with racial homogeneity reinforced by differential counseling for Negro and white children.

(5) Token and quota admission of Negro students to "desegregated" schools.

(6) The provision of "private" schools for white students while maintaining "public" schools for Negro students.

An effective decree would have to be specific in order to prevent the widespread utilization of any or all of the above devices. It should be added that the quicker the implementation of the desegregation decision, the less is the likelihood of the utilization of any of these evasive techniques. In addition, other techniques of evasion to subvert the desegregation process entail the misuse of academic achievement test results as the basis for assigning children to particular schools, of psychological and psychiatric information, and of public opinion polls (6).

The disturbingly uncanny accuracy of these predictions of evasion techniques can best be observed by an examination of the criteria used by boards of education in deciding where to place Negro children whose parents request transfers from segregated to desegregated schools. Nine states — Alabama, Arkansas, Florida, Louisiana, North Carolina, South Carolina, Tennessee, Texas, and Virginia — have since 1955, adopted pupil assignment statutes which illustrate these devices, all made possible largely through the ambiguity of the implementation decree by the Supreme Court.

Among the factors and criteria which these new statutes require the local, county, or state school boards to take into account in the assignment of pupils are the following:

The effect of the admission of new pupils upon established or proposed academic programs;

The suitability of established curricula for particular pupils;

The adequacy of a pupil's academic preparation for admission to a particular school and curriculum;

The scholastic aptitude and relative intelligence or mental ability of the pupil;

The psychological qualification of the pupil for the type of teaching and associations involved;

The effect of admission of the pupil upon the academic progress of other students in a particular school or facility;

The effect of admission upon prevailing academic standards at a particular school;

The psychological effect upon the pupil of attendance at a particular school;

The possibility or threat of friction or disorder among pupils or others.

One or more of these criteria is found in the statutes of each of these nine states. The pupil assignment laws of Alabama, Arkansas, Louisiana, Tennessee, and Texas contain almost all of them.

The way these criteria are used shows a clear design to exclude Negro students from white schools or to reduce the number of Negro students to a token few. The effective use of these laws to evade desegregation or to effect evasive token compliance is predicated primarily upon the psychological criteria indicated. Perhaps the controlling authorities in these resistant states reasoned that since the original Supreme Court decision seemed based upon psychological findings, an effective evasion of both the letter and the spirit of the decision could also be based upon "psychological" data and techniques. This problem defines the present major and, hopefully, the final legal obstacle which must be solved to obtain effective desegregation of the nation's public schools. In this regard, it should be noted that a group of social psychologists and specialists in tests and measurements are at present collaborating with lawyers in the preparation of an effective attack on these aspects of the pupil assignment laws. Some of the propositions which must be presented in legally effective ways on the trial and appellate levels are the following:

That differences in intelligence and academic achievement are not determined by inherent racial factors;

That there is some overlap in the intelligence and achievement test scores of random samples of white and Negro children in a given school district;

That intelligence and achievement test scores reflect, among other factors, educational opportunity and stimulation;

That there are some psychological traits and characteristics which are subject to standardized and objective measurements but others which, at present, psychologists are not able to measure objectively. Judgments of these latter traits lend themselves to the biases and preconceptions of those who are required to make the evaluations;

That the results of intelligence and achievement tests and other psychological methods of evaluation, even when these instruments are used adequately and with the necessary scientific precautions, should not be used for purposes of exclusion or rejection of children, but should be used for diagnosis and stimulation.

Work groups on the uses and abuses of psychological tests and methods established by the Society for the Psychological Study of Social Issues, are now busy with this last problem. We may look forward confidently to their contributions within the next year.

In evaluating the effects of the pupil placement laws, the following facts should be noted: Of the five states in which not a single school district has desegregated — Alabama, Georgia, Louisiana, Mississippi, and South Carolina — three have adopted pupil placement plans. Only Mississippi and Georgia deemed it unnecessary to maintain segregation through the use of this device. Probably the controlling political authorities in these two states considered it beneath them to resort to any subterfuge which would contaminate the purity of their open and flagrant defiance of the United States Constitution.

Of equal interest is the fact that of the remaining six states with pupil placement statutes, only one, Texas, shows any appreciable degree of public school desegregation (8), almost all of which has occurred in the western part of the state. For the other five states, statistics indicate that in the school years of 1959-1960, Arkansas had desegregated eight of its 228 school districts; Florida, one of 67; North Carolina, seven out of 174; Tennessee, four out of 142, and Virginia, six of 128.

For that same year, a total of 4,212 Negro students were distributed through "desegregated" schools in each of these six states as follows: Arkansas, 94; Florida, 512; North Carolina, 34; Tennessee, 169; Texas, 3,300, and Virginia, 103.

These data clearly reveal that the pupil assignment statutes are designed, intended, and used not as instruments of desegregation, but as effective instruments for token evasion at best, and, at worst, the perpetuation of segregated public schools.

In an attempt to understand some of the significance of this regional pattern of defiance, it may be of interest to recall the following observation (5), published originally in April, 1955.

Already, a regional pattern in initial reactions to the demand for desegregation appears to be emerging. Some communities in the border states of Kansas, Missouri, Maryland, West Virginia, Delaware, and the District of Columbia have taken steps to desegregate their schools before being required to do so by the specific decree of the Supreme Court.

On the other hand, a hard core of resistance to public school desegregation is being stimulated or reinforced by political figures in such states as Georgia, Mississippi, South Carolina, and, to some extent, also in Virginia, Florida, Alabama, and Louisiana, It is difficult at present to determine the degree of resistance to or acceptance of desegregation in Arkansas, Oklahoma, Texas, Tennessee, Kentucky, and North Carolina. The political leaders in these states have not assumed an openly defiant attitude toward public desegregation.

When the governor of Arkansas did assume an attitude of defiance and obstruction, however, it markedly slowed the pace of desegregation in Arkansas and probably elsewhere. On the other hand, the more accepting attitude of the governor of Kentucky (and presumably other political officials of that state) made desegregation easier there. North Carolina presents an enigma. Certainly this is not one of the states which has been marked by overt defiance and shouts of "interposition" and "nullification." Unlike Virginia, which was required to make some retreat from its earlier stand of massive resistance, and South Carolina, which so far has made no retreat from its extreme position of defiance and rebellion, North Carolina has been characterized by a quiet, somewhat gentlemanly, verbal acceptance of the Supreme Court's decision but has been most effective in evading any effective implementation. Actually, North Carolina may be viewed as the truly brilliant leader of effective evasion, setting the pattern of "voluntarism" and "gradualism" which has been adopted by the other more reasonable states such as Virginia, Florida, and Tennessee. The effectiveness of the gentleman's approach for the evasion of the desegregation decrees is indicated by the fact that in spite of the strident defiance of Faubus and the dramatic chaos of Little Rock, Arkansas had a total of 94 Negro students in desegregated schools in the 1959-1960 school year, while North Carolina had only 34 Negro students in desegregated schools.

GRADUALISM

Gradualism has a superficial attractiveness, counteracted by the findings of the social scientists at the time of the Supreme Court's consideration of the desegregation issue. In general, the gradualist approach is subject to at least five serious limitations. First, it tends to increase the resentment of those whites who are immediately involved in the desegregation process. They resent the role of guinea pigs singled out for special observation. Second, as a result, there is an increased likelihood that minor incidents may occur, be exaggerated, and then used as evidence that desegregation won't work. Third, the occurrence of incidents during the slow, "gradualistic" introduction of desegregation tends to increase the anxieties and resistances of white people who are not immediately involved but who anticipate their being caught up in the process eventually. Fourth, the "gradual" approach provides time for the opposition to desegregation to become mobilized and to subvert the social enterprise in a planned fashion. Finally, such approaches are likely to be interpreted by the general public, white and Negro alike, as evidence of vacillation and indecision among the authorities and as a reflection of, in some quarters, a confirmation of the belief that there is something inherently dangerous in desegregation. Those who rely heavily on authority are particularly vulnerable to this kind of interpretation, and individuals who would otherwise be inclined to ride contentedly with the change become doubtful and hesitant, whereas those originally opposed to desegregation find new encouragement and support for their resistance.

It appears, then, that the most effective method of desegregation is not of the gradualistic or piecemeal type, but one which fulfills the following criteria:

(1) The abolition of all segregated facilities which are so inadequate that it would be economically and otherwise inefficient to attempt to use them.

(2) The assignment of all remaining facilities to all individuals without regard to such arbitrary distinctions as race.

(3) The restriction of the time allowed for this transition to the minimum required for the necessary administrative adjustments to insure effectiveness and impartiality.

(4) The specification of an inflexible deadline, based upon the particulars (not necessarily determined by the court) of the administrative adjustments which will take place during the interval.

Empirical study indicates that the desegregation of one school or one class at a time tends to increase anxieties and doubts rather than allay them, and to intensify resistance among the whites immediately affected. The one-grade-at-a-time, stair-step plan brings with it in most cases the major psychological problems of having some all-white classes and some racially mixed classes in the same school. The disadvantages of such segmentalized, "gradual" approaches outweigh the advantages that may be claimed for them.

In spite of these findings, various types of gradual approaches remain popular in certain states. Nashville, Tennessee, has been the chief exponent of the stair-step, one-grade-at-a-time movement toward desegregation. This plan is further complicated by a "voluntary" or "choice" provision wherein a Negro parent can decide whether to send his child to the desegregated or segregated school. Within the past four years since this plan has been in effect in Nashville, less than 10 per cent of the eligible Negro parents have chosen to send their children to desegregated schools. And the gradual, voluntary approach did not prevent the violence fomented by racial extremists.

At Little Rock, another type of gradual plan was instituted. The violence and prolonged resistance there are too well known to require comment. Indeed, every instance of violence or prolonged resistance to desegregation which has occurred during the past five years has involved some type of gradual, "segmentalized," or "token" form of desegregation. This fact tends to confirm the findings that gradualism does not insure effectiveness or increase desegregation's chances of acceptance. Immediate enforcement is, at worst, no more likely to lead to resistance of either violent or nonviolent kinds than are the various forms of gradualism.

The first legal breakthrough on the one-grade-at-a-time, twelve-year, gradual desegregation plan came a few months ago, when a Federal United States Court of Appeals rejected a plan submitted by the Delaware State Board of Education. The plan was originally approved by a Federal District Judge after a hearing in which a psychologist testified concerning the arbitrary basis of this form of desegregation and the fact that differences in the average intelligence of Negro and white children were not relevant to the process and method of effective public school desegregation. The Court of Appeals summarily rejected the arguments advanced by the Board in support of its plan. Two of the three judges did not agree that the plan was necessary because of differences in intelligence between whites and Negroes and that the emotional impact of a more immediate integration plan upon a predominantly southern society would be detrimental. An important step toward clarification of the implementation decree of the Supreme Court was taken by the decision of these three judges when they held that this stair-step plan did not meet the "deliberate speed" requirement. Whether the Supreme Court is tending to strengthen or soften its position on effective implementation will be determined by its reaction and decision when and if this case reaches it on appeal.

SUMMARY EVALUATION

In general, the social scientists who studied and analyzed the desegregation process seemed to be accurate in their predictions and anticipations of the process of public school desegregation. Events during the past five years tend to confirm the following general propositions:

1. Certain factors are related to effective desegregation, particularly the crucial role of strong leadership and effective enforcement.

2. Certain factors are related to ineffective desegregation, prolonged resistance, and violence. The role of ambiguity, equivocation, inconsistency, and evasiveness on the part of political authorities was clearly supported by the many negative events surrounding desegregation during the past five years.

3. Specific evasive techniques are ready to hand. The misuse of achievement, intelligence, and other psychological tests and of psychiatric assumptions and widespread "token" desegregation are the most obvious and persistent examples of the validity of this prediction.

4. Gradual forms of desegregation are no more likely to be effective, do not reduce resistance to desegregation, and do not decrease the chances of violence.

A number of factors which were not clearly foreseen by the social scientists emerged with greater clarity and significance from the actual events and trends of the past five years — for example, the use of the pupil assignment statutes of various states to avoid desegregation or to reduce it to a token compliance. This is accomplished by laws imposing special burdens and harassments upon only those Negro parents and students who seek transfers to desegregated schools. Only these children are given special tests, psychiatric and psychological examinations, and prolonged interviews. The effect, if not the intent, of these bureaucratic hurdles is to discourage the number of Negro parents who seek to enroll their children in non-Negro schools. It is a question whether this is not primarily a legal problem which should be challenged in the Courts under non-discrimination or equal-protection laws.

Second, there are the varieties of physical and psychological cruelties and harassments inflicted upon those few Negro children who are assigned as "tokens" to desegregated schools. The indignities inflicted upon the handful of Negro children in Little Rock's Central High School and the one or two Negro children in schools in North Carolina by a few highly organized racist adolescents may set a pattern for effective discouragement of school desegregation in some places.

Third, effective intimidation and immobilization of nonsegregationist whites through threats of economic reprisals, social ostracism, and political retaliation has occurred with unexpected frequency.

Finally, there is the dominance of the wave of moderation as a reaction to the dramatic and violent forms of resistance to desegregation in Little Rock and elsewhere. The role of President Eisenhower's ambiguity and vagueness on the desegregation issue must be seen as a major factor in this mood of moderation, retreat, and loss of initiative to the pro-segregationists.

Generally, the social scientists underestimated the intensity and deviousness of the opposition, the effectiveness of pro-segregationists propaganda outside the South, the lack of deep effective moral commitment in the nation as a whole and particularly in the executive and legislative branches of the Federal Government, and the ease with which the initiative would be seized by pro-segregationists.

The significant counterbalancing factor is the continued high morale, indomitable courage, and persistence of a significant proportion of Negroes. These individuals seem willing to endure any and all hardships for themselves and their children if it is necessary to obtain their adjudicated rights as American citizens. The sit-in movement among Negro students in the South, an effective technique of appropriate assertion, gives all indications of regaining the desegregation initiative and taking the pace of racial change out of the hands of the moderates and the segregationists. It offers additional evidence that although the pace can be slowed and the process postponed, the fact of desegregation is inevitable. The desire for human dignity and equality provides an irresistible human force.

A PROGRAM FOR THE FUTURE

In thinking of the contributions which must be made to facilitate orderly, lawful, constructive, and democratic changes in the pattern of race relations in America, one is confronted with the necessity for an action program on many levels. There is still some mopping-up which must be done at law. The attorneys must find some way of demonstrating effectively before the Federal Courts and the Supreme Court that the pupil placement laws are not "compliance in good faith" with the 1954 decision, and that these laws are designed and used to block and evade desegregation rather than to implement or facilitate it. The lawyers must also demonstrate before the Courts, and more forcefully before the public, that in two of the original public school desegregation cases (Clarendon County, South Carolina, and Prince Edward County, Virginia) there is at present, six years after the Supreme Court's decision, an open and flagrant defiance of the orders of the nation's highest judicial body. This state of affairs constitutes a form of anarchy and lawlessness which is inimical to stable democratic and constitutional government.

Similarly, the Supreme Court must define with greater precision the meaning of "deliberate speed." This definition must be made in terms of specific factors involved in the change from segregated to nonsegregated schools, with a definite deadline for initiation and termination of the program of desegregation, and — most important — with a clear statement of the penalty involved for non-compliance or flagrant defiance. Failure here will not only weaken the prestige of the Court but will make a mockery before the world of the eloquence of its original decision.

On the level of community action, some program must be designed and implemented to encourage Negroes to seek and to obtain their adjudicated rights. Such a program must necessarily include safeguards and protections against retaliation, intimidation, and economic reprisals against either whites or Negroes involved in community action. The failure on the part of Negro organizations, church groups, and national social agencies to develop and institute enterprises of this type has contributed significantly to the loss of initiative. The over-all timidity of national educational societies and educators in general certainly has not been an asset in the current struggle for public school desegregation.

On the political level, there is a crying need for the election of a president of the United States who is clear, forthright, and knowledgeable on this problem. In this regard one may recall the sardonic observation by Brewster Smith (9):

. . . the rest of us may perhaps be excused when we sometimes wonder glumly whether we mightn't have contributed more to the solution of the social issue if, instead of applying ourselves as psychologists to the problem of how intelligent and well-intentioned authority might be used to make desegregation effective, we had devoted ourselves more earnestly as citizens to electing the right president . . . or the right governor of Arkansas.

Civil rights are not the only issues which must concern our Chief Executive, but they are pivotal in the domestic and international constellation of problems. A president who equivocates on this issue does not have the vision or breadth of perspective to be clear, definitive, and just in his handling of other and related social problems. Such considerations seem to hold with equal force in evaluating the fitness of members of Congress from nonsouthern states. The problem of political realism, as opposed to fantasy and racial demagoguery, in the southern states seems inherently related to the struggle of Negroes to obtain safeguards for and to exercise their right to vote. When this is accomplished, it may precipitate surprisingly rapid changes in the social, economic, and racial climate of even such states as Mississippi, Alabama, and Georgia.

Finally, there are some specific tasks which remain in the social scientist's collaboration with the lawyers who are continuing the legal battle against the last vestiges of racial segregation and discrimination in American life. For instance, there is the need for psychologists as citizens and as professionals to help the public and its leaders to understand the difference between *desegregation* and *integration*. The President of the United States has repeatedly made statements which betray a basic confusion of these two social and psychological processes. When he talks about the "need for time" and that we cannot hope to "change men's hearts and minds overnight," he demonstrates that he does not understand the difference between desegregation, an objective social, legal, and political process, and integration, a subjective, psychological, and attitudinal process.

Because this confusion is likely to be widely shared, psychologists and educators must seek to clarify the issues involved. Desegregation involves a pattern of changes in the organization of social institutions. It has been defined (4) as "the process of change in social situations or institutions from a system of organization in terms of separate facilities for whites and Negroes, exclusion of Negroes, or a deliberate restriction of the extent or area of participation of Negroes, to a system wherein distinctions, exclusion, or restriction of participation based upon race no longer prevail." So defined, desegregation is a more descriptive, objective, and empirical term and does not involve the complexity of subjective, attitudinal, and individual adjustments which are inherent in the more evaluative term, "integration." Desegregation is the social, political, legal, judicial, administrative, or community processes by which racial barriers to the enjoyment of full and equal civil rights are removed. Desegregation can be and usually is brought about by laws and governmental authority. Desegregation can therefore be accomplished within the limited time required for the necessary administrative decisions and changes and their execution and enforcement.

Integration, as a subjective and individual process, involves attitudinal changes and the removal of fears, hatreds, suspicions, stereotypes, and superstitions. Integration involves problems of personal choice, personal readiness, and personal stability. Its achievement necessarily requires a longer period of time. It cannot come about "overnight." It requires education and deals poignantly with the problems of changing men's hearts and minds. Integration cannot be coerced by law or governmental authority. But psychologists and educators can understand and help to educate the general public to understand that there can be no *integration* before *desegregation.* There has been no known case of desegregation wherein the objective social and situational changes came as a consequence of subjective, individual, and attitudinal changes. On the contrary, the objective, situational changes are necessary antecedents to subjective, attitudinal alterations in the personalities of men. Being contributors to this confusion through their earlier emphasis on the convenient, isolated, and practically irrelevant preoccupation with attitude research, social scientists should now assume the responsibility for clearing up this misconception. They must now concentrate their studies and their public communications on the truth that in the process of social change, situational and determined behavioral changes precede and probably govern affective and attitudinal changes.

Another public educational responsibility is that of helping to change the general perspective toward the desegregation process. Up to the present, it has been generally believed that desegregation will benefit primarily, if not exclusively, Negro children. Obviously, these children have been the chief victims of the more flagrant inequities in a system of segregated education. It is not true, however, that white children will be harmed or will not benefit from desegregated schools. Segregated education is inferior and nonadaptive for whites as well as Negroes. Put simply, no child can receive a democratic education in a nondemocratic school. A white youngster in a homogeneous, isolated, "hot house" type of school situation is not being prepared for the realities of the contemporary and future world. Such a child may have brilliant college entrance scores, be extraordinary in his mathematical ability, or read and speak a foreign language with skill and precision, but he is likely to be blocked in many circumstances in his ability to use these intellectual abilities with the poise and effectiveness essential to personal and social creativity. A racially segregated school imposes upon white children the inevitable stultifying burdens of petty provincialism, irrational fears and hatreds of people who are different, and a distorted image of themselves. Psychologically, the racially segregated school at this period of American and world history is an anachronism which our nation cannot afford. This point must be made over and over again until it is understood by those who have the power to make the decisions which control our destiny.

Social scientists must continue to offer their skills, knowledge, insight, and techniques to a society in desperate need of an effective approach to the solution of many and complex social problems. Pure, applied, and action research findings must be made available to those forces in our society which are working toward the goals consistent with scientific facts and the values of human dignity and justice.

FOOTNOTES

¹ A tape recording of the entire discussion and proceedings of this conference may have some future historical value.

² See the briefs for the appellants in *Brown vs. Board of Education,* Topeka, Kansas, Nos. 1, 2, and 3, and for the respondents on further argument, Supreme Court of the United States, October term, 1954.

³ See also unpublished memoranda and other material in the files of the Legal Defense and Educational Fund of the National Association for the Advancement of Colored People.

REFERENCES

1. Ashmore, H. *The Negro and the schools.* Chapel Hill: Univ. of North Carolina Press, 1954.

2. Ball, W. B. Lawyers and social scientists: Guiding the guides. *Villanova Law Rev.,* 1959, 5, 215-223.

3. Clark, K. B. A non-legal analysis of the May 31, 1955, decree of the United States Supreme Court. Unpublished MS.

4. Clark, K. B. Desegregation: An appraisal of the evidence. *J. soc. Issues,* 1953, 9, 1-76.

5. Clark, K. B. Desegregation in the public schools. *Social Problems,* 1955, 2, 197-235.

6. Clark, K. B. Desegregation of the American public schools. In *Current problems and issues in human relations education.* New York: Anti-Defamation League, 1955. Pp. 17-23.

7. Clark, K. B. The desegregation cases: Criticism of the social scientists' role. *Villanova Law Rev.,* 1959, 5, 224-240.

8. School desegregation: The first six years. *New South,* 1960, 15, 1-35.

9. Smith, M. B. Rationality and social process. *J. individ. Psychol.,* 1960, 16, 25-35.

10. The effects of segregation and the consequences of desegregation: A social science statement. Appendix to Appellant's Brief, Supreme Court of the United States, October term, 1952.

Bibliography

Abel, T. M. "Dominant Behavior of Institutionalized Sub-normal Negro Girls: An Experimental Study," *American Journal of Mental Deficiency* (1943), 47:429-436.

Ackerman, N. W.; Jahoda, M. *Anti-Semitism and Emotional Disorder.* New York: Harper, 1950.

Adams, E. L., *et al.* "Attitudes with Regard to Minority Groups of a Sampling of University Men Students from the Upper Socio-economic Level," *Journal of Educational Sociology* (1948), 21:328-338.

Adorno, T. W.; Frenkel-Brunswik, E.; Levinson, D. J.; Sanford, R. N. *The Authoritarian Personality.* New York: Harper, 1950.

Allport, G. W. *The A B C's of Scapegoating.* Chicago: Central YMCA College, 1944.

Allport, G. W. *The Nature of Prejudice.* Boston: Beacon Press, 1954.

Allport, G. W.; Kramer, B. M. "Some Roots of Prejudice," *Journal of Psychology* (1946), 22:9-39.

Ashmore, H. S. *The Negro and the Schools.* Chapel Hill: University of North Carolina Press, 1954.

Bauer, C. "Some Questions in Housing and Community Planning," *Journal of Social Issues* (1951), 7:1-34.

Bayton, J. A. "The Racial Stereotypes of Negro College Students," *Journal of Abnormal and Social Psychology* (1941), 36:97-102.

Bayton, J. A.; Byoune, E. F. "Racio-national Stereotypes Held by Negroes," *Journal of Negro Education* (1947), 16:49-56.

Berenda, R. W. *The Influence of the Group on the Judgments of Children.* New York: King's Crown Press, 1950.

Bettelheim, B.; Janowitz, M. "Dynamics of Prejudice," *Scientific American* (1950), 183:11-13.

Bettelheim, B.; Janowitz, M. *Dynamics of Prejudice.* New York: Harper, 1950.

Blake, R.; Dennis, W. "The Development of Stereotypes Concerning the Negro," *Journal of Abnormal and Social Psychology* (1943), 38:525-531.

Bovell, G. B. "Psychological Considerations of Color Conflicts Among Negroes," *Psychoanalytic Review* (1943), 30:447-459.

Brief Survey of the Major Agencies in the Field of Cultural Education. New York: American Jewish Committee, 1950.

Brenman, M. "Minority Group Membership and Religious, Psychosexual and Social Patterns in a Group of Middle Class Negro Girls," *Journal of Social Psychology* (1940), 12:179-196.

Brenman, M. "The Relationship between Minority Group Membership and Group Identification in a Group of Urban Middle Class Negro Girls," *Journal of Social Psychology* (1940), 11:171-197.

Brenman, M. "Urban Lower Class Negro Girls," *Journal of Psychiatry* (1943), 6:307-324.

Brown, F. "An Experimental Study of Parental Attitudes and Their Effects on Child Adjustment," *American Journal of Orthopsychiatry* (1942), 12:224-231.

Brown, J. F. "Social and Psychological Factors in the Anti-Semitic Attitude," *Journal of Educational Sociology* (1943), 16:351-354.

Bryant, G. E. "Recent Trends in Racial Attitudes of Negro College Students," *Journal of Negro Education* (1941), 10:43-50.

Cantril, H. "Toward a Scientific Morality," *Journal of Psychology* (1949), 27:363-376.

Caroll, R. E. "Relation of Social Environment to the Morale, Ideology, and the Personal Aspiration of Negro Boys and Girls," *School Review* (1945), 53:30-38.

Charles, C. V. "Optimism and Frustration in the American Negro," *Psychoanalytic Review* (1942), 29:270-299.

Chein, I. Personal communication, October 1950.

Chein, I. "Towards a Science of Morality," *Journal of Social Psychology* (1947), 25:235-238.

Chein, I.; Hurwitz, J. "A Study of Minority Group Membership: The Reactions of Jewish Boys to Various Aspects of Being Jewish," *American Psychologist* (1949), 4:260-261.

Chess, S.; Clark, K. B.; and Thomas, A. "The Importance of Cultural Evaluation in Psychiatric Diagnosis and Treatment," *Psychiatric Quarterly* (Jan. 1953), pp. 1-13.

Clark, K. B. "Desegregation: An Appraisal of the Evidence," *Journal of Social Issues* (1953), 9 (No. 4): 1-75.

Clark, K. B. "Group Violence: A Preliminary Study of the 1943 Harlem Riot," *Journal of Social Psychology* (1944), 19:319-337.

Clark, K. B. "Racial Prejudices among American Minorities," *International Social Science Bulletin,* Winter 1950.

Clark, K. B. "Social Science and Social Tensions," *Mental Hygiene* (1948), 32:15-26.

Clark, K. B.; Barker, J. "The Zoot Effect in Personality: A Race Riot Participant," *Journal of Abnormal and Social Psychology* (1945), 40:143-148.

Clark, K. B.; Clark, M. P. "The Development of Consciousness of Self and the Emergence of Racial Indentification in Negro Pre-school Children," *Journal of Social Psychology* (1939), 10:591-599.

Clark, K. B.; Clark, M. P. "Emotional Factors in Racial Identification and Preference in Negro Children," *Journal of Negro Education* (1950), 19:341-350.

Clark, K. B.; Clark, M. P. "Racial Identification and Preference in Negro Children," *Readings in Social Psychology,* edited by T. M. Newcomb and E. L. Hartley. New York: Henry Holt, 1947.

Clark, K. B.; Clark, M. P. "Segregation as a Factor in the Racial Identification of Negro Pre-school Children," *Journal of Experimental Education* (1939), 8:161-163.

Clark, K. B.; Clark, M. P. "Skin Color as a Factor in Racial Identification of Negro Pre-school Children," *Journal of Social Psychology* (1940), 11:159-169.

Cox, O. C. *Caste, Class and Race.* New York: Doubleday, 1948.

Crown, S. "Some Personality Correlates of War Mindedness and Anti-Semitism," *Journal of Social Psychology* (1950), 31:131-143.

Davis, A. "Racial Status and Personality Development," *Scientific Monthly* (1943), 57:354-362.

Davis, A. *Social Class Influences upon Learning.* Cambridge: Harvard University Press, 1948.

Davis, A. "The Socialization of the American Negro Child and Adolescent," *Journal of Negro Education* (1939), 8:264-275.

Davis, A.; Dollard, J. *Children of Bondage.* Washington: American Council on Education, 1940.

Davis, A.; Havighurst, R. J. "Social Class and Color Difference in Child Rearing," *American Sociological Review* (1946), 11:698-710.

Deutsch, M.; Collins, M. E. *Interracial Housing: A Psychological Study of a Social Experiment.* Minneapolis: University of Minnesota Press, 1951.

Deutscher, M.; Chein, I. "The Psychological Effects of Enforced Segregation: A Survey of Social Science Opinion," *Journal of Psychology* (1948), 26:259-287.

Directory of Agencies in Intergroup Relations. Chicago: American Council on Race Relations, 1950.

Dollard, J.; Doob, N. E., *et al. Frustration and Aggression.* New Haven: Yale University Press, 1939.

Engle, T. L. "Personality Adjustments of Children Belonging to Two Minority Groups," *Journal of Educational Psychology* (1945), 36: 543-560.

Flowerman, S. H. "The Use of Propaganda to Reduce Prejudice: A Refutation," *International Journal of Opinion and Attitude Research* (1949), 3:99-108.

Frazier, E. Franklin. *The Negro in the United States.* New York: Macmillan, 1949.

Frenkel-Brunswik, E. "Studies of Social Discrimination in Children," *American Psychologist* (1946), 1:456.

Frenkel-Brunswik, E. "A Study of Prejudice in Children," *Human Relations* (1948), 1:295-306.

"Froebel School Strike, Fall 1945, and Emerson School Strike, Fall 1947." Confidential report. American Jewish Congress: Commission on Community Interrelations.

Gardiner, E. E.; Aaron, S. "The Childhood and Adolescent Adjustment of Negro Psychiatric Casualties," *American Journal of Orthopsychiatry* (1946), 16:481-495.

Gesell, A.; Ilg, F. L. *Infant and Child in the Culture of Today.* New York: Harper, 1943.

Goff, M. R. *Problems and Emotional Difficulties of Negro Children.* Teachers College, Columbia University: Bureau of Publications, 1949.

Goodman, M. E. "Evidence Concerning the Genesis of Interracial Attitudes," *American Anthropologist* (1946), 48:624-630.

Goodman, M. E. *Race Awareness in Young Children.* Cambridge: Addison-Wesley, 1952.

Gould, K. M. *They Got the Blame: The Story of Scapegoats in History.* New York: Association Press, 1944.

Gruesser, Sister M. J. "Categorical Valuations of Jews among Catholic Parochial School Children," *Catholic University of America Studies in Sociology,* 34:1-162. Washington, D. C.: Catholic University of America Press, 1950.

Harris, A.; Watson, G. "Are Jewish or Gentile Children More Clannish?" *Journal of Social Psychology* (1946), 24:71-76.

Hartley, E. L. *Problems in Prejudice.* New York: King's Crown Press, 1946.

Hartley, E. L.; Rosenbaum, M.; Schwartz, S. "Children's Perceptions of Ethnic Group Membership," *Journal of Psychology* (1948), 26:387-398.

Hartley, E. L.; Rosenbaum, M.; Schwartz, S. "Children's Use of Ethnic Frames of Reference: An Exploratory Study of Ethnic Group Membership," *Journal of Psychology* (1948), 26:367-386.

Heyman, D. "Manifestations of Psychoneurosis in Negroes," *Mental Hygiene* (1945), 29:231-235.

Horowitz, E. L. "Attitudes in Children" in *Characteristics of the American Negro,* edited by O. Klineberg. New York: Harper, 1944.

Horowitz, E. L. "The Development of Attitude toward the Negro," *Archives of Psychology* (1936), No. 194.

Horowitz, R. "Racial Aspects of Self-identification in Nursery School Children," *Journal of Psychology* (1939), 7:91-99.

Houwink, E. "Color Is an Additional Problem," *Mental Hygiene* (1948), 32:596-604.

Hunt, W. A. "The Relative Incidence of Psychoneurosis among Negroes," *Journal of Consulting Psychology* (1947), 11:133-136.

Ivey, J. W. "American Negro Problem in European Press," *Crisis* (1950), 57:413-418.

Jenkins, M. D.; Randall, C. "Differential Characteristics of Superior and Unselected Negro College Students," *Journal of Social Psychology* (1945), 27:187-202.

Johnson, C. S. "National Organizations in the Field of Race Relations," *The Annals of the American Academy of Political and Social Science* (1946), 244:117.

Johnson, G. B. "Personality in White-Indian-Negro Community," *American Sociological Review* (1939), 4:516-523.

Kardiner, A.; Oversey, L. *The Mark of Oppression.* New York: W. W. Norton, 1951.

Ketcham, G., editor. *Yearbook of American Churches.* National Council of Churches, 1951.

Klineberg, O., editor. *Characteristics of the American Negro.* (Part 3, Chap. 1: "Experimental Studies of Negro Personality.") New York: Harper, 1944.

Klineberg, O. *Negro Intelligence and Selective Migration.* New York, 1935.

Lasker, B. *Race Attitudes in Children.* New York, 1935.

Lazarsfeld, P. F. "Techniques for Testing Educational Material Directed against Group Prejudice." Unpublished manuscript. Columbia University: Bureau of Applied Social Research.

Lee, J. O. "The Protestant Churches and Race Relations: Significant Trends," *Social Progress* (Feb. 1950), pp. 1-6.

Lehamn, H. C.; Witty, P. A. "Some Compensatory Mechanisms of the Negro," *Journal of Abnormal and Social Psychology* (1928), 23:28-37.

Lehrer, L. "The Jewish Elements in the Psychology of the Jewish Child in America," *YIVO Annual of Jewish Social Science* (1946), 1:195-216.

Lewin, K. "Psycho-sociological Problems of a Minority Group," *Character and Personality* (1935), 3:175-187.

Lewin, K. "Self Hatred among Jews," *Contemporary Jewish Record,* (June 1941), 4:219-232. Reprinted in K. Lewin's *Resolving Social Conflicts.* New York: Harper, 1948.

Long, H. H. "Tested Personality Adjustment in Jewish and Non-Jewish Groups," *Journal of Negro Education* (1944), 13:64-69.

McLean, H. V. "The Emotional Health of Negroes," *Journal of Negro Education* (1949), 18:283-290.

Malzberg, B. "Mental Disease among American Negroes," in *Characteristics of the American Negro,* edited by O. Klineberg. New York: Harper, 1944.

Marks, E. S. "Factors Affecting Skin Color Judgments of Negro College Students," *Psychological Bulletin* (1942), 39:577.

Marks, E. S. "Skin Color Judgments of Negro College Students," *Journal of Abnormal and Social Psychology* (1943), 38:370-376.

Marrow, Alfred J. *Living Without Hate: Scientific Approaches to Human Relations.* New York: Harper, 1951.

Maslow, A. H. "The Authoritarian Character Structure," *Journal of Social Psychology* (1943), 18:401-411.

Meltzer, H. "Nationality Preference and Stereotypes of Colored Children," *Journal of Genetic Psychology* (1939), 54:403-424.

Merton, R. K.; West, P. S.; Jahoda, M. "Social Fictions and Social Facts: The Dynamics of Race Relations in Hilltown." Mimeographed manuscript. Columbia University: Bureau of Applied Social Research.

Metreaux, A. *Race and Civilization.* UNESCO, 1950.

Murphy, G.; Likert, R. *Public Opinion and the Individual.* New York: Harper, 1938.

Mussen, P. H. "Some Personality and Social Factors Related to Changes in Children's Attitudes toward Negroes," *Journal of Abnormal and Social Psychology* (1950), 45:425-441.

Myers, H. J.; Yochelson, L. "Color Denial in the Negro: A Preliminary Report," *Psychiatry* (1948), 11:39-46.

Myrdal, G.; *et al. An American Dilemma.* New York: Harper, 1944.

Newcomb, T. M. "Autistic Hostility and Social Reality," *Human Relations* (1949), 1:69-86.

Nichols, L. *Breakthrough on the Color Front.* New York: Random House, 1954.

O'Malley. "Psychosis in Colored Race," *American Journal of Insanity,* 71:309-337.

Plotkin, L.; Colbert, M. "Anti-Semitism and Its Relation to Range of Interests and Interests Preference." Unpublished master's thesis. College of City of New York: Department of Psychology, 1950.

Powdermaker, H. "The Channeling of Negro Aggression by the Cultural Process," *American Journal of Sociology* (1943), 48:750-758.

Radke, M. "Group Belonging of Jewish Children in Relation to Their Age." Unpublished document. American Jewish Congress: Commission on Community Interrelations.

Radke, M. "The Meaning of Minority Group Membership to Jewish College Students." Unpublished document. American Jewish Congress: Commission on Community Interrelations.

Radke, M., Trager, H. G. "Children's Perceptions of the Social Roles of Negroes and Whites," *Journal of Psychology* (1950), 29:3-33.

Radke, M.; Trager, H. G. "Children's Perceptions of the Social Roles of Children," *Genetic Psychology Monographs* (1949), 40:327-447.

Radke, M.; Davis, H.; Hurwitz, J.; Pollack, P. "Group Belonging among Various Sub-groups of Jewish Children." Unpublished document. American Jewish Congress: Commission on Community Interrelations.

Reichard, S. "Rorschach Study of Prejudiced Personality," *American Journal of Orthopsychiatry* (1948), 18:280-286.

Ripley, H. S.; Wolf, S. "Mental Illness among Negro Troops Overseas," *American Journal of Psychology* (1947), 103:499-512.

Rokeach, M. "The Effect of Perception·Time upon Rigidity and Concreteness of Thinking," *Journal of Experimental Psychology* (1950), 40:206-216.

Rokeach, M. "Generalized Mental Rigidity as a Factor in Ethnocentrism," *Journal of Abnormal and Social Psychology* (1948), 43:259-278.

Rose, A. M. *The Negro's Morale.* Minneapolis: University of Minnesota Press, 1949.

Rose, A. M. *Studies in the Reduction of Prejudices.* Chicago: American Council on Race Relations, 1948.

Rose, A. M. "The Use of Propaganda to Reduce Prejudice," *International Journal of Opinion and Attitude Research* (Summer 1948), pp. 220-229.

Russell, D. H.; Robertson, I. "Influencing Attitudes toward Minority Groups in a Junior High School," *School Review* (1947), 55:205-213.

Saenger, G. *The Social Psychology of Prejudice: Achieving Intercultural Understanding and Cooperation in a Democracy.* New York: Harper, 1953.

Saenger, G.; Gordon, N. S. "The Influence of Discrimination on Minority Group Members in Its Relation to Attempts to Combat Discrimination," *Journal of Social Psychology* (1950), 31:95-120.

Sanford, R. N.; Levinson, D. J. "Ethnocentrism in Relation to Some Religious Attitudes and Practices," *American Psychologist* (1948), 3:350-351.

Seeman, M. "Skin Color Values in Three All-Negro School Classes," *American Sociological Review* (1946), 11:315-321.

Seidman, J. "Unstructured Sentence Completion Technique for the Measurement of Stereotypes." Unpublished manuscript.

Shuey, A. M. "Personality Traits of Jewish and Non-Jewish Students," *Archives of Psychology* (1944), 290:38.

Smith, L. *Killers of the Dream.* New York: W. W. Norton, 1949.

Sperling, A. P. "A Comparison between Jews and Non-Jews with Respect to Several Traits of Personality," *Journal of Applied Psychology* (1942), 26:828-840.

Steinbaum, J. "A Study of Jewishness of Twenty New York Families," *Yivo Bleter,* 31-32:208-323. In Yiddish.

Sterba, R. "Some Psychological Factors in Negro Race Hatred and in Anti-Negro Riots," in *Psychoanalysis and the Social Sciences,* edited by G. Roheim. New York: International Universities Press, 1947.

Stevens, R. "Racial Aspects of Emotional Problems of Negro Soldiers," *American Journal of Psychology* (1947), 103:393-398.

Sukov, W.; Williamson, E. G. "Personality Traits and Attitudes of Jewish and Non-Jewish Students," *Journal of Applied Psychology* (1938), 22:487-492.

Taba, H. "The Contributions of Workshops to Intercultural Education," *Harvard Educational Review* (March 1945), pp. 122-128.

Taba, H. Introduction to "The Story of a Project." Unpublished document. University of Chicago: Center for Intergroup Education.

Tait, J. W. "Race Prejudice and Personality," *School* (1946), 34:795-798.

Trager, H. G.; Yarrow, M. R. *They Learn What They Live: Prejudice in Young Children.* New York: Harper, 1952.

Verin, O. "Manifestations of Racial Conflict in Negro Clients of a Child Guidance Clinic," *Smith College Studies in Social Work* (1944), 15:126-127.

Warner, W. L.; Junker, B. H.; Adams, W. A. *Color and Human Nature.* Washington: American Council on Education, 1941.

Watson, G. *Action for Unity.* New York: Harper, 1947.

Watts, F. P. "A Comparative Clinical Study of Delinquent and Nondelinquent Negro Boys," *Journal of Negro Education* (1941), 10:190-207.

Whitman, H. "Is Prejudice Poisoning Our Children?" *Woman's Home Companion,* October 1949.

Williams, R. M., Jr. "The Reduction of Intergroup Tensions: A Survey of Research on Problems of Ethnic, Racial and Religious Group Relations," *Social Science Research Council Bulletin* (1947), 11:153.

Williams, R. M., Jr.; Ryan, M. W. *Schools in Transition*. Chapel Hill: University of North Carolina Press, 1954.

Wirth, L. Foreword to *Studies in Reduction of Prejudice*, by Arnold Rose. Chicago: American Council on Race Relations, 1948.

Zawadszki, B. "Limitations of the Scapegoat Theory of Prejudice," *Journal of Abnormal and Social Psychology* (1948), 43:127-141.

Zborowski, M. Unpublished manuscript. American Jewish Committee: Division of Scientific Research.

Zeligs, R. "Children's Intergroup Attitudes," *Journal of Genetic Psychology* (1948), 72:101-110.

Zilboorg, G. "Psychopathology and Social Prejudice," *Psychoanalytic Quarterly* (1947), 16:303-324.

This bibliography contains for the most part material published since 1940. For material prior to 1940, see the extensive bibliography in Klineberg's *Characteristics of the American Negro*. New York: Harper, 1944.

Index